EARLY LANGUAGE DEVELOPMENT
IN
FULL-TERM AND PREMATURE INFANTS

EARLY LANGUAGE DEVELOPMENT
IN
FULL-TERM AND PREMATURE INFANTS

Paula Menyuk
Boston University

Jacqueline W. Liebergott
Emerson College

Martin C. Schultz
Southern Illinois University

 LAWRENCE ERLBAUM ASSOCIATES, PUBLISHERS
1995   Hillsdale, New Jersey   Hove, UK

Lawrence Erlbaum Associates, Inc., Publishers
365 Broadway
Hillsdale, New Jersey 07642

Library of Congress Cataloging-in-Publication Data

Menyuk, Paula.
   Early language development in full term and premature infants /
Paula Menyuk, Jacqueline W. Liebergott, Martin C. Schultz.
      p.   cm.
   Includes bibliographical references and index.
   ISBN 0-8058-1772-7 (c). — ISBN 0-8058-1773-5 (p)
   1. Language acquisition.   I. Liebergott, Jacqueline W.
II. Schultz, Martin C., 1926–   .   III. Title.
P118.M399   1995
401 '.93—dc20   94-36167
                                                         CIP

Books published by Lawrence Erlbaum Associates are printed
on acid-free paper, and their bindings are chosen for strength
and durability.

Printed in the United States of America
10 9 8 7 6 5 4 3 2 1

Contents

Preface

This book is designed to provide practical information to those who are concerned with the development of young children. First, the authors wish to acquaint these investigators, educators, and clinicians with details about patterns of language development over the first 3 years of life. Although intensive studies have been carried out by examining from 1 to 20 children in the age range of 0 to 3 years, there has been no longitudinal study of a population as large as 53 children, nor have as many measures of language development been obtained from the same children. Examining language development from a broad perspective in this size sample allows us to see what generalizations can be made about patterns of language development.

The second purpose of the book is to examine the impact of such factors as biology, cognition, communication input, and the interaction of these factors, which traditionally have been held to play an important role, on the course of language development. Biological factors and risk were considered by selecting half of the infants from a premature group and the other half from a group of full-term infants. A fairly detailed medical history was obtained on all the premature infants. Thus, the fact of prematurity and the conditions that stem from prematurity allowed us to study some of the effects of the biological state of the infant on language development. The cognitive development of all the children was measured periodically over the 3 years, and the effect of cognitive variation on language development was observed. Finally, a detailed analysis of mothers' language to and conversational interaction with their infants was carried out to determine those input factors that seem most important for language development. The comparative influence of each and the interaction of all three were examined statistically from children's scores on standard language tests at age 3.

The third purpose of the book is to provide information to beginning investigators, early childhood educators, and clinicians that can help them in their practice. There is information about what appear to be good early predictors of language development at 3 years of age. There is also information about language assessment procedures that can be used with children below age 3, how these procedures can be used, what they tell us about the language development of young children, and which warning signs should probably be attended to and which can most likely be ignored. In addition, some suggestions are made about what patterns of communicative interaction during the different periods of development seem to be most successful in terms of language development outcomes at 3 years of age, and what the study indicates overall about appropriate intervention.

ACKNOWLEDGMENTS

The material reported in this book was, in its original form, a final report to the U. S. Department of Education, Office of Special Education and Rehabilitative Services (OSERS) Field-initiated Research Grant G008006727, entitled "A Prescriptive Manual for Parents and Teachers of Children At Risk for Language Disorders from Zero to Three Years of Age." The study that was the basis for the report was supported in part by the OSERS grant just named to M. C. Schultz, principal investigator and to J. W. Liebergott and P. Menyuk as co-investigators, and partially by funding to the principal investigator from the Esther S. & Joseph M. Shapiro Fund.

Our heartfelt thanks go to the families that participated in the study. We also thank the members of the research staff for their fine work. In particular, we thank Marie Chesnick and Linda Ferrier, who played a principal role in gathering the data and in keeping the families in the study.

Paula Menyuk
Jacqueline W. Liebergott
Martin C. Schultz

CHAPTER 1

The Study

Study of language development has been the focus of attention of a number of professions concerned with early childhood. Because language development plays a crucial role in social and cognitive development it has attracted the attention of educators and clinicians. Social and cognitive development, in turn, play a role in language development. In addition, the effect of biological state and maturation on language development has been a focus of attention. Researchers have studied premature as compared to full-term infants in hopes of determining the effects of biological state on development. Many studies have explored speech and language mastery in both full-term and premature infants as a way of examining whether or not there are early and late differences that can be found in this development due to prematurity per se or to the complicating medical or social factors that accompany prematurity. As stated, language development has been a focus of attention because of the important role it plays in social and academic development, although other aspects of development can be affected by prematurity and accompanying factors. (For further information on recent studies of the effect of prematurity on a number of aspects of development, outside of language development, during the early years of life, readers can look at Rosenblith, 1992.)

The questions of the comparative effect of social, cognitive, and biological factors and their interaction on language development has been examined in many studies. The answer to these questions are of theoretical and applied interest. The theoretical interest is that of explanation of this important development. The applied interest is to determine what may be important early deviations from normal patterns so that intervention may be planned. The study reported on in this volume was undertaken also to examine these

1

theoretical and applied questions. The primary study took place from 1982 to 1985. Although a great deal has been learned from many studies before and after the study, the questions have still not been thoroughly answered. The results of this study, we believe, contribute to the answers.

In this chapter we summarize some of the results of studies that have examined the question of the effect of prematurity and the factors that accompany the premature state on language development, and indicate why we think the questions still remain unanswered. We then describe how we carried out our study: who the paticipants in the study were (the infants and their families), how we got them to participate in the study, and the methodology we used to collect and code data on the children's language development. In subsequent chapters we discuss how we measured the children's cognitive and linguistic development, and what we found out about their cognitive and linguistic development over the first 3 years of their lives. In the final chapter we present a summary and what we think the implications of these findings are. As an epilogue, we present our findings on a follow-up study of some of the children. Finally, we indicate what we think are the most promising questions that remain to be asked.

CONTRASTING LANGUAGE DEVELOPMENT IN
FULL-TERM AND PREMATURE INFANTS

A large number of studies have focused on the question of the effect of prematurity on language development alone. Both older and recent studies of the language development of premature infants have found that they were comparatively delayed in the language they understood and the language they produced. These were the findings in a study carried out in the 1960s (DeHirsch, Jansky, & Langford, 1964), and in studies in the 1980s (Bailey & Wolery, 1989; Field, Dempsey, & Shumar, 1981; Siegel, 1982) and even in 1990s (McCormick & Schiefelbusch, 1990). Thus, over a period of almost 30 years, researchers have found that prematurity negatively affects language development, and for the most part, it delays it.

Although all of the studies just mentioned indicate a negative effect of prematurity on language development, which apparently places great importance on the effect of biological factors on this development, other studies indicate no such effect. Some studies comparing the language develoment of premature and full-term infants have found that early differences disappear at 2 to 3 years of age (Greenberg & Crnic, 1988; Ungerer & Sigman, 1983). A quite sizeable study reported (Aram, Hack, Hawkins, Weissman, & Borawski-Clark, 1991) concludes that specific language impairment (SLI), as defined and measured by certain standard tests, is not more frequent among the low birthweight children (infants weighing 1,500 grams or less at birth) than full-term children, at age 8. The children in both the very low birthweight (VLBW) and full weight populations were randomly selected from a community. There were more than 200 children in the low birthweight group and more than 300 children in the control group. Aram et al. (1991) also reviewed some 20 other studies that had examined this question and further concluded that the studies overall present a less than convincing argument that low birthweight is causally related to disordered speech and language. However, although the presence of a language disorder could not be attributed to low birthweight, there were significant differences between the low birthweight children and their controls on a number of measures of language development and the WISC–R, a standard measure of intelligence. Thus, one could conclude that, although language disorder was not related to birthweight, linguistic and cognitive delay might be.

Recent studies have asked whether or not prematurity affects other aspects of language development such as reading and writing. If such an effect is found it implies that early delays in oral language development, which may or may not disappear at 2 to 3 years of age, might affect later academic performance. Again the findings have been mixed. Some studies have found differences in the reading scores of prematurely born children, whereas others have found no such differences (Barsky & Siegel, 1992). In a study (Menyuk et al., 1991) that included some of the children who were infants in this study, it was found that some of the children who were born prematurely did have subtle oral language difficulties that were not evident when they spoke and, also, that they were not only significantly different from their age peers on a test of early reading development, but could be classified as *at risk* for reading. The emphasis is on the word some. Of the 27 premature infants who participated in the study, 4 performed as poorly as children diagnosed as having an SLI on standard tests of oral language development at 5 years old, 9 did as poorly as SLI children on an experimental oral language processing battery, and all of these 9 were identified as being at risk for reading failure at age 8. These latter findings are discussed at length in the final chapter of this book.

As can be seen, different studies have obtained widely different answers to the question. The reasons for the differences in findings are multiple. First, there is a wide diversity in the biological state of premature infants, regardless of their weight, although these two aspects of prematurity are related. Such biological risk factors as fetal distress, infection or sepsis, respiratory distress syndrome (RDS), metabolic problems and intraventricular hemorrhaging (IVH) may accompany low birthweight. The incidence of biological insult is greater, the smaller the infant. Such factors appear to play an important role in language development outcomes for premature infants. Another consideration is that infants who are premature and their full weight controls are born into families that vary widely in terms of socioeconomic status (SES) and cultural background, although, again, there is a trend. Premature births are more prevalent among poor women due to differences in nutrition and health–care delivery. Obviously, such socioeconomic and sociocultural differences can affect children's performance on standard measures of language development. Biological factors associated with prematurity and social factors, in interaction with each other, might differentially affect language development.

Another complexity leading to differences in findings of studies might be that the prematurity of the infant affects mother–child interaction, and does so in differing ways depending on the personalities of an individual dyad (mother–infant pair) as well as the factors just cited. Some mothers perceive their premature children as being handicapped, and this can lead to differences in mother–child interaction (Brown & Bakeman, 1980; Sameroff & Chandler, 1975). Some mothers of premature children have been found to try harder. In one study of the first year of life of premature children, it was found that their mothers were more active and offered more stimulation than mothers of full–term infants, but that the infants themselves were less responsive as well as less competent than their full–term age peers (Crnic, Ragozin, Greenberg, Robinson, & Basham, 1983). This lack of responsiveness might have been the result of overstimulation. Clearly, studies finding differences when examining the effect of prematurity on language development versus the findings of no differences might be due to individual mother–child communicative interaction factors as well as to the biological and social factors discussed previously.

Differences in the measures of language development used in different studies might be one last factor to explain these variable findings. That is, which aspects of language were being measured, how they are measured, and what ages they were being measured at. In the Aram et al. (1991) study reported previously, a number of studies are briefly reviewed. In 15 studies listed, no two are alike in the measures used. In some, assessment of language takes place at one point and in others over a period of time, and at different ages from 9 months to 9 years. Measured IQ, vocabulary, articulation, or sentence comprehension and production (to mention a few developmental aspects) are different outcome measures reported on in different studies.

To summarize, there is a significant interest in explanations of language development and in detailing positive and negative influences on its rate and course. Many researchers have chosen to contrast development in premature and full–term children because prematurity may be expressed through differences in biological integrity, in cognitive maturity, and in caregiver–infant interaction. That is, the accompaniments of prematurity can be viewed as challenges to normal development so that a study population including premature as well as full–term children provides examples of various normal but differing paths as well as the course or courses of troubled children. Through careful documentation of the biological and environmental factors, plus when and how language learning deviates from the normal course, researchers have hoped to sort out the individual influences, their interactions, and their relative potencies.

The review of research findings provides some sense of how each of several influences impacts development but most studies followed too few children for too short a period, and the measures that were used varied by study. Therefore, the results of comparative research with premature and full-term infants have not led to assured or useful answers to the questions about comparative effects of biological, social, and cognitive influences on language development and their possible interaction.

There seemed to be a clear need for a study that would redress as many of these inadequacies as could reasonably be taken into consideration with a limited set of resources. Although many of the questions were straightforward, it could not be expected that the answers would be simple. The necessities were to observe developmental speech and language behaviors in a variety of children of differing backgrounds, under conditions that were as minimally artificial as could be managed. Those data would then have to be coupled with information on the biological integrity of the child, the child's cognitive abilities, and important characteristics of the child's environment, notably the infants' interactions with their primary caregivers. All measures had to be acquired under stringent conditions of quality control, without having the need for rigor impact on the in-home behaviors of child or caregiver.

GENERAL CHARACTERISTICS OF THE STUDY

The specific measures that were scheduled and taken are discussed in a later section, but first the overall plan. The research was designed to obtain high quality recordings and observations of each child's vocal behaviors and language growth, and of the associated, simultaneous environmental influences, from routine and periodic home visits. The goal was to collect samples of the child's language emergence, and caregiver–child interaction, as well as what the child had not yet mastered.

Although it was desirable to observe each child continually from birth to 3 years of age (when standard tests can be used to assess and predict language development), the available funding was insufficient to support the total period required to recruit families into the study, watch 3 years of development, and then have time to evaluate the data. As an alternative, half the children were recruited into the study at birth and followed through 30 months of age, the other half were recruited into the study beginning at 9 months of age and exited after their 36-month evaluation. By synthesizing the trends of the findings, we expected to obtain a coherent view of the course of the first 3 years. The younger and older groups were equal in size and there were equal numbers of premature and full-term children in each.

Home visits were scheduled periodically and so as to accomodate the rhythms of both primary caregiver (mother mostly) and infant. Each family was linked with a specific member of the study group. That person was the regular and expected visitor and she established a close personal relationship with mother and infant and, often, with other family members as well. Family members were made full partners in the ongoing study to minimize the practice of any withholding behaviors from any party.

The full-term children in the study were recruited because they were born in a university medical school teaching hospital. This introduced some subtle selection criteria (unconscious on our part). Their families resided in or near a large metropolitan center and mothers chose obstetricians who delivered in a teaching hospital of a university medical school. Not so for the premature babies. Many of them were sent from various parts of the state to the medical school teaching hospital after birth because of prematurity and required special care. These babies were unselected by us, except for having been born very early and were not subject to the same sampling bias.

HOW THE STUDY WAS CARRIED OUT

To find out what the development of language looks like over the first 3 years of life, we chose to visit the infants in their homes. We felt that only by observing the children as they interacted and conversed spontaneously with their caregivers and their siblings would we be able to describe their language as it emerged. Recording the children in their homes also allowed us to observe, measure, and describe the natural interactions that might influence the children's patterns of language development. We originally scheduled visits with each family a minimumof 23 times and a maximum of 28 times over a 2 1/2-year period but actually the children were seen more frequently than this. We often attended birthday parties and other family events. Also, on occasion the recordings were terrible or we missed recording all together because the tape recorders were broken or had weak batteries, or the child refused to talk very much or play some games with us. In cases such as this we went back to visit.

An average visit lasted 2 hours. Most often, one of the hours was spent with the caregiver (most frequently the mother) and child while they did what infants and their caregivers do during the day. The activities they engaged in varied depending on the time of day and the individual dyad. We did not ask the mothers to do anything special and we tried to schedule the visit at a convenient time for the family. Some visits involved our playing with and testing the children. These tests were experimenter-designed measures of speech sound discrimination and comprehension of multiword phrases and sentences. These are described in detail in chapter 2. When the children were 2 1/2 to 3 years of age they were brought to a speech clinic at a metropolitan hospital for a full diagnostic battery of standardized tests. These tests were administered by a certified speech and language pathologist.

Who the Children Were

In this section of the chapter we describe how we found the children in the study, what criteria we used to admit them, and what their birth conditions were. Some background information on their families will be given.

Locating the Children. We began the study by entering 56 different children and their families, 28 premature and 28 full-term babies. The number of babies was determined by two factors. First, we needed to have a large enough number from which to make meaningful generalizations about patterns of language development. Because many previous intensive studies of language development had had as few as 3 children in their population, and most studies had fewer then 20, we were confident that we had a substantial number. Second, the population had to be small enough so that, given the resources of the project and its time course (3 years), we could not only maintain personal contact and knowledge of each family but, also, have the time to analyze carefully the massive amount of data we were going to collect from each child and family.

Half of each group of children, full-term and premature, entered the study when they were born, and were seen for their first home visit during their first month of life. This, of course was not true for some of the premature infants who were kept in hospital for a number of months. The other half of each group was seen for the first time when they were 9 months of age and recording begun at 10 months. We followed the younger children from birth through 30 months of age, and followed the older children from 9 through 36 months of age. This was done so that we would have the time in the 3-year course of the study to examine the course of language development over the first 3 years of life. If all the children had been entered at birth we would only have been able to study language development over the first 2 1/2 years of life. Many standard tests of language development are appropriate for use only with children 3 years old or older.

Premature children were equated with the full-term children by using their gestational age birth date. For several of our premature newborns this meant that they were in an intensive care unit while we waited for them to reach their gestational birth date.

Of the 56 families, 53 completed the study. One family left the study because they moved out of the state, the other because the mother returned to full-time employment and did not want to be visited at night or on weekends. A third dropped out after a change in family status. Thus, data obtained at the beginning of the study include all 56 children, whereas data obtained at later stages report on from 53 to 56 children,

A different procedure was used to locate the children in the younger and older age groups. To find the younger infants, members of the project staff first checked the birth records of two large metropolitan hospitals. If an infant and his or her family met our criteria, a member of the team would explain the purposes and goals of the project to the mother. Often we would return at a later time so that we could meet both parents and sometimes grandparents and other members of the family. If the parents indicated that they were interested, we would visit the family in their home, review the goals of the project, answer questions, collect background information, and have the parents sign a consent form.

The older group of children in our study were recruited by mail. First the hospital records were checked for the names of children who were the right age and met our subject criteria. We then sent a letter to the homes of each of these children explaining the project goals and telling the parents that we would call in a few days to discuss their participation. At the time of the phone call, if the parents expressed interest we made an appointment to visit them in their homes.

Characteristics of the Babies.   The babies differed markedly in their status as newborns. The characteristics of the premature group and the full-term group are summarized in Table 1.1. This table describes the significant differences between the two groups of infants in birthweight, weeks of gestation and their 1- and 5-minute Apgar scores. All of these differences between premature and

TABLE 1.1
Newborn Characteristics of Premature and Full-Term Infants

Birthweight		Weeks Premature	1-Minute Apgar	5-Minute Apgar
Full-term				
Means	3,476.7 grams	0	7.6	8.7
Range	2,693–4,933	0	2–9	7–10
SD	560.5	0	1.80	.12
Premature				
Means	1,575.2	7.9	5.7	7.6
Range	794–2,500	3–13	1–9	1–9
SD	435.3	2.60	2.39	2.2

full-term babies were significantly different at $p < .01$. The groups were not different in terms of sex as each group had an approximately equal number of boys and girls. The premature group consisted of 14 boys and 14 girls and the full-term group had 15 girls and 13 boys.

Half the children entered the project at birth and half entered at 9 months of age, thus we contrasted the older and younger infants in each group on all of the birth measures to determine that they were not significantly different. Table 1.2 describes the birth measures of the younger and the older groups. On each measure, statistical tests revealed no significant differences. Therefore, unless we indicate otherwise, we discuss language development in both younger and older premature infants together, and we do the same for all the full-term children.

Prematurity alone does not appear to be a good predictor of language development outcomes, as we indicated in a previous section of this chapter, As we also indicated, other biological measures appear to be related to poor language outcomes for some premature infants. Health-care professionals and researchers have developed some broadly based indices to identify children at risk, regardless of prematurity. Some of these indices have been successful in predicting how the infant will function at a very young age (1 year) and are less successful in predicting developmental status at a later age (3 years). Because one of our goals was to determine those biological and environmental factors that might affect patterns of language development, in conjunction with prematurity, we developed a risk index that included reproductive, perinatal, and environmental variables, despite the inconclusive findings. Table 1.3 defines each of the risk indicators, and displays its incidence in the full-term and premature groups. As can be seen in this table, and as might be expected, some biological risk factors were much more frequent in the premature than in the full-term group.

The Families. The families who participated in the project were distributed among four social classes. None of the families was at the poverty level, and there was a reasonably equal distribution of social class across groups. The families were assigned to a particular class based on the father's occupation,

TABLE 1.2
Comparison of Characteristics of Younger and Older Groups

	Premature		Full-Term	
Means of	*Younger*	*Older*	*Younger*	*Older*
Birthweight	1,514.5	1,685.9	3,430.6	3,511.4
Weeks premature	8.5	7.1	0	0
1-minute Apgar	5.3	6.4	7.7	7.6
5-minute Apgar	7.2	8.1	8.8	8.8

TABLE 1.3
Risk Index

Risk Indicators	Risk Definitions	Full-Term	Premature
Reproductive risk			
Smoking	More than 30 cigarettes per day	3	3
Previous abortions	Any pregnancy terminating before 20 weeks or a birthweight less than 500 grams	0	1
Previous prematures	Previous babies born at less that 37 weeks gestation or less than 2,500 grams	0	3
Previous stillbirths	Any occurrence of the birth of an infant born dead who is greater than 20 weeks gestational age and heavier than 500 grams at birth	1	1
Parity	Firstborn or seventh born child	16	16
Maternal age	Younger than 18 years or older than 30 years	1	9
Maternal chronic disease	Illnesses such as diabetes and hypertension that begin prior to conception and continue through pregnancy	1	2
Chronic drug use	Illegal use of drugs, or use of approved medication in an abusive fashion	0	0
Chronic alcohol use	Alcohol used in an abusive fashion. Child reported as showing signs of fetal alcohol syndrome	1	1
Environmental risk			
Social class	Member of lowest socioeconomic class	3	6
Gender	Male child	12	15
Maternal education	Less than high school	0	1
Paternal education	Less than high school	1	1
Perinatal risk			
Birthweight	Less than 2,500 grams	0	28
Gestational age	Less than 37 weeks	0	28
1-minute Apgar	Less than 6	4	15
5-Minute Apgar	Less than 6	0	3
Hyperbilirubinemia	Bilirubin greater than 14mg./100	0	8
Respiratory distress	Presence of one of the following for more than 1 hour (a) grunting, (b) retractions, (c) respiratory rate greater than 60,0, (d) nasal flaring	1	16
Ventilation	Assisted ventilation by mask or tube, continuous positive pressure air way	1	13
CNS—hemorrhage	Medical documentation of hemorrhage	0	2
Noninfectious diseases	All other major illnesses	0	5

source of income, dwelling area, and amount of parental education. There were no statistical differences in the numbers of premature and full-term, younger and older children who could be assigned to each of the four SES status groups. There were 8 children in the upper middle-class group (3 younger full-term, 2 younger premature, 1 older full-term and 2 older premature). There were 20 children in the middle-class group (6 younger full-term, 4 younger premature, 5 older full-term, and 5 premature). There were 21 children in the lower middle-class group (4 younger full-term, 6 younger premature, 7 older full-term, and 4 premature). There were 7 children in the lower class group (1 younger full-term, 2 younger premature, 1 older full-term, and 3 older premature). There were also no differences among the four groups when their families were compared for age, education level, level of occupation, and number of siblings. These data are shown in Table 1.4.

The Babies' Hearing.   Because hearing plays a crucial role in vocal language development, we felt it was necessary to assess as carefully as possible, the hearing of the children in the study. Two procedures were used to assess their hearing. All of the children who entered the study as newborns had their

TABLE 1.4
Family Descriptions

Group	N	Mother's Age	Father's Age	Mother's Educ.	Father's Educ.	Mother's Occup.	Father' Occup	Older Sibs
Young full-term	14							
Mean		31.00	34.71	15.43	17.07	2.50[a]	3.00[a]	0.93
Range		25-37	29-43	13-17	13-20	2-8	1-5	0-5
SD		2.91	3.84	1.28	1.98	1.45	1.41	1.38
Young Premature	14							
Mean		30.21	32.78	14.86	14.50	1.93	2.70	0.64
Range		23-36	28-39	12-18	10-19	1-8	1-6	0-3
SD		3.62	3.42	1.99	2.65	2.65	1.27	.84
Old full-term	14							
Mean		29.86	30.64	15.57	15.64	3.00	2.36.	0.64
Range		24-35	25-36	12-17	10-18	2-8	1-6	0-2
SD		3.30	3.10	1.34	2.65	0.96	1.72	0.74
Old Premature	14							
Mean		28.93	32.14	14.57	15.43	2.43	2.00	0.36
Range		16-37	27-52	7-17	12-19	1-8	1-6	0-2
SD		6.30	7.66	2.79	2.71	2.17	1.03	0.63

[a]Occupations are assigned numerical scores with values from 1 to 4, according to the Warner Scales. A value of 1 is the highest score on the scales.

hearing evaluated using auditory brainstem response (ABR) procedures. For most of this group of 28 children the ABR was done prior to their leaving the hospital. For the rest, it was completed during the first few months of life. All of the children's hearing was found to be within normal limits. The entire group of children also had their hearing evaluated at a children's hospital during the second year of life. The children had their hearing screened at 10 dB ML at 500, 1000, 2000 and 4000 Hz. All children passed this hearing screening, although three initially failed. These three children were found to have otitis media (middle ear infection) and had fluid in their middle ears. They were referred to otologists for medical management, subsequently rescreened, and found to have hearing within the same normal limits as the rest of the children.

During the project, many children had episodes of recurring otitis media. The pediatricians of 17 of the children we studied reported prescribing medication two or more times for treatment. Of these 17 children, 5 had a tube or tubes surgically placed into their eardrums to allow the fluid to drain from the middle ear. The consequences of this experience are discussed to some extent in the final chapters of the book when the exit data are discussed.

Recording Procedures

We used an audio system to ensure good quality recordings of the infant, mother, and other people in the home without limiting their freedom of movement. Each recording visit involved a full-time member of the research staff and an assistant. Three portable battery-powered tape recorders were used: one to record the vocalizations and speech of the infant, a second one to record the mother's speech, and a third to record a continuous commentary on the ongoing activity in the environment in which the infant's and the mother's communicative interactions were taking place. The recording set-up is shown in Fig. 1.1. We went to great lengths In order to ensure that accurate recordings were made in less than an ideal situation. We describe in some detail the instruments that were used to make the home recordings so that those who wish to undertake similar studies can have some idea of what was done to make those recordings as accurate as possible.

The infants' utterances (labeled 1 in Fig.1.1) were recorded on a Sony TC-D5M cassette recorder with an AKG C-451 EB/CK-8 shotgun directional microphone hand held by one team member. The microphone was held between 12 inches and 4 feet in front of the infant's face. At the very earliest ages the infants appeared to ignore the microphone. At 6 months of age many of the infants spent time reaching and grasping for the microphone. At one meeting of the research team there was a discussion of marketing a replica of the microphone as a new infant toy, and donating the proceeds to the research project. However, for approximately the next 6 to 8 months, most of the children ignored the equipment. Sometime around 14 months each of the

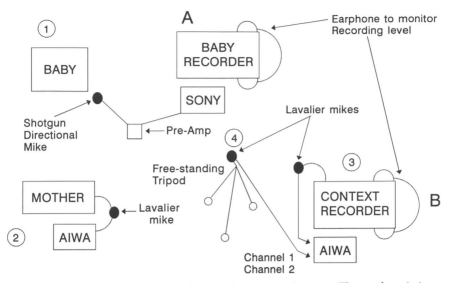

FIG. 1.1 Recording set-up. A and B are the two experimenters. The numbers 1–4 represent the four acoustic signals being recorded into the portable recorders. The diagram illustrates the approximate spatial relationships of the participants.

babies developed his or her own game with the microphone and the person at the other end of it. They would run from one end of the room or house to the other, and laugh at the home visitor who was desperately trying to keep up. As soon as possible after this, we replaced the hand-held unit with a set-up similar to the one used with the mothers. This is described later. For the most part, the infants enjoyed wearing "recording things like their moms," and usually quickly became interested in other toys and objects that were in the home after the visitor set up the equipment.

Two smaller high quality AIWA stereo cassette tape recorders were used to record the mother's utterances and a contextual commentary made by the second team member. The mother (labeled 2 in Fig. 1.1) wore one of these lightweight recorders on a shoulder strap, with a small lavalier miocrophone that clipped onto her blouse. This external microphone played into one channel of the stereophonic recorder. The internal microphone of this recorder acted as a back-up system in case the external microphone failed. This arrangement allowed the mother unrestricted movement and provided clear recordings of her speech. The other AIWA cassette recorder was worn by the other team member (labeled 3 in Fig. 1.1), acting as the recorder of the context, events, and objects in the environment. The context recorder spoke *sotto voce* into a Shure directional microphone that was attached to a headset holding the microphone close to the mouth. This ensured that the commentary about the context did not interfere with the infant or mother recording that needed to remain as free as possible from the background noise.

Finally, to allow synchronization of the contextual commentary with both mother's and infant's speech, a lavalier external microphone was clipped to a free-standing tripod (labeled 4 in Fig. 1.1), placed as close as possible to both infant and mother. This signal was recorded onto the second channel of the AIWA recorder carried by the context recorder. The tripod was sturdy enough to withstand crawling infants but was portable enough to be moved around the house. Both team members wore earphones to monitor sound levels and make necessary adjustments as the recordings were made.

When the infants were 12, 22, and 29 months old, we made 30-minute videotape recordings in addition to the audio recordings. Currently, video rather than audio recordings are standardly used to record mother–child communicative interaction. However, given the auditory fidelity of the video equipment at the time, it was felt that because information on vocal language development and interaction was the focus of the study, great efforts should be made to obtain as good quality audio recordings as possible.

Transcribing and Coding the Recordings

Our original plan was to have one of the members of the research team who had visited with the family for that session transcribe the tape. We felt that this would give us the most accurate transcription. We found, however, that the schedule of our research assistants and the huge amount of tape we had to transcribe made this impractical. Therefore, the original transcripts were made by a variety of project personnel. The tapes were transcribed in ordinary English orthography. A second member of the research project staff checked the transcriptions. Different amounts of the tape recordings we had obtained were transcribed each month depending on the types of analyses to be carried out. In all, we transcribed and analyzed more than 300 utterances from each of more than 550 recording sessions. Our rule for tape transcriptions was to begin transcribing each tape 15 minutes into the sessions. This allowed time for the mothers to show us their children's newest accomplishments, for everyone to get reacquainted and for everyone, once again, to get used to the introduction of the recording equipment. There were times when we could not follow this procedure. This occurred when we needed samples of a specified length (e.g., the proportion of babbled utterances within a sample of 100 utterances) and when a particular child did not talk very much. In these instances we would use the first 15 minutes rather than analyze fewer utterances.

Portions of several months' tapes were transcribed phonetically to examine phonological or speech sound development in the children. The trained phonetician on the project did the phonetic transcription. The words selected for analysis were transcribed into International Phonetic Alphabet (IPA) symbols with the modifications described by researchers on the Stanford Child Phonology Project (referred to in Ferguson & Farwell, 1975). Half of the samples were coded by one assistant and the other half were coded by a second assistant. Coding reliability was obtained by having 20% of the words from each sample transcribed a second time by the alternate assistant. The percentage of agreement per consonantal phoneme or sound (vowels were excluded and not used in the analyses) was calculated. It was found that there was 85% agreement between the coders in the categorization of all sounds of all the children across the ages at which phonological production was analyzed.

Each month's tapes were coded by members of the project staff specifically trained to use the scoring procedures. The procedure used to ensure reliability was to have two or more members of the staff practice coding several transcipts together. During this time, a series of rules to follow for the coding of a particular aspect of language was developed and recorded. For each aspect, a member of the research staff was selected as the quality control person. This person established the reliability of coding across each coder of that particular aspect of language. A level of at least 80% agreement across coders was set as the standard. The quality control person rescored 10% of each sample for this aspect. If interjudge agreement on this aspect was less than 80%, the data on this aspect would be rescored by the quality control person.

Summary

In summary, we were able to follow the language development of 53 children over a 30-month period. Half of the children were born prematurely and half were full-term. We began studying half of them at birth and half when they were 9 months of age. We continued to study the newborns until they were 2 1/2 years old and the older children were 3. We measured many aspects of their cognitive and language development, and we also measured how their mothers (primarily) and other caregivers spoke to them. We used these measures to describe patterns of development in the children as a whole, and in the premature and full-term children separately. We also examined how these developments and types of language input were related to standard test performance at the end of the study. One set of questions we asked in the study was concerned with the effects of differences in biological state on the course of language development. To that end we selected a group of premature and a group of full-term infants to study where differences in biological state were guaranteed. Another set of questions was concerned with the effects of mother language input and communication interaction on the course of language development. A third set of questions was concerned with the effect of cognitive development on the course of language development. We then asked about the effect of the interaction of these factors on language development. We were also interested in determining what early language behaviors on the part of the infant or mother might signal later language problems.

CHAPTER 2

Description of
Measures Used

Measures of cognitive and speech and language development were obtained from the infants in our study. We also obtained a number of measures of caregivers' interactions with the children. Most often the measures of the children that we selected were those frequently used by both practitioners and researchers with children in the age range of 0 to 3 years. We also used measures that we ourselves developed based on the research literature. The source of a particular measurement, be it standard or developed by us, is indicated so that interested readers can examine the original data. In one instance, a research measure has been developed into a test and we provide the reference for this test. Measures of speech and language development are discussed separately. Although speech and language development are intimately related to each other they also represent distinct aspects of development. Speech is perceived and produced earlier than recognized categories of language such as words and sentences, and speech perception and production require somewhat different abilities than language production and perception.

Many methods for coding and analyzing speech and language perception and production had been developed before this study was carried out. Since the time of the study, methods for coding data for computer input and quantification have become available (MacWhinney, 1991). This is a giant step forward and allows a number of researchers to share the same or similar bodies of data. However, computerization and quantification of data do not bypass the need for careful transcription nor selection of particular language categories for quantification (MacWhinney & Snow, 1992). The measures we selected to use are those that we believe are, for the most part, easily obtainable by educators and clinicians but, nevertheless, yield important data.

Further, we think that during the first 3 years of life there are particular language categories of speech and language behavior that should be measured to determine the infant's course of language development and we think we did this. Because we thought that other measures that can impact on this development, cognitive maturation and maternal input over time should be obtained simultaneously, we have measures of these developmental changes as well.

MEASURES OF COGNITIVE DEVELOPMENT

The children's cognitive development was assessed several times over the course of the project. Table 2.1 lists the measures and the ages at which they were administered to the children who entered the study at birth (Group 1) and those who entered at 9 months (Group 2). Each of these measures is standardized, and from them we obtained age-equivalent scores that were both corrected and noncorrected for prematurity.

In doing our assessment of the children's cognitive ability, we used different measures for several reasons. We used the Ordinal Scales of Psychological Development (Uzgiris & Hunt, 1975), an instrument based on the work of Jean Piaget. We gave this test because previous research had suggested that what it measured was related to language development. The scales assess children's acquisition of sensory and motor behavior that, according to Piaget, underpins the development of representation. This development has been said to be related to language development either as a precursor to development of aspects of language (Nicolich, 1981) or as a simultaneous development (Gopnik & Meltzoff, 1986). We also used the Bayley Scales (Bayley, 1969) for two reasons. Although some of the behaviors on the Ordinal Scales are also measured by the Bayley Scales, the latter scales presumably are designed to give a much broader assessment of cognitive functioning that appraises mental and motor development separately. Fur-

TABLE 2.1
Tests of Cognitive Development

	Age of Assessment	
Test	Group 1	Group 2
Bayley Scales of Infant Development	13 months	13 months
Uzgiris and Hunt:		
Ordinal Scales of Psychological Development	19 months	19 months
Bayley Scales of Infant Development	28 months	28 months
McCarthy Scales of Children's Mental Ability	30 months	36 months

ther, these latter scales are the ones that were used most frequently by other researchers to measure cognition during the early years of life. These scales have been revised very recently and have become available for general use (Bayley, 1993). The revised Bayley Scales are advertised as being appropriate for infants from 1 to 42 months. The last measure we used was a substitute for the Bayley and its selection was based on the fact that it was more age appropriate. The McCarthy Scales (McCarthy, 1970) also yield general measures of children's cognitive abilities, and are comparable to the Bayley Scales. We switched to the McCarthy Scales from the original Bayley because the latter measure is an inappropriate test for children much beyond 2 years.

MEASURES OF SPEECH DEVELOPMENT

Our primary interest in the babies' acquisition of speech, like their acquisition of other aspects of language, was to determine what similarities or differences existed between the speech development of premature and full-term infants. Further we wished to determine if earlier behaviors predicted later behaviors. The behaviors sampled were numerous and differed according to the children's stage of development. Table 2.2 is a summary of the various measures we derived and the ages at which they were taken. Most of the measures discussed here were obtained from the audio recordings. The later phonetic measures are based on Ingram's (1981) procedures for analyzing the speech sound units and sequences in natural speech samples. These procedures focus on the child's ability to reach phoneme target articulations (e.g., to make a /t/ when he or she means to say a word that has a /t/, such as "table"), and they primarily concern consonant production.

TABLE 2.2
Measures of Speech Development by Age and Group

Procedure	Age of Administration	
	Group 1	Group 2
Elicited cry	1 & 3 months	
Agony ratio	8, 10, & 12 months	10 & 12 months
Structured vocalizations	8, 10, & 12 months	10 & 12 months
Proportion of words to total vocalizations	16 months	16 months
Proportion of closed syllables	22 & 29 months	22, 29, & 35 months
Articulation score	22 & 29 months	22, 29, & 35 months
Phonetic score	22 & 29 months	22, 29, & 35 months
Match score	22 & 29 months	22, 29, & 35 months
Match indices	22 & 29 months	22, 29, & 35 months
Acoustic analysis	12, 14, 16, 19, 22 months	12, 14, 16, 19, 22 months
Speech discrimination	18 to 29 months	18 to 35 months

We also measured speech sound discrimination at a later age. Speech discrimination during infancy is an area of research that has flourished tremendously from the time of our study until the present (Menyuk, 1992; Yeni-Komshian, 1993). However, procedures for the testing of infant speech discrimination require laboratory testing conditions and a great deal of expenditure of time on the part of infants and mothers. Frequently, a large number of infants within a study population do not provide clear data. Given these factors, very young infant's speech discrimination was not part of our study. The infant's ability to discriminate among speech sounds and to segment speech sequences during the early months of life can have bearing on later speech and language development (Morgan & Saffron, 1992). However, the relation between these abilities and these later developments have yet to be clarified.

Elicited Cry

Measurement of infants' crying has for a long time been looked at as a possible very early measure that might predict later developmental speech and language problems. Early crying is unlikely to show environmental influences; it reflects the biological state of the infant. Like others, we were interested in determining if early cry behaviors could be used to tell us anything about the later speech and language development of the infants.

To obtain this measure from our babies, we elicited three cries from each infant in Group 1 during the home visits made in Months 1 and 3. We got the babies to cry by snapping an elastic band against the sole of the infant's foot using a sling-shot type device. Our sling-shots allowed us to be sure that each baby was stimulated with approximately equal intensity. The cries were tape-recorded, and the first three cry exhalations from each of the three cries obtained in each month were analyzed acoustically.

Agony Ratio

This measure assessed the proportion of involuntary nonspeech vocalizations that the babies made during the 8th, 10th, and 12th month of life. It included all crying, coughing, hiccupping, sneezing, and so on, that the babies produced, unless we had evidence that the vocalizations were intentional. As an example of intention, some of the children played imitation games with their mothers. The mother would cough, then the baby would cough, and then the mother would cough, and so on.

Structured Vocalizations

This was a measure of the proportion of syllabic vocalizations to the total vocalizations produced by the baby. Syllabic vocalizations are those composed of a sequence of a consonant alternating with a vowel (CV or VC or CVC or VCV). Subcategories of structured vocalizations include reduplicated babble, variegated babble, and something we called gibberish. A reduplicated babble is a multisyllabic utterance in which all syllables are alike. /Mamama/ is a reduplicated babble. Variegated babbles are also multisyllabic but the syllables differ. Something like /mapa/ or /dagi/ would be considered a variegated babble. Gibberish is a sequence of vocalizations that contains both syllables and nonsyllabic vocalizations. An example is hard to come up with. The baby sounds as if she is making a short serious speech. Our babies' vocalizations were examined for the presence of syllabic structures and the subcategories of these structures. These subcategorizations are based on those discussed in Oller (1981).

Proportion of Words to Vocalizations

This measure is the proportion of utterances that contain words in a sample of 100 consecutive utterances. The measure is a relatively simple one to calculate as it requires merely counting from the transcript the number of utterances from the total sample of 100 that the transcribers could interpret. This measure and the previous one could be considered as developmental changes in the articulation abilities of the children. The increasing number of syllabic utterances indicates increasing control of the speech production mechanism. This latter development, increasing number of recognizable words among structured vocalizations, not only indicates increasing control of the vocal mechanism, but also the coordination of speech with meanings in the language the child hears. Therefore, we felt that this behavior measures lexical development as well as speech development. For this reason we also refer to it when we discuss language development.

Sound Development in Words

Children's abilities to produce sounds in words were measured in various ways. Table 2.3 defines how we calculated each of these measures from the phonetically transcribed language samples we obtained from the children at 22, 29, and 35 months of age. These were the measures taken from Ingram (1981).

Acoustic Analyses

The speech of young children during the period in which they were acquiring words was examined acoustically. For each child, five utterances from the spontaneous speech samples, during five consecutive home recoding sessions, were analyzed. The sessions were spaced at intervals of 2 or 3 months.

TABLE 2.3
Measures of Speech Sound Development

Measure	Definition
Proportion of closed syllables	The number of words in which the child produced a final consonant divided by the number of words that required a final consonant
Articulation score	The number of initial and final consonant sounds that reached some preset minimum count.
Phonetic ability	The number of consonants produced out of 43 possible consonants. This measure and the one above assess sound production ability irrespective of the adult target.
Matches	Three match scores were calculated. They were the number of initial sounds that matched the adult target, the number of final sounds that matched, and the total number of sounds that matched. The number of sounds matched was always determined as a proportion of the number of different sounds attempted.
Match index	This score was derived by cumulating the number of sounds matched over the two or three time periods sampled and multiplying this score times the match score. That is, we multiplied the cumulative number of sounds matched in the initial position by the initial match score, the cumulative number of sounds matched in the final position by the final match score and the total cumulative number of sounds matched by the total match score.

The first session was defined arbitrarily as the session in which the child first produced at least five words containing the vowels /i/ as in bee, /I/ as in kit, u as in boot, /ʊ/ as in book, /ɑ/ as in pot, and /ɔ/ as in bought. We chose these sounds for two reasons. Vowels are, on the whole, mastered before consonants and these vowels represent different places of articulation in the mouth, from front to back and from high to low. The vowel sounds /i/. /I/, /u/ and /ʊ/ are made high in the mouth, whereas /a/ and /ɔ/ are made low. The sounds /i/ and /I/ are made in the front of the mouth, whereas /u/, /ʊ/, /ɑ/, and /ɔ/ are made in the back. We, therefore, could assess the time and order in which children were able to target these positions for articulation.

For some children, those who said words early in our late first-year visits, the speech sampling sequence consisted of Months 12, 14, 16, 19, and 22. For other children, who began lexical development later, we began sampling their speech at 14 months or, in some instances, later still. The selection of utterances was based on the vowels and consonants in the words that were glossed by the person doing the transcription, rather than a phonetic transcription of the sounds in the utterance. For example, if the child's utterance was glossed as /gɔg/ for "dog", the word was treated as containing the sound /ɔ/. In this way, the child's approximations to the production of the sound /ɔ/ could be determined. Only words with known referents were used so that target vowels could be determined. The acoustic measurements were taken from the spectrograms (pictures of sounds) that were the result of the children's production of utterances. Although these pictures were quite crude, measures of the duration of a vowel and its frequency characteristics (fundamental frequency and first and second formant frequencies) could be obtained. Examples of what a child's spectrogram looks like can be found in Lieberman (1980).

Speech Discrimination

The last measure of speech assessed children's ability to hear the difference between sounds in words. The children were asked to discriminate between six contrasting pairs of words. The order in which they were presented was varied. One member of the pair was a familiar word, and the other was a nonsense word. Children were asked to identify the object that the speech sound sequence referred to. The pairs of sequences were very similar in that they differed by only one sound. We selected the pairs on the basis of the order of speech sound discriminations as reported in previous studies. Two pairs were said to develop early (rock–zock and lock–dock), two late (cup–gup and duck–juck) and two in the middle (sock–shock and book–dook).

We tested the children at 3-month intervals, beginning when they were a 18 months old. The procedure we used is described in Eilers and Oller (1975). We used familiar objects to represent the real words and showed them unfamiliar objects to represent the nonsense words. The children were encouraged to play with the toys and to name them. In this way some unknown words were learned. When we were sure the children at least recognized the name of the familar object, we placed that object on top of a container and the unfamiliar object on top of another container. One of the containers held a treat, usually cereal or raisins. The child was then told to find the treat in the container on which the real object was placed or in the container with the nonsense object. In order to be credited with making the discrimination the child had to make the right choice seven out of eight times and order of presentation was randomized. Specific information on the presentation and scoring of this speech discrimination test is presented in Appendix F.

MEASURES OF LANGUAGE DEVELOPMENT

Table 2.4 summarizes the categories of measures we obtained to assess the children's development of language. Some of these measures were obtained from the language produced by the children during our visits and others from the results of small tasks that we gave the children. Most of these measures have been used by other investigators, and when possible, we attempted to follow their descriptions on how to codify these measures. We did this so that we could compare our findings with those of other studies and in this way

TABLE 2.4
Measures of Language Development by Age and Group

Procedure	Age of Administration	
	Group 1	Group 2
Lexical diary	8–24 months	10–24 months
Vocabulary diversity	22, 25, & 29 months	22, 25, 29, & 35 months
Two-part sentence comprehension	14–30 months	14–32 months
Multiword comprehension	27 months	27 months
MLU	22, 25, & 29 months	22, 25, 29, & 35 months
Syntactic structures	25 & 29 months	25, 29, & 35 months
Morpheme development	25 & 29 months	25, 29, & 35 months
Semantic roles	25 months	25 months
Pragmatic functions	25 & 29 months	22, 29, & 35 months
Participation in conversation	25 & 29 months	25, 29, & 35 months
Imitation-expansion paraphrase	25 & 29 months	25, 29, & 35 months

examine the consistency of results with nonstandardized measures. Specific references to previous work are included with our description of each measure so that, as stated, those who are interested may consult the original references for additional information. The appendices to this book contain the protocols and coding instructions that were developed by the project staff. Each of the 11 measures that we used and the way in which we obtained each measure can be considered a mini-test of an aspect of language development. In the final chapter we review the findings of our and other studies using these measures wherever possible. The usefulness of each measure in predicting language outcome measures at 3 years and later is discussed then.

Word Acquisition

A very crucial aspect of language development is word acquisition. Recent research indicates that children not only acquire knowledge of the meanings of words per se but, also, at some point simultaneously acquire knowledge of the sentential contexts in which these words can appear and, therefore, not only know what category of experience the word denotes but also the syntactic uses to which it can be put (Markman, 1991; Waxman, 1990). Word acquisition was measured in several ways.

Lexical Diary. Parents kept a diary of their child's first words so that we could assess the children's acquisition of a first lexicon. The diaries were given to the mothers of the babies who entered the project at birth when either the mother told us that their child understood some words, or when we observed at our monthly home visit that the baby appeared to understand words. The mothers' of the children who entered the study when they were older were given diaries during the initial (10th month) recording session. Each mother continued to make entries in the diaries until her child comprehended 100 words and produced 50 words. Each month when we visited the family, we checked the new entries and obtained contextual information about the circumstances under which each new word was comprehended or produced so that we could code each diary entry. Appendix A contains a copy of the diary that we gave to the parents, and a description of the coding procedure used by us and by Benedict (1979).

A test has now been developed to measure this aspect of language development, the MacArthur Communicative Development Inventories (Fenson et al., 1993). The inventory elicits parental report on lexical development by questioning parents about the presence of particular vocabulary much as we did when we probed parents on their diary entries. Plans are underway to use the inventory with special populations. The development of this inventory has indicated that mothers are quite accurate in their assessments of their children's vocabulary, as we also found when we checked the diaries each month. An attitude previously held by a number of researchers was that mothers were inaccurate, and tended to inflate the numbers of words understood and produced. Now there is evidence that this is not the case. This helps us to better understand that, on the whole, mothers' have good knowledge of their children's vocabulary development.

Although most of the diaries were completed by the babies' mothers, some were kept by fathers. We found that keeping the diary not only allowed us to obtain measures of vocabulary development but also played a role in focusing both mothers' and fathers' attention on their children's language development. We think it played a motivating role in encouraging communicative interaction on the part of some parents to see that vocabulary did increase. From these diaries we obtained the following measures: age of comprehending 10, 50, and 100 words, age of producing 10 and 50 words, rate of lexical acquisition, distribution of acquired words according to semantic and grammatical categories, and the correlation between these measures and other measures.

Vocabulary Diversity.   To assess the sophistication of the children's vocabularies we counted the number of different words used in 50 consecutive utterances. We also calculated a type/token measure (number of different words used over the total number of words) in an attempt not to underate the complexity of the vocabularies used by children whose utterance lengths were shorter than others. We eliminated from our counting all utterances that were repetitions or imitations. These measures of lexical development have been used over decades and with special populations as well as normally developing children. A very early reference to this aspect of language development is McCarthy (1930).

Sentence Comprehension

We felt it was important to assess both comprehension and production of utterances that contained more than one word and to do so at an early age. We began by measuring two word combination comprehension and then moved on to multiword comprehension.

Two-Word Comprehension. To assess the child's comprehension of two-word utterances, we wrote our own sentence comprehension test. A copy of the test and directions for administration and scoring are contained in Appendix B. The test consists of a series of sentences said to the child while he or she is playing with a specially chosen group of toys. The child is expected to select the appropriate toy from the group and perform the action requested.

Because we wanted to measure sentence comprehension and not vocabulary comprehension, we purchased an identical set of inexpensive toys for each child and left the set in their homes. These toys were given to the babies during the 11th month home visit to ensure that they would become familiar with the names of the objects. At that time, we told the parents to feel free to let their babies play with the toys in any way they chose. The parents also watched us play with the babies and the toys at each subsequent visit, and we assume that they tried to get their children to manipulate the objects in the ways that we did.

The child's ability to understand three different types of sentences was evaluated. The first type of sentence (semantically predictable) was obvious from the context. So, for example, we asked the children to "Blow the horn" and "Smell the flower." The second type of sentence (Agent–Action) was also obvious from the context but changed the possible agent from the child to another as in "Make the bunny kiss." The third type of sentence (anomalous) required that the children perform unusual actions with objects and, therefore, the children could not rely on context alone. They had to "Push flowers" and "Smell trucks."

Children were asked to respond to anomalous sentences only after they could perform successfully with semantically predictable sentences containing the items used in the anomalous sentence. For example, a child would be asked to "Hug the horn" only after he or she could respond correcty to "Hug the bunny" and "Blow the horn." Once a child responded correctly to an item he or she was not asked to do that item again. We did not keep repeating items at each session for two reasons. First, we wished to maintain the children's willingness to cooperate and second we wished to maintain their interest. Some of the children, with a tremendous drive for independence, interpreted the sentences as demands to follow orders and resented this. Others became bored after a half dozen items had been presented. We decided it was best not to use the little time during which they were willing to cooperate, getting them to do things they had already demonstrated they could do.

From this procedure the following measures were derived: the age of completion for each type of sentence and for the test as a whole, the proportion of correct responses at ages 16, 22, 25, and 29 months, and the rate of item completion. We also calculated the correlation between these and other measures. This procedure was loosely based on a study carried out by Sachs and Truswell (1978).

Multiword Comprehension. We were interested in the children's production and comprehension of utterances that would require understanding of word order, and the relation between categories in phrases (actor, action–object relations, adjective–noun relations, etc.). There is now evidence from a series of studies that comprehension of subject–verb and object word order rules in the language can be found many months before multiword utterances are produced (Golinkoff, Hirsh-Pasek, Cauley, & Gordon, 1987). However, when this study was undertaken little such evidence was available. When the children were 27 months old we gave them an investigator-designed sentence comprehension test. This test, we felt, represented a logical progression from the two-word comprehension test we had devised as an earlier measure of multiword comprehension, and also, a leap from comprehension based on word meaning to comprehension based on understanding syntactic relations. We measured their ability to demonstrate their understanding of agent–action–object constructions in Part A and their ability to comprehend more complex constructions such as modifier + agent + action + object (Big doll push truck) and Agent + action + object + prepositional phrase (Doll push truck on the box). In Part B we devised sentences that employed the names of the toys we had left many months before. A complete list of the sentences plus the scoring procedure are indicated in Appendix E. Responses were scored as correct, incorrect, did not do, or noncontingent. Noncontingent responses were those where the child did something unrelated to the sentence presented.

Sentence Production

Many of the measures of language development that readers will be most familiar with are those described now. They are varying measures of sentence production. Those researchers concerned with language development have been interested in how many words a child knows as a sign of developmental change. They have also been interested in how many words a child can put together in a single utterance at what age, also as a sign of development. But it is not amount or size alone that they are interested in. The contents of these utterances in terms of their structure, meaning, and function is also a matter of interest. These contents are also signs of developmental change.

Mean Length of Utterances (MLU).   This measure was one of several used as an index of the child's syntactic development. It is calculated by determining the average number of morphemes (meaningful units) in a series of utterances. If a child produced 50 utterances the MLU for that child at that time would be the addition of all the morphemes in each of these 50 utterances divided by 50. Other investigators have found this measure to be a better predictor of children's development of syntax than chronological age. In computing MLU we followed Brown's (1973) procedures, with the modifications suggested by Miller (1981). Unless otherwise indicated we used language samples of 100 utterances in length.

Syntactic Structures.   Some time around the child's second birthday, a few months after he or she begins to use recognizeable words, multiword utterances appear. These produced multiword utterances increase in both length and complexity as the child develops. We measured the syntactic development of the children in several ways. The measures we chose were simple and easy to code. Our first series of measures considered the utterance as a whole. We considered the grammaticality of the utterances, what sentence types they represented, whether they were simple or complex, what types of complex sentences were produced, and whether or not the sentence contained morphological markers. These measures were calculated on 100 consecutive utterances taken from the 25-, 29-, and 35-month transcripts. These measures are described in Table 2.5.

Another group of measures we made were adapted from the work of Tyack and Gottslaben (1974). These measures allowed us to assign each of 100 consecutive multimorpheme utterances to a structural type that indicated the syntactic category or categories that composed each utterance. The

TABLE 2.5
Measures of Sentence Development

Measure	*Description*
Percentage of grammatically correct sentences	The percentage of sentences considered grammatically correct by conversational usage in a 100 utterance sample.
Types of sentences	The distribution of sentences according to type: declaratives, yes–no questions, Wh- questions, imperatives, and indicators.
Percentage of simple and complex sentences	Complex sentences included both conjoined and embedded.
Different types of complex sentences	Number of different types of complex sentences used more than once in a 100 utterance sample.
Percentage of sentences marked for tense	Sentences were categorized as referring to the present, immediate past, remote past, immediate future, and remote future.

structural types are described in Table 2.6. The examples given are all taken from children age 25 months.

Morphology.   As our final measure of the syntactic aspects of children's language, we calculated the percentage of correct use of the series of morphemes described by Brown (1973). We calculated this measure at 25, 29, and 35 months in a sequence of 100 utterances at each age period. The morphemes are listed in Table 2.7 according to the general order observed by Brown in the three children he studied. We required that a child use a morpheme twice in obligatory contexts before including it in the score.

Both similar and somewhat dissimilar orders have been observed by other investigators who have analyzed the sequence of appearance of these items in the language of children from differing populations. One of the populations that has been studied in terms of their use of these morphemes are specifically language-disordered children. Children with language problems appear to have particular difficulty with those morphemes that are bound (attached to nouns and verbs) in the list (Leonard, 1989). However, even with these children, the sequence of appearance of the 14 morphemes is somewhat similar. We did not measure the sequence in which these morphemes appeared. Rather, we measured the percentage of correct usage in obligatory contexts for each of the 14 morphemes at each of the three ages, and the

TABLE 2.6
Structural Types Used to Classify Multimorpheme Utterances

Type	Example[a]	Gloss
Noun	Pickles	
Modifier & noun	Red glasses	
Verb	Take out	(Take out the toyman)
Verb & noun	Open it	
Noun & verb	I close	(I'm closing it)
Noun & copula omission & noun/adj.	Handle red	(The handle is red)
Verb & modifier & noun	Got "eye" book	(I've got the "Eye" book)
Noun & verb & noun	I drop it	(I dropped it)
Verb & noun & noun	Turn top on floor	(Turn the top on the floor)
Modal & verb & noun	Can't pick him up	
Noun & verb & noun & noun	I put some cars in there	(I'm going to put some cars in there)
Noun & cop & noun/adj.	This is Snoopy	
Noun & modal & verb	It doesn't work	
Noun & modal & verb & noun	I gonna push it	
Noun & adj. & noun	They are both circles	
Complex	I think I do	
Unanalyzable	fast down	(I went fast down the slide)

[a]All of these examples are taken from children who are 25 months old.

TABLE 2.7
Acquisition Order of 14 Morphemes and Examples of Their Use

Order	Morphemes	Examples
1	Present progressive:ing	I washing clothes
2	Preposition:in	Put (them) in (the) pots
3	Preposition:on	(Wave) bye (to) Daddy on the street
4	Plural: s	Get more books, mommy
5	Past irregular: e.g., fall	(he) fell down
6	Possessives: 's	Scott's toys
7	Uncontractible copula: be	Is it green?
8	Articles: the, a	Get a napkin
9	Past regular: ed	(I) 'dropped it
10	Third person regular: s	(He) falls down
11	Third person irregular: e.g., have	She has
12	Uncontractible auxilary: be	Is she crying?
13	Contractible copula: be	What's that
14	Contractible auxilliary: be	She's crying

percentage of children who used each of these morphemes correctly in two obligatory contexts at each month.

Semantic Roles. In addition to the syntactic structures produced by the children, we were also interested in the semantic relations expressed in their utterances. By the time most children reach the age of 2 they begin to combine words together to talk about people, objects, events and the relations among these. Although the children's utterances at age 2 are longer than they were at 18 months, on average two words instead of one, they are still talking about the same things as when they were younger. However, at age 2, the children verbally make explicit the relations among objects and events instead of using the context or gesture to describe a relation. To measure what children talk about, we analyzed the semantic roles that the children used when they produced multiword utterances at 25 months of age. The specific roles we used to code the utterances were described by Retherford, Schwartz, and Chapman (1981). Table 2.8 contains examples of some multiword utterances that we obtained from one of the children, and how we coded the semantic roles in these utterances.

Appendix C contains a summary of the coding instructions we followed. To measure semantic roles we coded the first 75 multiword utterances produced by the baby at 25 months. We excluded complex sentences, conversational devices, and routines. We also ignored the syntactic categories of the items produced in these 75 utterances as these were coded separately. Just as in the coding of MLU, we did not score any self-repetitions or imitations. For each semantic role we calculated the number of times we found it in the utterances we analyzed.

TABLE 2.8
Semantic Roles in Adam's Multiword Utterances

Roles	Example	Context
Agent & action & location	Truck hit wall	Referring to the toy truck that had just crashed into the wall
Experience & state & entity	I love it	Referring to soda his mom handed him
Action & created object	Make a house	Playing with his mom and some blocks
Action & location	Move over there	Pushing his mom aside
Attribute & entity	Happy dog	Hugging his toy dog

Functions of Language Before children acquire recognizeable words they are able to communicate with their parents and others in their environment. Some time during the second half of their first year of life they appear to accomplish this communication intentionally through a series of vocalizations that have different stress and intonation patterns and that are accompanied by different facial expressions and gestures. With these vocalizations and by bringing and showing things to others, as well as reaching and pointing, they get those around them to do what they want. As the children grow, these gestures, facial expressions, and intonation and stress are combined with words, not just vocalizations. Their communicative effectiveness grows. We were interested in describing the functions of the language that the children used as they moved from single word to multiword utterances. Using procedures described by Dore (1974) and Folger and Chapman (1978), we coded the functions of the language the children produced from ages 2 to 3. Table 2.9 provides a series of examples from one of the children, a precocious 35-month-old girl.

To determine how the children used language in the third year we coded 100 consecutive child utterances taken from the 25-, 29-, and 35-month tapes. The specific coding instructions are included in Appendix D. We used the same coding procedures for child utterances to others as we did for

TABLE 2.9
Functions of Language in Lisa's Speech at 35 Months Old

Function	Example	Context
Statement	One time Nicole came here and her mommy didn't and Nicole cried	Talking to her mom while having a tea party
Description	I make your coffee	Pretending to make coffee
Request for action	You drink it for pretend	Passing her mother a pretend cup of coffee
Request for permission	Mom, can I have a coffee roll?	Asking for a block she put on a plate
Request for information	Want some?	Holding up coffee pot

caregivers' utterances to children. For each linguistic function we calculated the percentage of occurrence, and then compared our findings to those investigators from whom we had taken the coding instructions.

Participation in Conversation

Although each utterance can be categorized according to its structures and to the purpose or function it serves, it may also be described in relation to the utterances it precedes and follows. So, for example, when someone asks, "Where's the book?", the person is both requesting information (the function of the utterance) and producing an utterance that attempts to elicit a response from a conversational partner (a type of conversational move). The producer of the utterance simultaneously carries out an intention (to get information) and sets up a conversational situation (a response is required). In addition to coding the utterances of the children in terms of structure and function we also coded them in terms of their conversational moves. We designed this measure using information reported on by Wells, MacLure, and Montgomery (1979). Table 2.10 defines and gives examples of the coding system as we applied it to the utterances of another 35-month-old girl. Each category, as we have defined it, represents a different type of conversational move.

One hundred consecutive child utterances obtained at 25, 29, and 35 months were coded in terms of the conversational moves they represented.

TABLE 2.10
Conversational Moves of Sarah at 35 Months Old

Move	Definition	Example	Context
Elicit	An utterance that expects a response.	Where my stickers of valentines?	Said to her mom while looking for her sticker book
Continue	An utterance that is a response to the previous utterance and expects a response	Where are we gonna put it?	Said in response to her mom's request for a sticker
Response	An utterance that supplies requested information	Today is Thursday after night	Said in response to her mom's question "What's today?"
Acknowledge	An utterance that recognizes and evaluates responses and nonrequests	Okay	Said after mom tells her that the doll is asleep
Give	An utterance that supplies information	Let me find another little cake	Said while looking for a pretend cake for her doll

The measures we obtained from this procedure were compared over time and related to other measures we obtained.

Imitation, Expansion, and Paraphrase

The role of imitation in language acquisition remains controversial to the present day. Many have argued that its major function is to facilitate the acquisition of vocabulary and sentence structures. Others have argued that it is the child's way of testing hypotheses about whether or not they have got it right. Still others argue that imitation is more related to the development of conversational skills than to the acquisition of the words and structures in the language. The role that the child's use of expansion and paraphrase plays in language acquisition has been argued about in a similar fashion. Not only do children imitate, expand, and paraphrase what others say but they also repeat, expand, and modify what they themselves say. The role of this kind of behavior is also unclear but from a functional point of view this repetition and modification allows the child to do the following: hold on to his or her turn, clarify his or her utterances, interrupt the conversation of others, and initiate a conversation. Thus, we viewed it as playing an important part, at least, in conversational development. One of our children repeated "mommy" 87 times, while his mother tried to have a phone conversation. Table 2.11 summarizes the types of repetition, expansion, paraphrase, and imitation we coded. For this measure, like the previous ones, we coded 100 consecutive utterances at 25, 29, and 35 months.

MEASURES OF INTERACTION AND INPUT

We were interested in determining what mothers do that may be responsible for variations in the rate of development of their infants' language. The way in which caregivers interact with babies might have an effect. We, therefore, measured two specific aspects of mother–infant interaction: early turn-taking and direction giving. The way in which caregivers talk to babies may also have an effect. Therefore, we measured multiple aspects of the speech that mothers addressed to their children. In chapter 6 we discuss what others have found about the possible effects of early interaction, and what we found about the effects of this interaction and input on language development. Because this is such an important topic, and a matter of some controversy we felt it merited a separate chapter.

Turn-Taking

From the very beginning, mothers talk to their children and encourage them to take part in conversations. They help them to take turns being both speaker

TABLE 2.11
Imitation and Repetition

Type	Example	Context
Exact imitation of other	Mom: Who's this? What's this person's name? Child: Vocalizes. Mom: Big who? Big Big Bird. Child: Big Bird.	Mom and child reading book. Mom points at picture.
Partial imitation	Mom: What is that? Child: /wit/(Sleep?) Mom: What? That's a blanket. Child: Blanket.	Child is holding a piece of puzzle
Expansion of others	Mom: Down to the basement with you Child: Down to the basement with you, rotten orphan. We gotta do what Ms. Annigan says.	Pretending the musical "Annie"
Paraphrase of other	Mom: Are you with spiders now? Child: I'm with them now.	Still pretending "Annie"
Exact repetition self	Child: Dog. A dog. Dog Dog. Mom: Mary, that's a dog.	Picks up piece of puzzle and shows it to his mom
Partial repetition of self	Mom: We're going to California on Sunday. Child: Tomorrow is gonna be Sunday. Tomorrow is Sunday.	Talking with mom about her trip to California
Expansion of self	Child: Cake for you. Here's some cake for you. Mom: Thank you very much, sir.	Serving his mom some cake
Paraphrase of self	Mom: What are you looking for? Child: I want my coloring book. I want my goose one.	Searching for his coloring book

and listener. Early on, mothers make into turns all sorts of things that their children do. It is quite common to hear a mother say to her infant after a burp, "and what else do you have to say?". As children mature, mothers expect, as turns, behavior that is more sophisticated. But in our society they are quite willing to accept minimal cues that a turn has been taken until the baby gives some evidence that they can do better. Burping is replaced by sound making, which is replaced by sound making plus gesture and action, which is replaced by words, phrases, and sentences.

We measured the early turn–taking behaviors of our infants and their mothers when the babies were 8, 10, and 12 months old. Detailed instructions on how we coded turns are included in Appendix G. We counted as turns both vocal and nonvocal behaviors. If the mother said, "Look at that" while pointing to a picture in a book, and the baby looked, this was counted as two turns, one for baby and one for the mother. Turns were grouped into sequences according to topic, and we counted the number of turns in which mother and baby interacted at each sampling. Turns in interactive sequences were contrasted with those that were not interactive. The following is an example:

(Michael is playing with a toy when a dog enters the room)

Michael: (Looks at dog)

Mom: Oh you see Lucky. Wanna pat him?

Michael: (crawls over to the dog)
  (says) /ɑgɑ/ (and pats)

Mom: Nice Lucky

Michael: (moves back to toy and plays for a while)

Mom: Michael pat the dog. Pat him. Michael pat him.

Michael: Raspberries (3 times)

The dialogue just described would be analyzed as follows. There was one interactional sequence that began with Michael looking up at the dog and ended with Mom saying, "Nice Lucky." This sequence was initiated by Michael and terminated by Mom and consisted of 6 turns, 3 by each participant. Somewhat later there were 6 turns that were noninteractive. Mom spoke three times and baby produced three raspberries that were unrelated to what mom said. We constructed a measure of interaction that was the proportion of interactional turns to total turns for each sampling. In this case there were 6 interactional turns and a total number of 12 turns, so that the interaction score was .50. Using this measurement procedure we analyzed 25 minutes of interaction from each dyad for each month.

Directives

A very frequent early behavior on the part of mothers is to request that their children act or stop acting. Mother's requests for behavior from their children provide an opportunity to examine what mothers believe about their children's ability to respond, and what children can actually do in these communicative situations. Further, it allows for the study of the devices that mothers use to help their children learn conversational rules. The data for this measure were obtained from 30-minute video recordings that we made in our families' homes when the babies were 12, 22, and 29 months old. Each mother was asked to play with her child in ways that she was accustomed to (i.e., use familiar toys in familiar activities).

From these videotapes we transcribed and coded each directive or request of the mothers. We considered each of these to be an episode that contained one or more verbal directions, all accompanying gestures and repetitions, and the child's subsequent response. Each episode was then categorized according to type of directive. There were three types: protodirective, in-focus directives and out-of-focus directives.

Protodirectives are those that occur when mothers tell their children to do some activity that the child is already doing. An example of a protodirective is a mother asking her child to put a block in a shape sorter just as the child is about to drop in the block. Mothers also give protodirectives while they physically guide the child through a requested action or perform the action themselves.

In-focus directives are those that occur when the mothers ask their children to perform a new action using an object they are already playing with or looking at. For example, the child picks up a spoon and puts it in his or her mouth and the mother says, "Give the spoon to momma." These directives are more complex for the child than protodirectives because they elicit actions from the child that he or she was not in the process of performing. They do, however, offer contextual support because the child has already focused on the object or action.

Out-of-focus directives are those that require the most independent linguistic ability on the part of the child. They require that the child change focus. An example is when a mother asks her child to put on his or her shoes when the child is playing with a truck.

Each of these directive episodes was then analyzed for outcome or the nature of the response on the part of the child. Responses to protodirectives were considered irrelevant because the child was already in the process of carrying out the action. All other outcomes were scored as appropriate or inappropriate. A refusal was considered an appropriate response, whereas ignoring the request was considered inappropriate. Our babies, like all babies, did a fair amount of both types of responding. Finally, each episode was examined for the presence of gestural cues, the degree of explicitness of the syntactic form used by the mother, the presence of final rising intonation on the utterance or utterances of the mother , and the number of repetitions. These behaviors are all said to play an important role in getting and keeping the baby's attention on the utterance and the situation. This, in turn, is said to play an important role in encouraging conversational participation if not in helping language acquisition per se. Coding information for the directive measure is available in Appendix I.

Mothers' Speech

To examine how our mothers talked to their children and the potential influence of this talk on the children, we analyzed 100 consecutive mother utterances to their children. We did this when the children were 8, 12, 16, 22, and 25 months old. In other words, we began this analysis around the time when the children were beginning to comprehend and some were beginning to produce words, and continued the analysis to the time when the children were primarily producing multiword utterances. We coded each of the 100 utterances for aspects that were said to be important to language acquiring children by a number of investigators. These included various categories of mothers' simplification of language (e.g., MLU and sentence type) the pragmatic intent of the utterance (e.g., request for action and information), the discourse relations represented (e.g., repetitions and expansions) and conversational parameters (like topic intiation and continuation). Specific information on the coding is presented in Appendix H.

OUTCOME LANGUAGE MEASURES

When the children in Group 1 reached 2 1/2 years of age and when the children in Group 2 reached 3 years, they were brought to a metropolitan hospital for a full diagnostic battery of standardized tests. These tests were administered by a certified speech and language pathologist. As much as possible, both groups of children received the same tests. Some differences in testing were necessary to accomodate the 6-month difference in the ages of the two groups. Many speech and language tests are not appropriate or are not normed for children below age 3. The test battery was designed to assess multiple aspects of language, and to explore both the comprehension and production of language. They included the PPVT (Dunn & Dunn, 1981), the SICD (Hedrick, Prather, & Tobin, 1975), the NSST (Lee, 1969), the DSS (Lee & Canter, 1970), and Reynell (1969). Table 2.12 lists the tests we gave.

From each of these tests we obtained a raw score that was converted into a language age score. We also compared the scores of the children in our study to those of children on whom the tests had been normed to determine how far ahead or behind each of our children performed on each of the tests. When appropriate, we averaged the results of the expressive language battery into a single measure and did the same for the receptive language tests. We used these two scores as our primary outcome measures, and attempted to determine what earlier measure or measures might predict each of them.

SUMMARY

The children over the course of our study ranged in age from 1 to 36 months. Over this time, various measures of cognitive and linguistic development were taken. Over this same time, the ways in which the mothers spoke to

TABLE 2.12
Standardized Battery

Aspect of Language Assessed	Tests Administered	
	Group 1	Group 2
Receptive vocabulary	Peabody Picture Vocabulary Test	Peabody Picture Vocabulary Test
Expressive vocabulary	Picture Vocabulary Subtest of Binet	Picture Vocabulary Subtest of Binet
Receptive language	Sequenced Inventory of Communication Development	Sequenced Inventory of Communication Development Northwestern Syntax Screening Test
Expressive language	Developmental Sentence Scoring Sequenced Inventory of Communication Development Reynell Language Expression	Developmental Sentence Scoring Sequenced Inventory of Communication Development

their children and how they communicatively interacted with them were also measured. When the children exited the study they were given a battery of standardized language tests that allowed comparison among them and with the children on whom these tests had been normed.

Most of the speech measures obtained from the children were measures of their production, cry, babble, order of contrasts among vocalic sounds, mastery of consonantal sounds within words. They were, however, given a speech discrimination test beginning when they were 18 months old and continuing until they were just about to exit the study.

Single-word comprehension and production were assessed by employing parental (primarily mother's) report. Measures of multiword comprehension were used to assess comprehension of nouns and verbs to begin with and then comprehension of subject–verb and object utterances and expansion of these utterances into more complex subjects and objects. Specifically, comprehension of actor–action and action–object relations and then actor–action–object and actor–action–adjective–object and actor–action–object–prepositional phrase was also assessed. Multiword production was used to assess MLU, acquisition of particular structural relations in these utterances, use of different sentence types, and morphological development. In addition, the semantic relations and functions expressed in their utterances were observed. Finally, children's use of language (their pragmatic knowledge) over time was measured by describing how they participated in discourse.

Parental (mother primarily) interaction and input was measured in various ways. Their turn-taking behavior, their use of directives and the functions of their language as well as the structure of their language to their children was measured. Thus, not only was the child's language development over time measured but also how they were spoken to as they were developing language.

When the children in the younger group were 30 months old, and when the children in the older group were 36 months old, they were given a battery of standardized tests that measured both their comprehension and production of language. One purpose of all these measures was to observe the course of language development in this group of infants and factors that might influence this development. Another purpose was to determine if there were early language behaviors and other factors that might predict language performance at 3 years of age. A final purpose was to see if these early language behaviors and other factors could predict possible delay or difference in language performance at 3 years of age.

CHAPTER 3

From the Beginning: The First Year

This chapter is divided into two parts. The first part is an introduction to our findings. The problem and challenge of individual differences among the children and in the communication interaction between them and their families is discussed first, hence the subtitle, "Prologue." We discuss individual differences by giving some examples. From our point of view this is an important perspective to take on the language development of the children in our study. Although much of the time, in subsequent chapters, we discuss patterns of development across children, and behaviors across caregivers, we would like the reader to be aware of the fact that there were marked individual differences among our children and in the families in which they were growing up.

The second part of the chapter deals with our findings during the first year of life. Language development during this period is quite different than the development that occurs over the following 2 years. Few infants produce recognizeable words even at the end of the year. However, this first year is extremely important in laying the groundwork for what follows. Infants learn a great deal about communication through crying and babbling even though they have no words, and they also learn a lot about how meaning is conveyed in the language they hear. We examined those aspects of language development occurring during this period that the literature had indicated might be predictive of later developmental problems. The literature on infant speech sound production and, more importantly, perception during the first year of life has grown enormously since the time of our study. However, there are few studies that have been carried out subsequently that point to additional aspects of languge development during Year 1 that are more predictive of later development than the ones we originally selected.

PROLOGUE: DIFFERENCES AMONG CHILDREN
AND FAMILIES

The children and their families differed in many ways. In addition to the ways that children described in manuals and books such as this one usually differ (by gender, family income level, number of siblings, etc.), these children differed in the likelihood with which they could be expected to develop language normally. Half of the children were at risk for developmental disorders due to medical reasons. As a group, the children were premature, but the extent of their prematurity, and the other conditions that surrounded their birth differed greatly. Some of the premature infants were very small; they weighed less than 1,000 grams. Some were not so small and weighed closer to 4 pounds. Some had breathing difficulties at birth, whereas others did not. Although all of the premature babies required special medical attention at birth, none of them appeared to have severe handicapping conditions. The children were, rather, what has been termed *at risk* for the mild and moderate problems that frequently go undetected during the first 2 years of life. But we were not sure that this would be the case with these children.

Not only were the children in our study different from each other in terms of risk factors, their caregivers were different from each other as well. For example, 2-month-old Alex squeaks and wiggles and moves slightly. His mother reaches for him and tells him he's a little squirt. She picks him up.

Alex: (Vocalizes)

Mom: Come on! You wanna do some excercise? Oow.
(She pulls him up, keeping his head supported with the palms of her hands)
Huh?
Oow.

Alex: (vocalizes)

Mom: Huh? A couple more times? Okay.
(She pulls Alex up again)
Stretch.
(she moves his arms away from his body)
(pause)

Mom: (She props him up on the couch)
What are you doing sitting up?
Are you sitting up?
Look at you.

This kind of interaction takes place in varying amounts between babies and caregivers from the beginning. For Alex, this type of interaction takes place many times during Alex's day as his mother, father, and the rest of the family reach out to communicate with him. They will provide him with numerous opportunities to participate in conversations, to display newly acquired competencies, and to learn more about the world of people and objects. As the quality and quantity of his contributions change, the nature of his family's communicative interactions with him changes as well.

The kinds of behavior we observed between Alex and his caregivers from the earliest months of life was not what we observed in all families. There were differences among the parents in how they communicatively interacted with their children. They varied in the degree to which they allowed their children to participate in conversation, and in the degree to which they acknowledged their contributions. Their responsiveness to developmental changes in the children varied from family to family. Further, the behavior of the mother, just described, of treating Alex's vocalizations as if he were actually taking part in the conversation did not occur with all mothers.

Although we were aware that there would be differences in the ways children developed, and in how their parents dealt with their development, we were not prepared for the diversity we found. For example, Adam's mother reported that he was saying "dog" when shown a picture of a dog and calling his brother Sam "am" when he was 6 1/2 months old. It then took him a full 11 months more before he could say 50 different words and another 5 months before he could put two words together with some regularity. Sarah, on the other hand, began saying her first words close to her first birthday and had 50 different words by 14 1/2 months of age. Her average sentence length was 4 words long before she was 2 years old.

This rather remarkable diversity was the rule rather than the exception in these children's language development, and so it is no wonder that early detection of language problems is so difficult. Early identification of children with language problems, and intervention to help them overcome their problems is felt to reduce the number and severity of the academic and social difficulties faced by the language-delayed or impaired child as he or she enters school. However, knowing when to intervene and how to intervene remains a problem. It is important, therefore, for parents, clinicians, and teachers to be familiar with the wide range of behaviors and differences in rate of development that turn out to be normal. This is what we hope to explicate in this book. We also hope to point to factors that might be early signs of later language problems.

To give the reader an overview of what we mean by differences, we present here a description of the behavior of four babies (two full-term and two premature) and their mothers.

Some Examples of Individual Variation

Nicole and Her Mother.   Nicole's parents were a little apprehensive during the prenatal months. Her mother had already had two miscarriages and both parents very much wanted to start a family. Nicole was born precisely on schedule. She weighed 7 pounds 13 ounces at birth. Her mother was in labor for 10 hours, and Nicole was born by vaginal delivery with assistance from forceps. Nicole and her mother spent 2 1/2 days in the hospital and came home to continue their adventure of getting to know each other.

Nicole's mother had been an office worker who chose to stay home with Nicole during her early years. Her father worked for the city of Boston. He had a college degree and some additional schooling beyond that, while her mom had completed 2 years of schooling beyond high school.

Nicole's early months were easy. She ate well and slept well. During our visit when Nicole was 2 months old, she played happily with her mother for about 15 minutes, cried for the next 5 minutes, and then went to sleep. At 3 months old, she stayed awake for our whole visit, making some nice cooing sounds and burping, hiccupping, and sneezing when she wasn't being breast-fed.

At 8 months old, we began to measure her communicative interaction with her mother. Nicole and her mother took fewer turns than did most of the infants and their mothers that we studied. They engaged in less verbal and nonverbal communicative interaction than the average mother and baby. Within their interactions the mother was doing more work than Nicole, but less than some other mothers were doing. Nicole was offering her mother fewer vocalizations on which to build a conversation.

Given this somewhat depressed communicative interaction, one might expect that Nicole would be slow in understanding and producing words. But this is not what happened. Nicole's ability to comprehend and say words was very much like other children her age. She could understand 50 words by 13 1/2 months old and could say 50 words by 18 months, so she was right on target. An interesting question is, then, was Nicole doing anything prior to her word acquisition that could indicate that she would be on target?

One indication Nicole gave us that word acquisition would not be a problem was her ability to produce syllablelike utterances. At 10 and 12 months of age she was producing more syllablelike utterances than the average child. She could repeat the same syllable over and over again "ba-ba-ba" or repeat it with some changes "ba–ga."

Just as one might ask, was Nicole doing anything that told us she would have an easy time using words, we could ask if her mother was doing anything within their interaction to help her. We have already said that Nicole's mother was not particularly assertive within their communications. We view the situation as being much like driving a car. For a car to start it must have some gas (but you can give it more or less gas) and the car must be in relatively good working order. (Relatively, because there are some things for which you can compensate. Using the same metaphor, you can always "pop" the clutch to get a car with a dead, battery going.) Next you must turn the key and push down on the accelerator. Although giving the car more gas will get it to move faster so will going down a hill, even a small one, and no matter how fast the car travels, if it travels it will get to its destination just the same.

In Nicole's case, there was lots of gas in the car, the car was in working order, and her mother knew how to start the car. She gave it enough gas to get it going. At some points during Nicole's development her mother may have helped her more than at other points (i.e., given her more gas). Early on, Nicole's mother wasn't in a hurry and did not push very hard.

The last time we saw Nicole she was 2 1/2 years old. She was talking, playing, and enjoying being a 2-year-old. When we tested her, she did beautifully. She was similar to the other children we had followed, and was more than 6 months ahead of the children who were used to standardize the tests we gave her as she left the study.

Sam and His Mother. Sam was a first child and he was big. He weighed more than 9 1/2 pounds at birth. He was delivered vaginally after a 6–hour uneventful labor. He had an Apgar score of 9 at 1 minute, and 10 at 5 minutes. He and his mother left the hospital after 1 week. Sam's father finished the 10th grade and worked as a meat packer. His mother graduated from high school and, before Sam was born, she had worked as a secretary.

The first time we saw Sam he was 10 months old. At that time he was not a particularly active child. He could sit by himself alone, and he crept around the room. He could not pull himself up to a standing position nor stand holding onto furniture. His slow motor development was verified by his performance on the Bayley Scales of Infant Development that we administered to him at 13 months of age. He scored 118 on the Mental Development Index and 66 on the Motor Development Index. (An average score is between 85 and 115, and the more advanced the child the higher the score.)

During our 10- and 12-month home visits we noted that Sam and his mother interacted communicatively as much as our average dyads. However, at 10 months of age they were less successful than other dyads at establishing and maintaining topics. By Sam's 12th month they were doing fine. Both mother and Sam contributed to the interaction taking approximately the same number of turns as other babies and their mothers. Like Nicole, Sam did not contribute as much as the most talkative of the children, nor did his mother "pick up" on as many of his contributions as the most responsive mothers. In general, there was little difference in their communicative interactions from what we had seen in other dyads.

When we visited with Sam and his mother at 10 months of age, we gave his mother a diary to write down the first 100 words he understood and the first 50 words he could say. (All mothers were asked to keep diaries in the same way.) On the average, our mothers reported that their children could comprehend 50 words by 13 1/2 to 14 months of age. It was not until 14 1/2 months of age that Sam's mother told us that he could understand 10 words, and he could not understand 50 words until he was 17 months old. Shortly after he understood 50 words he was able to say 10 words. Then it took him almost 6 months more to learn to say 40 additional different words, and he did not say the 50th until close to his second birthday. Certainly his communicative interaction with his mother at 10 and 12 months would not have led us to suspect that he would struggle so long to learn words. As we later realized, his ability to produce syllablelike utterances gave us a hint of what was to come. He produced very few of them, significantly fewer than other children his age. Although he could repeat the same syllables over and over, he did this less frequently than other infants and also he seldom repeated an utterance including a change (like da-ga).

At 19 months we administered the Dunst version of the Uzgiris and Hunt Scales (a widely accepted test of children's cognitive development) to Sam. When we compared his total score to the norm he was performing at age level. His ability to perform on the object permanence subscale was at the 22-month level (+3 months) and his ability to do means–ends tasks was at the 26–month level (+7 months). He was 4 to 5 months below age level on the vocalization subscale and the schematic scale. Sam did not imitate unfamiliar sounds or words, although he happily repeated words he knew. He did not say words spontaneously, nor did he use objects symbolically.

Some of his problems became more obvious when we began testing his comprehension month by month. Sam could not follow even one request to perform unusual actions on objects until he was more than 2 years old. Most of the babies his age could do several. When he was 25 months old, he finallly agreed to "smell the horn" rather than blow it. He also was more than 2 years old before he showed us both how to "kiss the bunny" and "make the bunny kiss." It actually took Sam 8 months longer than it took, on the average, for our other babies to perform all of the unusual items on this test.

By the time Sam was 27 months old we decided that a formal clinical speech and language evaluation was appropriate. He was seen by a speech and language clinician who administered some standardized tests to him, and did some informal observation. The testing resulted in a recommendation that Sam be enrolled in an early intervention program. As is sometimes the case with very young children who need help, that help is not always immediately available. Sam's parents lived very far from public transportation, and Sam's mother could not drive. The federal law, 94–142, applied to children 3 years of age and older. As a result, Sam could not be provided transportation through the state. It was 9 months before Sam began to attend a preschool program for language-impaired children 5 mornings a week. He was now 3 years old and covered by the law that guarantees all children from 3 to 21 a free and appropriate education. At that time, the school evaluation team did their own assessment of Sam. They reported that he had normal intellectual potential, with an expressive language delay. The school psychologist and resource room teacher both said that they felt Sam was quite active and displayed a limited attention span. Sam remained in that preschool program until he was deemed ready for school entrance.

Some indications that Sam would have later difficulties in language development were that Sam was markedly delayed in production of structured vocalizations, word comprehension and production, and sentence comprehension and production. In summary, Sam evidenced both perceptive and productive difficulties. As indicated by his performance on the Bayley, his early perceptual–motor development was delayed but he performed well within the range of normal on the later tests of cognitive development.

A question of interest is, what role did Sam's environment play in the development of his language problem? Many things happened to Sam during his early developmental years, but they seem no different than things that happened to other children. When Sam was 20 months old his sister was born. This took a lot of his mother's time and energy, but does not explain Sam's problem. Sam was showing signs of trouble well before his sister was born. Another thing that happened to Sam is a little more difficult to interpret. Two months after Sam's first birthday he began to have middle ear infections (otitis media) a couple of times each year. The infections were severe enough to require medical treatment with antibiotics. Sam's hearing was monitored periodically, but there was never any hearing loss noted once the infection had subsided.

How these infections interacted with Sam's developmental language impairment is difficult to know. Clearly there are children with middle ear problems who have no difficulty acquiring language. There are also children with language learning problems who have had a series of middle ear infections during this developmental period, that is, the first 3 years of life. In fact there is some indication that such episodes of infection during the first 6 months may have a negative effect on later development (Teele, Klein, Chase, Menyuk, & Rosner, 1990). There have been many papers and several books written on this topic. Otitis media occurs at least once with most children during the first year of life, and occurs with very great frequency for some children. One of the many books dedicated to this topic is Kavanaugh and Jenkins (1986).

Sam's family was concerned about Sam's earaches, which sometimes hurt and at other times made him uncomfortable. The family would quickly take Sam to the doctor who would put him on antibiotics to treat the infection.

Another potential source of environmental influence on a child's language development is the language the child hears. One needs to question whether there were systematic differences in the way Sam's mother talked to him and the way other children are talked to. In Sam's case, we can begin by stating that whatever differences we found were not big. Sam's mother talked and played with him a great deal. She did not read him books very much or spend time with him looking at pictures. One of his earliest words was "car" and Sam and his mother spent time with cars. She was not a mother who introduced many new items and themes into their play, but this must be viewed in the context of Sam's way of playing. He did not play very long with things, and was easily distracted by almost anything.

The complex problem of who leads whom in early language development is nicely illustrated in the following interchange between Sam and his mother. Sam was 35 months old when we recorded this.

(Sam dumps a Linus puzzle on the floor)

Sam: /gɑuh pɑl/ (we think he said another puzzle) (He picks up a piece and shows it to his mother)

Sam: Boy. /gog/ a /gog/. Dog. Dog. Dog a dog

Mom: That's not a dog.

Sam: (Says something no one can understand.)

Mom: What is that?

Sam: Dog

Mom: Thats

_____ .(pause) It's not a dog

Sam: Dog

Mom: No that's not a dog. What is that?

Sam: /weet/ (Could be sleep)

Mom: What?

Sam: /Kohu/ (unintelligible)

Mom: That's a blanket.

Sam: Blanket (an approximation to the word)

This interaction typified some of the communicative difficulties that Sam and his mother had. Although certain aspects of his mother's speech to Sam may have influenced his language development, two other facts need to be kept in mind. The first is that there seems to be nothing in this interchange nor others like it that was of sufficient magnitude to "give" Sam a language problem. Second, Sam's depressed language skills and his behavior clearly affected how Sam's mother or any other mother would talk to him. It was difficult for Sam's mother to pick up on what he was saying because it was often difficult to understand what he was saying. Given these conditions it would be wrong to suggest that Sam's problem was caused by his mother's language input. It may not have been helped by this input but it isn't clear that it could be helped by input alone.

Kate and Her Mother. Kate was really tiny. She weighed 1,000 grams when she was born, which is a little over 2 pounds, 3 ounces. She was born 11 weeks early, after a 96-hour labor. A review of her hospital records (which were larger and fatter when we saw them than she was at birth) recorded an Apgar score of 2 at 7 minutes and 4 at 10 minutes. At 5 hours of age she was moved from the local hospital where she was born to the neonatal intensive care unit at a children's hospital so that she could be treated appropriately for severe respiratory distress syndrome (RDS; hyaline membrane disease). While at the children's hospital she was incubated and received assisted ventilation (and oxygen as high as 100%). She spent the first 3 months of her life in the hospital.

Kate was the second child in the family. She had a 6-year-old brother when she was born. He had a speech and language problem for which he received therapy. Another child had been stillborn after a 6-month pregnancy, a result of placenta previa. Kate had several respiratory infections during her first year of life, and repeated middle ear infections from 6 months of life. Her mother reported giving her Ampicillin every 2 weeks, each time for 10 days, since she was 10 months of age. Her physician reported fewer occurrences than did mother, but not many fewer. Clearly, there were multiple reasons why Kate might be classified as a child at risk for a language problem or other developmental problems.

The very first time we recorded Kate she was 10 months old. Her chaotic early months were behind her, and her mother was feeling confident of her ability to handle Kate. Her mother was 32 years old and a housewife who had completed 2 years of college. Her father also had completed 2 years of college, and worked as a salesman.

Kate and her mother interacted a lot during our visits with them when Kate was 10 and 12 months of age. Both of them took more verbal and nonverbal turns than many of our other babies and their mothers. Her mother's interactive style was to wait for Kate to do something and then to use the baby's actions to set the topic of the interaction.

Kate: (Begins to walk holding on to the edge of the table)

Mom: What are you gonna do now?

Kate: (picks up a tape box and looks at it)

Mom: Oh you see yourself. That's like a mirror.

Kate: (vocalizes looking at the tape box)

Mom: Is that like a mirror? (Mom points at the tape box)

That's Kate. (Mom points at Kate)

There's Kate (She laughs)

Kate: (She moves the tape box toward her mouth)

Mom: You kissing Kate? Can you kiss Kate?

Kate: (vocalizes)

Mom: Can you kiss? (smacks lips)

As this exchange indicates, Kate's mother uses what Kate is attending to to set-up the communicative interchanges, and encouraged Kate to participate.

When Kate was 13 months old we gave her the Bayley Scales of Infant Development. Kate scored 100 on the Mental Development Index, and 104 on the Psychomotor Developmental Index. Her cognitive and motor development were within normal limits, and repeated testing with the same and different tests over the next 2 years gave similar results. It is important to note that these scores were corrected for her prematurity by changing her actual birth date by the number of weeks she was born prematurely. The result is called her gestational age birthday and was most often used when evaluating her performance during the first year of her life. For example Kate was 11 weeks premature. She was born March 15, 1980, which we called her chronological age birth date. If we move 11 calendar weeks to a full-term pregnancy birth date it would be May 31, 1980, 2 months later. This made her gestational age 2 months younger than her chronological age. Using chronological birth dates as a basis for scoring results in lower scores than using gestational age birth dates, because the child is older chronologically than gestationally. The older child must do more than a younger merely to reach the same numerical score. The practice of correcting for prematurity is common, although somewhat controversial. It is difficult to determine a premature infant's gestational age, and different procedures often yield different results. Throughout the book we sometimes talk about our premature children's performance corrected for gestational age and sometimes their uncorrected performance. We indicate which we are referring to.

Kate's progress toward saying words occurred right on schedule. The diary kept by her mother showed that she understood 10 words when she was 11 months old and 50 words early in the 12th month of life. She could say 10 words shortly after understanding 50, and could say 50 different words by the time she was about 16 1/2 months old. By 22 months old she was regularly putting two words together. Her language development over the next year progressed steadily.

She was, like most children, faster at developing some aspects of language than others. For example, Kate's average sentence length increased by about 1 word from 22 to 35 months of age. Most of our babies increased their sentence length by two words during this period. On the other hand, Kate's ability to learn the grammatical aspects of the language developed very rapidly. For example, at 25 months she was using plural endings, talking about what she was doing using the "ing" form (walking, sleeping, etc.), and talking about what she had done before by using past tense. She had even learned to use the word "is" in some of her utterances.

> Mom: (Hides a small farm animal in her hand)
>
> Kate: Where is it? (She points at her Mom's hand)
>
> There it is!
>
> Mom: There it is.
>
> Kate: Again!
>
> Mom: Again?
>
> Kate: (Laughs)
>
> Mom: Gonna mix it up? (Shakes hands back and forth)
>
> Kate: Where'd it go? There it is. (Points to Mom's hand)
>
> There it is. I will do it.

Her rapid development of word endings was accompanied by her equally rapid development of the ability to control different sounds. Kate was a child who was very easy to understand, and her speech was intelligible to strangers when she was 2.

At 35 months, Kate was given an extensive battery of language and cognitive tests. She performed much like Nicole on these tests. She was about 6 months ahead of other children who had been given these tests and in the middle of the group of children we had studied.

A comparison of Sam's and Kate's development leads to more questions than answers. It appeared as if Sam's development might have been delayed by frequent episodes of otitis media but Kate had these as well. Sam seemed to have difficulties in both production of speech sounds and words and in producing symbolic acts (symbolic play). Other researchers (Rescorla & Goosens, 1992) found that children with expressive language delay also have fewer occurrences of symbolic play transformations (pretending with an object) than children without such delay. Although one can speculate, it not clear what the relations between these behaviors might be. Kate, on the other hand, despite frequent middle ear infections, was early in speech sound realization and in producing endings on words that indicate tense and plural. Kate's and Sam's mothers interacted somewhat differently with them but Sam's mother had little to work with for a long time. A number of factors in interaction with each other, not singly, appeared to be playing a role in bringing about differences in the patterns of these children's language development. Among them were otitis media, ability to realize motor acts, and communication interaction. These factors are discussed further in the final chapter.

Dom and His Mother.   Dom's early months, like Kate's, were very difficult. He weighed about 1,000 grams. His Apgar scores at 1 and 5 minutes were both 1, and improved to 5 at 10 minutes. His mother's labor lasted 2 1/2 days. Dom had severe RDS. He needed to be fully resuscitated (and was given 100% oxygen). He remained intubated for 7 days. During his stay in the hospital he developed pneumonia, and his mother reported the presence of seizures during the neonatal period. A computerized axial tomography (CAT) scan revealed an intracranial hemorrhage. He spent 10 weeks in the hospital before he went home.

His mother had had no early indications that Dom's birth would be difficult. Her health during pregnancy was fine, and she had no previous miscarriages nor difficulty conceiving. No bleeding was reported during the first trimester of pregnancy. Dom's mother had one previous pregnancy, and delivered Dom's sister Susie who weighed 7 pounds, 3 ounces. That pregnancy, labor, and delivery were easy and uneventful (except, of course, for the arrival of Susie).

Dom's mother was 28 when Dom was born. Prior to the birth of her children she had worked as a medical technician. Dom's father was 35 years old. He taught at one of the local universities. Dom's sister was almost 5 years old when he was born and was attending nursery school.

Our earliest visits with Dom, at 1 and 3 months gestational age, were quite pleasant. He would often lie awake in his playpen, happily sucking on his pacifier. His mother would often come over to the playpen, pat him, and talk to him softly. She would lift him up, hold him for a few minutes and talk with him, and then put him down. As he grew, their interactions became more lively. During our visit when he was 8 months old, they interacted less than other dyads, at 10 months as much, and by 12 months Dom and his mother were interacting more than most. The amount of successful communicative interaction was similar to that of our other babies and their mothers, with Dom's mother working hard to keep the interaction going. Like Kate's mother, Dom's mother picked up on Dom's actions and vocalizations and used them to set and maintain the topic. One apparent difference between this dyad and others was that Dom did not contribute as much to the interchanges as his mother, so that his mother worked harder than most to maintain conversations. We cited a study in chapter 1 that talked about this behavior. A frequent finding about interactions between mothers and their premature babies is that these mothers may work harder to keep interactions going. If the babies cannot handle a lot of stimulation, this will be difficult for them. If they can, this stimulation may be of benefit.

When Dom was 13 months old we gave him the Bayley Scales of Infant Development. At that time he scored 120 on the Mental Development Index and 99 on the Motor Index. His performance was clearly at or above normal and this was true even when we used his chronological age as the basis for comparison.

He was somewhat slower developing words than our other children. He understood 10 words at 15 months and 50 different words at 18 months. About 1 month after, he comprehended 50 words he could produce 10 words and he was almost 23 months of age before he could say 50 different words. He began putting two words together at about the same time that he reached 50 words. During our 22-month visit he said "see it," while looking at the light we were using with the video recorder. He also commented on the video recorder by saying "it going," which he repeated multiple times during the next half hour. He also said "see go" after his mother had told him it was his turn and said to him "go, Dom." By 29 months his average sentence length had progressed to two and a half words. When we compared this sentence length to that of other children the same age, Dom was about average. He was able to talk about people, actions, and objects, he could use noun–verb–noun constructions. Dom was a little slower than our other children in learning to use word endings. By 29 months he was using plural endings and the "ing" form of the verb for talking about ongoing actions. He could use, but frequently omitted, forms of the verb " to be," but this was no different than his peers. His parents could understand his speech, and an analysis of the sounds he used revealed nothing very different from our other children.

At 30 months of age, he was administered the McCarthy Scales of Mental Development, and seen at a childrens hospital for a formal outcome speech and language evaluation. He scored 115 on the McCarthy, which is a measure of general cognitive development. His performance was relatively the same across subscales, with the quantitative area showing a slight depression over his verbal perceptual, memory, and motor abilities, which were excellent. On all the various language measures he was given during the children's hospital evaluation, he did fine. Some examples may prove helpful. On the Peabody Picture Vocabulary Test, which measures receptive vocabulary knowledge, he scored 13 months above age level if we corrected for prematurity and 11 months above if we did not. On the Sequenced Inventory of Communicative Development he scored 2 months above age level both receptively and expressively if we corrected for prematurity, and 1 month behind if we did not. On the Reynell Language Expression Test he scored 5 months above age level if we corrected and 2 months above if we did not.

The single disturbing thing we found at this time was when we analyzed a language sample from Dom taken in his home while he was playing with his mother. We analyzed this sample using the Developmental Sentence Scoring procedure. On this measure Dom scored 7 months below age level when we corrected and 10 months below if we did not. This score is below the 10th percentile for children his age (i.e., less than 10% of all children his age do this poorly), but given his other test scores and the other information we had on Dom, we felt that there was not sufficient reason to institute intervention. Dom was only 2 1/2 years old and, although he was often a little delayed in achieving a language milestone, he was within the normal range.

When Dom was 38 months old, his mother called the hearing and speech division at the hospital and said that his pediatrician had requested another evaluation. He was given an appointment with the same clinician who had tested him previously, and was seen at 40 months of age. Her report of Dom at the time of the 30-month outcome evaluation began:

> Although Dom was at the lower end of the range of normal in the acquisition of speech skills, other measures of language acquisition such as the development of semantic skills (vocabulary and language concepts) were always advanced for his age. Even his articulation development appeared within normal limits for his gestational age.

At the time of the requested evaluation (40 months of age) Dom was reported to have "eagerly engaged in lengthy verbal discussions with his father and the examiner on a variety of topics." He was administered the Expressive One-Word Picture Vocabulary Test and scored at the 5-year 8-month level, and the examiner concluded that his single-word naming abilities were superior for his age.

Dom's speech skills were evaluated by asking him to label pictures and repeat words and sentences. He was reasonably successful. He was able to say correctly every sound in every position with the exception of /s/ and /z/, and /r/ when each was used in combination with other consonants. The examiner did not have a problem understanding Dom, except if he rapidly switched topics. His speech improved when he spoke more slowly, and the examiner felt that this might indicate a mild delay in the development of control of rapid oral motor movements for speech. She saw no reason at this time for intervention, but asked Dom's parents to bring him back in 6 months to assess his rate of progress.

As we review Dom's developmental history we see a pattern. Dom seems to start to do many new things slowly, but then catches up with the group. The examiner's recommendation to give Dom a little more time appears appropriate, but Dom would need to be re-evaluated. He has lots of internal and external resources to help him to solve the problems involved in learning language. So far the process appears not to have been easy for him, but he continues to progress. However, this pattern of development might signal later difficulties in reading. As indicated in chapter 1, there have been a number of studies that suggest that the catch-up in language development seen in premature children may hide their abiding difficulties in processing language. These hidden difficulties lead to problems in learning to read. This possibility is discussed at greater length in the final chapter.

Summary. In this section of the chapter we very briefly discussed possible sources of differences in patterns of language development among the children in our study. We then sketched four patterns of development that dramatically indicate the individual variation that exists in patterns of language development that are, on the whole, considered to be normal. These sketches also point up some of the difficulties parents, teachers and clinicians have in deciding whether a child is markedly different in their pattern of development. Nicole, a full-term baby, and Kate, a premature one, both exhibit patterns of development that are clearly normal, although they differ from each other. The fact that they are both developing normally might be accounted for by their internal competence and the kinds of input they are getting. Sam and Dom exhibit somewhat different patterns. Sam, a full-term baby, is delayed enough in comprehension and production of language to signal the need for intervention. There are also early signs that Sam may be delayed in lexical production. He begins to produce structured vocalizations at a late age. He also suffers from frequent bouts of otitis media. Dom, a premature baby, shows a much more irregular pattern of development. His speech skills were delayed and his spontaneous language production was significantly less mature than his peers. However, overall his language development was not delayed enough, even in the area of language production, to suggest that intervention should be instituted. Differences in internal resources might account for the differences in the language development of these two boys. Sam's language comprehension as well as production is delayed, whereas Dom is only delayed in language production. There seems to be no outstanding differences in the kinds of interactions that take place between these boys and their mothers and the interactions between the other mothers and children in our study. In the final chapter of this book we present a summary of our findings about factors that may lead to individual variation in the patterns of language development of all the children in the study.

THE DEVELOPMENT OF COMMUNICATION IN YEAR 1

It was held by many for a long time that language development began when babies understood and then produced their first words. It is now understood that months before this happy event occurs the baby is learning a great deal about communication, how to interact with the environment so that it produces appropriate responses. This early interaction includes both cry and noncry vocalizations. In this chapter, we discuss both these developments during the first year of life.

Cry Vocalizations

Short, soft, creaky door noises emerge from the crib. They grow louder. Harvey's father, who is having his first break from a busy day, sits watching the news. He begins to hope that the crying will not become louder until the commercial starts. Unfortunately, it gets louder. Before he can see the end of what started out to be a great editorial he gets up. He walks reluctantly into the child's room. He picks up Harvey, thinking what a cute baby he really is. He walks the baby around the room a few times. The crying continues. He takes him into the livingroom, and sits back down with him in front of the television. Harvey keeps crying. His dad gets up and carries the baby to the refrigerator. He takes out a bottle of milk, and begins to warm it. The longer it takes to warm the bottle, the louder Harvey cries. Finally it is ready and into the baby's mouth it goes. Silence at last. Harvey's father returns to the television, and turns it off. His favorite show is over. He talks to Harvey for a few seconds while he feeds him, and then he reaches for the evening paper while Harvey continues to suck on his bottle.

One of the most noticable things that infants do is cry. When the parent of a newborn hears one of these squeaky door noises, he or she flip through a mental list of possible reasons for the crying to try to figure out the cause. Usually the parent responds by doing something for the child. The parent might pick the child up, turn him or her over, feed or walk the child. The parent might have to try a variety of things before the baby quiets down.

It is from routine cycles of interaction like the one described between Harvey and his father that communication emerges. The baby cries and the parent responds. In this way, crying may be viewed as among the earliest communicative signals. The cry serves to bring the infant and the parent together, and the parent's response to the cry completes the communication interaction. As the child grows older, the crying becomes integrated into the child's other communicative behaviors.

Initially, the infant's cries are undifferentiated. The baby does not have a special cry to announce hunger, nor a different cry to say that he or she is wet. The parents are the ones who give meaning to the crying. They interpret what the baby says. The baby has not had his or her diaper changed in several hours, he or she must be wet. It is getting close to 5; he or she must be hungry. As the baby grows older, the process of putting meaning to the early cries and vocalizations becomes more accurate. The baby develops the ability to cry differentially. The baby also begins to vocalize. The parents become better able to interpret the cries because they have had lots of practice. All of this makes the process of communication easier.

Responding to Crying. Crying decreases as the children get older. This decrease occurs despite the fact that parents respond frequently and often quite promptly to their children's crying. It was once thought that frequent and prompt response to the baby's cry might "spoil" the child, and, in fact, increase the crying. Research has shown that this is not the case.

Frequent and prompt response does not mean accurate response. Some parents are better interpreters than others. Some are really good at responding when the baby is crying by feeding the baby because he or she is hungry, and putting the baby to bed when he or she is tired. All parents misread their children's cries some of the time and put their hungry infants to sleep, or try to play with their baby when the baby is tired. No matter how frequently the parents respond correctly to the crying, it decreases and is gradually replaced by other more sophisticated modes of communication.

Interestingly, some studies have shown that where babies are responded to more frequently and promptly in the early months, crying is more diminished in the later months, and is replaced by noncry vocalization (Bell & Ainsworth, 1972). Therefore, responding to crying frequently and promptly helps, rather than hinders, the development of communication. One might speculate that earlier notions of such responding spoiling the child might be due to the fact that inexperienced parents might wait and then only respond when the baby is crying very loudly and frantically. This might teach the baby that a response can be obtained only when loud and frantic cries are produced. This might make it seem as if response to crying leads to temper tantrums when, in fact, the inverse seems to be the case. The fact that all children cry shows that children do not have to be taught to use their voices to communicate. To facilitate the acquisition of babies' communicative skills, parents need to follow their natural tendencies and respond.

By the second year of life crying does not occur in most situations. The baby only begins to howl when other forms of communication fail, or when crying will get the child the exact response wanted (comfort, reassurance). The other forms of communication that the baby now has available include several different types of vocalization, a fair amount of gesturing, some wonderful facial expressions and, in some cases, some words and phrases.

Measurement of Crying.   In our project we examined several aspects of the infants' crying. First we studied what, if anything, we could learn about the status of the baby from the cry itself. The procedures we used to collect our cry samples were explained in chapter 2. We attempted to elicit three cries from each of the 28 babies in the younger group when they were 1 and 3 months old. At 1 month old, one of our babies was in the hospital so we did not make a recording. A second baby did not cry although we attempted to stimulate a cry several times. At 3 months of age, one of our parents asked us not to make her baby cry so we complied. Sometimes specific aspects of a cry could not be measured. Table 3.1 summarizes the number of cries we examined at each month.

Each cry was analyzed to yield measures of amplitude (loudness) and duration (length of cry) of each exhalation. The first two exhalations of each cry were further studied for differences in frequency (pitch). We found some interesting differences. There was a tendency for male and female cries to

TABLE 3.1
Number of Cry Samples Analyzed

Month		First Exhalation	Second Exhalation	Third Exhalation
1	First cry	22	20	16
	Second cry	23	22	18
	Third cry	22	20	1
3	First cry	24	20	14
	Second cry	21	19	15
	Third cry	17	14	8

differ in pitch. There was also a tendency for the cries of premature children to differ from the cries of full-term infants, and for the cries of high-risk infants to differ from those of low-risk infants. The high-risk infants were those who had several of the factors in their birth histories listed in the Risk Index in Table 1.3. This difference in cry was a difference in the tendency to disphonate the second exhalation of each cry. In crying the usual pattern is to get the sound going on the first exhalation, and then produce less sound or disphonate the second exhalation. In the 14 premature children (7 of whom constituted the high-risk group) there was less of a disphonation on the second exhalation. This implies that the premature babies' first exhalation was produced with less strength. A number of studies have found that infants with obvious birth defects produce cries that are different from those of infants presumed to be normal (Prechtl, Theorell, Gramsbergen, & Lind, 1969) .Other research indicates that there is a relation between risk factors and cry characteristics and between cry characteristics and later cognitive development (Lester, 1987)

It seems that babies' early crying might tell us two things. The first is it might tell us something about the more general status of the baby at the time the cry is elicited. The second is that it might be useful to determine if there is anything that the cry tells us about how the children will perform later. We looked at this question in three ways. We compared aspects of the cry—pitch, loudness, and duration—to the language scores obtained at the end of the project—the rate of acquiring the first 50 words—and to a speech and language clinician's judgment of developmental status at the end of the project. We found no relation between any aspect of cry and these later language measures. The elicited cries, as we analyzed them, appeared to tell us more about how the baby was than about how the baby would be. But, as we said, although the infants in our study might be at risk for later problems, none of them appeared to be severely impaired.

We next looked at what happened to crying as the children got older. As expected, the amount of crying decreased. To determine how much of the time the babies spent crying or making discomfort sounds, we calculated the proportion of cry and discomfort sounds in utterances to the total number of vocalizations that the baby made in a 25-minute sample. (See "Utterance Type" in Appendix G for codings.) These data are shown in Fig. 3.1.

As can be seen in the figure, by 8 months of age our babies cried very little during our visits and this proportion decreased to less than 10% of all vocalizations by 12 months of age. At 12 months of age, 11 of our babies did not cry or fuss at all during our visit, whereas 1 spent 40% of his time being unhappy. There was no significant relation between how much our babies cried during recording and how rapidly they began to say words.

Babbling

We examined some of the kinds of sounds very young children make that replace their crying. This sound making includes coughing, laughing, hiccupping, raspberries, as well as other physiologically produced sounds. In addition, babies begin to babble. It is this latter sound making that is most directly related to language development. We examined the development of the frequency of babbling and the relation between babbling and word production.

Frequency. We began by measuring how much the babies talked. To do this, we counted the number of utterances the babies made in a 25-minute

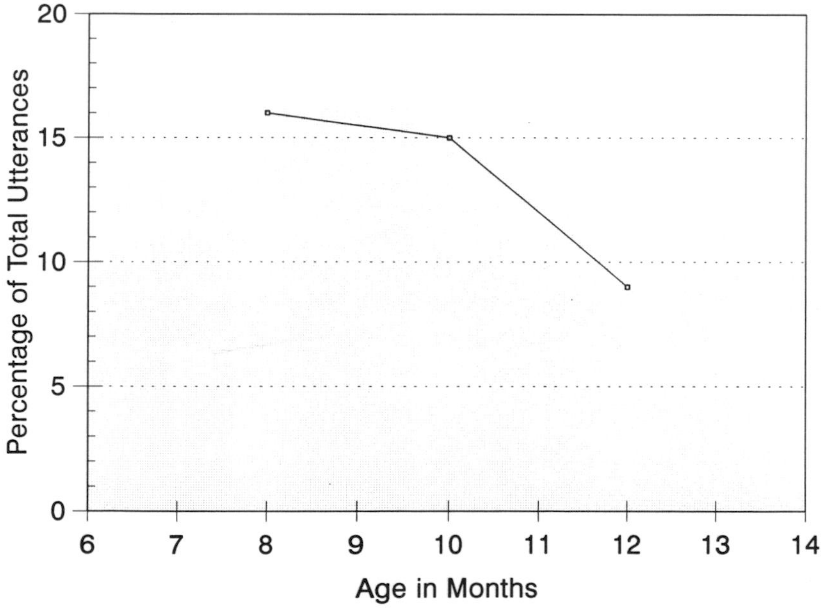

FIG. 3.1.   Proportion of cry and discomfort sounds in baby vocalizations (25-minute sample).

period of time while they interacted with their mothers. We excluded from this measure all crying and discomfort noises, physiological sounds, and laughing that was associated with tickling. The infant who talked the most produced 369 utterances, whereas our quietest infant talked 25 times. On the average, the babies spoke 155 times or about 6 times a minute. There was no difference between how frequently the boys and girls talked. The boys averaged 151 utterances, whereas the girls averaged 159 utterances. The premature children and the full-term children talked about the same as well. The full-term infants spoke on the average 156 times and the premature infants spoke 153 times.

We then examined how much our children babbled syllables. A babbled syllable was one that contained at least one consonant and a vowel. Another term we use is *structured vocalization* because these utterances require control over articulation. Table 3.2 describes what we found about the development of syllabic utterances when we analyzed 25 minutes of mother–infant interaction.

As can be seen, the proportion of syllabic utterances increases as the babies get older. It is also clear that there are wide differences between babies. Some infants made no syllablelike utterances during our sampling period, and others made quite a few. Interestingly, none of our children was unable to produce a syllabic vocalization although some did it very infrequently. There were two babies who made no syllablelike utterances at 12 months, but one of them had made four syllabic utterances at 10 months and the other baby had made two.

The connection between babbling and the acquisition of sounds in words was of interest to us. To examine this relation we selected 25 children who met specific criteria based on the age of acquisition and the rate of development of their first 50 words. The children were divided into three groups. The first group we called early fast developers (EFD). They were children who had acquired a 10-word vocabulary by 12 months and a 50-word vocabulary within the next 4 1/2 months. The second group we called late fast developers (LFD). These were children who did not acquire 10 words until after 15 months, but they proceeded to acquire the next 40 words rapidly, in less than 4 1/2 months. The third group were slow developers

TABLE 3.2
Proportion of Babbles to Vocalizations

Month	Children Tested	Proportion of Syllabic Utterances	Minimum	Maximum	SD
8	28	.09	.00	.47	.11
10	40	.19	.00	.48	.12
12	40	.25	.00	.66	.18

(SD). These children acquired their first 10 words after 15 months and took more than 5 months to reach 50 words. There were 8 EFD infants, 5 girls and 3 boys. Twelve infants were LFD, 8 boys and 4 girls; 5 boys were SD. Figure 3.2 indicates the differences between the groups by displaying each group's mean age when 10 and 50 words were produced, and the number of months between these two points.

We next examined the relation between production of syllabic utterances and word production. Figure 3.3 shows each group's use of syllablelike vocalizations, beginning at 10 months and up to the point where 50 words were produced. As can be seen in this figure the EFD babies had almost as high a percentage of structured vocalizations at 10 months as did the SD babies at 19 months. Of course, the total number of vocalizations per sampled period increased for all three groups.

No significant differences in the proportion of syllabic utterances were obtained between the LFD and SD groups in the months sampled so that these groups were combined to contrast both groups against the EFD. The results of these tests are shown in Table 3.3. The EFD are significantly different from the LFD and the SD during the early months. At 16 months of age the LFD begin to look like the EFD at 12 months of age in terms of the structure of their speech. The SD show this same pattern 3 months later. Given how rapidly changes occur in the composition of the vocalizations of infants, these differences of 4 months and of 7 months between the EFD and the other two groups are quite sizeable.

We next attempted to answer the question of whether children who began

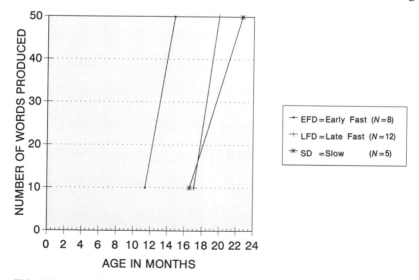

FIG. 3.2.   Age of production of 10 and 50 words for children categorized by learning rate.

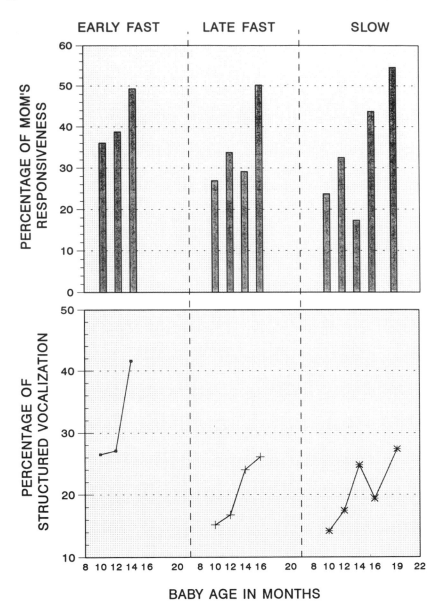

FIG. 3.3.   Relation of mother's responsiveness to baby's structured vocalizations.

to develop syllabic utterances late showed "catch-up" behavior. In other words, we wanted to know if children, who only later used greater numbers of syllablelike vocalizations, also increased their use of these vocalizations more rapidly so that they could catch-up to the children who started earlier. To examine this, we calculated the average percentage of syllabic vocaliza-

TABLE 3.3
Significance Levels for the EFD Percentage of Structured Vocalizations Contrasted with the
LFD and SD

Month	EFD	LFD/SD	t	p
10	26.5	14.9	2.16	<.04
12	27.1	16.9	1.68	<.01
14	41.6	24.2	2.52	<.01

tions gained per month. We found that the EFD group increased their mean percentage of syllabic utterances by 3.78% over the period of 10 to 14 months, the LFD by a mean of 1.82% and the SD by a mean of 1.47%. Thus, the EFD show the most rapid rate of structural acquisition, followed by the LFD, followed by the SD. Examination of the rate of structural gain from month to month for each of the groups revealed no evidence of catch-up behavior. The EFD started out ahead of the other groups and their rate of structural gain was twice that of the other two groups.

Finally, we were interested in determining the relation between the development of syllabic vocalizations and the development of a 50-word production vocabulary. To determine this, we correlated these two measures. Significant correlations were not found at 10 and 12 months, but were found at 14 months ($r = .43$, $p < .03$) and 16 months ($r = .52$, $p < .03$). The child's phonetic ability as measured by his production of syllabic utterances appears related to his lexical development. This makes good sense. Babies who could more rapidly conrol their articulations, as indicated by their early syllabic production, could more rapidly plan the production of words. It appeared to us that this might be a good predictor of later language production, and we examine whether or not this is the case in a later chapter. For now, as we indicated in the previous section of this chapter, two boys who appeared to be very slow in this development gave some signs of being delayed in language development at 3 or more years.

SUMMARY

During this first year of life we looked at crying and babbling. We found that by 8 months babies cried very little, at least when we were visiting them. By 12 months, cry only composed a mean 10% of all the vocalizations produced by the infants in our study at that month's visit. We also found that the measures of cry that we used (loudness, length, and pitch), and measure of change over a crying sequence (dysphonation over the second and third exhalation) indicated differences between boys and girls and between full-term and premature infants, but were not predictive of later aspects of language development.

We measured several aspects of babbling at 8, 10, and 12 months that we thought might differ between full-term and premature infants. What we found was that all of these measures varied across children but not across groups. We found no differences in frequency of occurrence of structured vocalizations between boys and girls or between full-term and premature infants. We did find that frequency of occurrence of these structured vocalizations steadily increased over these months from 9% at 8 months to 19% at 10 months to 25% at 12 months. Two of our babies had produced no syllabic utterances by 12 months and 2 were extraordinarily productive babblers. We found that we could characterize our sample of children into EFDs, LFDs and SDs. All the SDs were boys but not all were premature. Children remained members of their group throughout this first year.

Two aspects of this somewhat different pattern of development seemed important. First, when the proportion of responsiveness of mothers to babble in relation to rate of development of babble was examined, no relation was found. This is discussed further in chapter 6. Second, the children's proportion of syllabic utterances at the beginning of the second year was related to their rate of productive vocabulary development during the second year. Thus age and rate of production of syllabic utterances were related to age and rate of spoken vocabulary development. A possible predictor of later development might have been determined.

All in all, the most outstanding feature of structured vocalization development was variation in pattern across children. Two children in our study exemplify the variation in the rate of this aspect of language development. Thus, although rate of development of structured vocalizations is related to rate of development of words this may not always be the case.

Sarah was an incredible child. She was Judy and Paul's second child and there was one other child in the family from Paul's previous marriage. Sarah was all smiles and happiness. At 6 months old, when we visited, her mother sang to her and rocked her to sleep. When her mother would finish a rhythmic line she would pat Sarah on the back. Soon Sarah began to anticipate the phrase and would vocalize and pat her mother. At 8 months of age, she could clap her hands when asked. She did this for her mother, and for us too. When we asked we did not gesture, but that did not matter very much. Sarah was a big talker. She babbled a lot and made many syllablelike utterances. By the time she reached her first birthday, she could comprehend 50 words and say 10. She was well on her way.

Calvin was a second child. He was cute. He played alone a lot of the time, and developed numerous ways to keep himself happily occupied. He had a brother, Ben, who was 4 years older. Ben talked a lot, and it was sometimes hard for Calvin to get his share of the conversation. Calvin's mother returned to work when Calvin was quite young. Calvin's father had left home when Calvin was about 1 year old. Calvin spent most of his weekdays with a babysitter, but the family would have nights and weekends together. Calvin enjoyed being read to. He would sit and listen closely, and point to various pictures when asked. Although not always correct in his choices, hearing the same books over and over always resulted in a few new successes for Calvin. He could also make his needs known. Calvin would point and vocalize, and reach and ask. Calvin was quieter than Sarah. He vocalized less and there was less conversational interaction between Calvin and his mother, and Calvin and his sibling than between Sarah and her family. At 12 months, Calvin was very different from Sarah in his use of words. He could not yet understand 10 words nor could he say any. Although Sarah was able to direct her world with words, Calvin controlled his through his actions. Calvin's mother was not concerned about him and neither were we because he exhibited so much intention to communicate that we felt words were on their way, and they were.

The first year ends with much accomplished. All of our children are able to communicate. Some do so with words and gestures, others have not yet begun to talk. Interestingly, no matter whether they have words or not, they have all had numerous opportunities to participate successfully in conversation, and to learn its value. During the next year all of our babies would begin to use words.

SOME IMPLICATIONS FOR ASSESSMENT AND INTERVENTION

There were some language behaviors on the part of the infant during this first year of life that are important to note. These might be signposts of language development that observers should obtain. There are other behaviors on the part of caregivers that seem most supportive of language growth, and might be encouraged.

Although the production of structured vocalizations varied across children, we believe that there is an important relation between such productions and later lexical development. It was found that a mean 25% of our infants productions at 12 months were these structured vocalizations. An assessment of the proportion of such vocalizations in a sample obtained from the baby may be an important indication of the rate of development of articulation of language. A very low proportion of or absence of these vocalizations, together with a very small number or absence of words comprehended at 12 months may be signposts that these infants should be watched carefully or might have to have their hearing assessed again.

Caregiver behaviors that appear to support further language growth during this first year are response to cry behavior, and attention to the vocabulary development of the infants. The first observation is supported by data, the second by intuition. When crying is responded to promptly it is replaced by noncry vocalizations more rapidly. This indicates that there should be prompt and consistent response to cry vocalizations. Keeping a diary of lexical development seems to focus the caregiver's attention on that aspect of their infant's development and provide concrete rewards for this attention. It may be difficult for some caregivers to keep such a diary. If that is the case, then asking the caregiver to periodically assess the child's lexical development by using the diary materials in Appendix A may serve the same purpose.

CHAPTER 4

The Development
of a First Lexicon:
The Second Year

Jeff was having the time of his life. He had just discovered the swimming pool located in his garden apartment complex. Once a day, sometimes twice a day, his mother would take him for a swim. Jeff was one of those children without fears. In the early summer he would crawl to the pool edge, or in the late summer walk to the pool edge, and just keep going. This was his favorite game. It always brought his mother running at top speed out of her lounge chair. They finally resolved the game by confining Jeff's playing to the area around the children's pool. By the middle of the summer Jeff would stand on the side of the pool and throw himself in the water. But now his mother would watch with relative calm from the side. She clearly adored and enjoyed her first child.

In the house Jeff was just as active and assertive as he was outside. Some might have considered him a little terror. He would run down the narrow hall from the livingroom to the bedrooms all day long. Whenever anyone asked or told him to do something, down the hall he would go. Swimming became a part of his indoor life. If you said the word swim to Jeff, he would throw himself flat down on the floor, as if he were diving in the pool, and laugh.

At 15 months of age, Jeff began to learn the power of words. "Whatzat?" he would demand, pointing at the closest object. As soon as his mother would tell him, his finger would dart to another object and he would yell "Zat?" asking for yet another name. "Dat" he would scream with his arm stretched out to an object, commanding his mother to fetch. "No" he would assert when he was asked almost any question. "Do you want candy?" his mother would say. "No" he answered while his little hands pushed the candy

65

in his mouth. By his second birthday, however, Jeff could have provided the content for a book entitled, *The Power of Words.*

Jeff, like the rest of our babies, had spent his first year learning about the world. He learned which objects you shake to hear a noise, and which ones you throw. Learning about throwing was more difficult than learning about shaking. He learned how to get his mother to respond, and how to respond himself. Knowing all of this he was ready in the second year to put words to the music.

In many ways the phrase "putting words to the music" describes the process. The words serve as a more explicit means of making intentions clear. The young nonverbal child can indicate when he or she wants something through gesture and vocalizing, but the use of the words accompanied by the now well-practiced gestures works faster. Although the word "no" produces wonderful results, the child already knew other means for expressing his or her displeasure. Mapping words onto newly acquired knowledge about the world of objects and actions becomes a major activity for the second year of life.

A process that accompanies this mapping is the freeing of the word from the specific context in which it is spoken. Early in the mapping process the word is tied not only to the object, but also to the presence of that object. Later the word can be used when the object is not around. So, for example, the young child will begin by using the word "ball" when he sees the ball. Only later will he say "ball" when he is trying to decide on a game to play and there is no ball in sight. Being able to talk about objects and events in their absence allows for communication about not only what is present and ongoing but also about what happened in the past and what will happen in the future. The foundation for this ability is laid in the child's second year.

In this chapter we describe the cognitive development of the infants in the study. We do this first because claims have been made about the relation between cognitive and lexical development. We then discuss how the infants in the study acquired their first words. We discuss both similarities and differences among the children in the rate, amount, and content of their early words, and in the stategies that they seem to be using to acquire words. During this second year many infants begin to combine words. We end the chapter by talking about our assessment of the children's comprehension of some two-word phrases that indicate relations between the words.

COGNITIVE ABILITY

When our children reached their first birthday we measured their cognitive ability for the first time. Each child was given the Bayley Scales of Infant Development (Bayley, 1969). Table 4.1 summarizes the children's perfor-

TABLE 4.1
Performance on the Bayley Scales

Scale	N	M	SD	Minimum	Maximum
MDIGA	53	117.0	20.45	50	150
MDICA	53	109.3	20.84	50	150
PDIGA	53	99.9	20.50	50	136
PDICA	53	94.5	18.79	50	136

mance on the Mental Development scale (MDI) that measures perceptual and cognitive ability and the Motor Development scale (PDI) that measures gross and fine motor skills. Scores for the premature children are reported both corrected and uncorrected for prematurity. When a score is followed by GA, it means that it has been corrected; when followed by CA, it is uncorrected. For both scales, the mean is 100 and the standard deviation is 15 for the sample of children with whom the measure was standardized. Our children as a group were clearly within normal limits.

Figure 4.1 shows the distribution of scores on the MDIGA, and the PDIGA. The scores our babies obtained on the MDIGA were skewed toward the very high end, and those obtained on the PDIGA were normally distributed. We were somewhat concerned about the two children with the lowest MDI scores. Their PDI scores were below -1 standard deviation as well. One of the children was born prematurely and had a very stormy first couple of months. He had been in the hospital for 18 weeks after birth, and had required oxygen for several weeks after his discharge. At the request of his pediatrician, he was enrolled in an early intervention program. He attended 2 mornings a week and had done so since he was 6 months old. The other child was Jeff, the little boy described earlier. He too was slightly premature, but nothing about his early history appeared very different. He didn't enjoy being tested, and often refused tasks. He also spent most of the testing time running away down the hall. We decided that we should watch both children closely.

We next considered the differences between our full-term babies and our premature babies. A display of these data is seen in Table 4.2.

As seen in Table 4.2, statistical analyses of the Bayley score for both the full-term and premature children showed that the only difference between our premature and normal children was on the MDICA ($t = 3.32, p < .001$), and this difference disappeared when we corrected for prematurity. We also examined differences in results between boys and girls, and between socio-economic groups. We found no significant differences.

When the children were 19 months old, we tested them again using the Uzgiris and Hunt Ordinal Scales of Psychological Development as modified by Dunst (1980). These scales are designed to determine the child's level of cognitive development in six structurally related areas. The Dunst version of

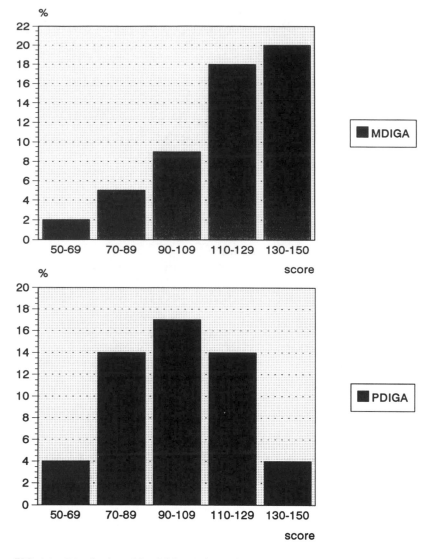

FIG. 4.1. Distribution of the children in the study on the MDIGA and PDIGA scales of
the Bayley.

these scales allows for conversion of the child's highest level of performance
within each area to an age score and subsequently a deviation score. We
discuss our children's performance in relation to age and stage. Table 4.3
presents a profile of our children's performance on each of the subscales.

Our children did exceedingly well on each of the measures. Ninety percent
of them reached at least Stage 5 on five of the six subscales. Only on the vocal

TABLE 4.2
Mean Bayley Scores for Full-Term and Premature Children

Score	Full-Term Children		Premature Children	
	M	SD	M	SD
MDIGA	117.9	17.94	116.0	23.09
MDICA	117.9	17.94	100.5	20.18*
PDIGA	97.6	19.02	102.4	22.03
PDICA	97.6	19.02	91.3	18.36

*$p < .001$.

TABLE 4.3
Percentage of Children Scoring at Each Stage on the Uzgiris–Hunt Scales

Subscales	Stages					
	1 (%)	2 (%)	3 (%)	4 (%)	5 (%)	6 (%)
Object Permanence						100
Means–ends					15	85
Vocal imitation			6	13	15	65
Gestural imitation			2	6	80	13
Operational Causality			2		27	71
Spatial				2	2	96
Schemes				2	8	90

imitation subscale were more than 10% of the children functioning below Stage 5. In addition, all of the children had achieved object permanance at the Stage 6 level and means–end relations at the Stage 5 level. To explore further the relation between these cognitive measures and the children's acquisition of language, we contrasted the mean age scores for the children who had not yet comprehended 100 words with the group means, and those who had not yet produced 50 words with the group means. These data are shown in Fig. 4.2. The data show that both slow comprehenders and slow producers perform below fast comprehenders and producers on all scales. Both slower groups are markedly below their faster peers on Vocal Imitation. Thus, slow comprehenders as well as producers have much lower mean scores on this scale. This suggests that slow comprehenders may result in slow producers. Slow production may, in turn, be related to delayed verbal imitation. Only slow comprehenders have markedly lower mean scores on the Relating to Objects scale. However, only 1 of the 12 children represented in the slower production group could imitate either an unfamiliar word or sound pattern, and only 5 played symbolically. Thus, on the whole, slow comprehension and delay in development of symbolic play go together. Slow production and

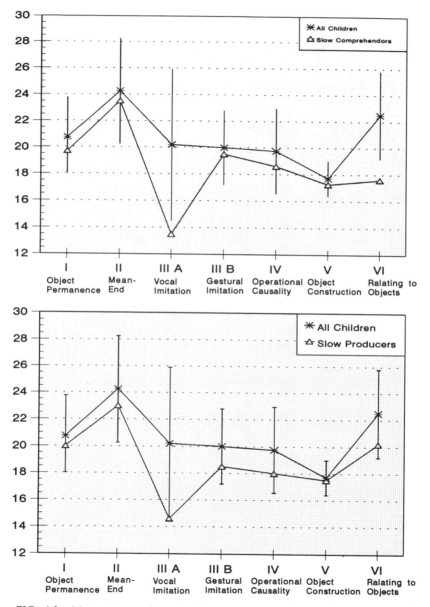

FIG. 4.2. Mean scores and standard deviations on the Uzgiris–Hunt Scales of all children compared to slow word comprehendors and slow producers.

delay in development of symbolic play may go together. As discussed in the previous chapter, other researchers (Rescorla & Goosens, 1992) found such a relation.

Table 4.4 describes the correlations between the subscale scores and measures of lexical development. These data indicate that there are some significant relations between age of comprehension and production of words and scale scores, and many that are not significantly related to each other. One explanation of these findings may be that in those cases when cognitive developments are simultaneous with language development (like some aspects of object permanance and means–ends referred to earlier; Gopnik & Meltzoff, 1986) these cognitive and linguistic behaviors mutually influence the rate of development in both areas. Other cognitive developments that are either verbal—like the ability to imitate—or are highly related to verbal behavior—like the ability to use an object to stand for another object (symbolic play) may be dependent on word knowledge, both word meaning and realization or production of a word. The data we obtained suggest that word acquisition and various aspects of cognition appear to be interdependent and influencing one another. Although the acquisition of words may require particular cognitive underpinnings, that are also required for knowledge of means–ends relations or object permanance, the ability to replicate novel verbal patterns, engage in symbolic play, and the proliferation of words used may be influenced by the child's linguistic competences.

Our children were now 7 months older than when we assessed their cognitive ability previously. We were interested in the relation between their earlier performance on the Bayley and their current performance on the Uzgiris–Hunt Scales. We assessed this relation, and the data are displayed in Table 4.5.

The children's performance on the Uzgiris and Hunt scales correlated significantly with both the PDI and MDI scores. Scores obtained on the PDI of the Bayley were more strongly related to the scales than the scores obtained on the MDI as far as the individual children were concerned. The two children whose performance was somewhat depressed on the Bayley Scales performed at age level on the Uzgiris and Hunt Scales. However, there were now two other children who performed more than 2 standard deviations below our group mean. One of these children had cerebral palsy, involving principally lower limbs. However, the cerebral palsy clearly affected his ability to manipulate the small objects. This is required in the Uzgiris and Hunt Scales. The other child, Billy, was quite interesting.

Billy was a full-term baby who had nothing remarkable in his birth history. He was a beautiful child with large dark eyes. His early progress was like that of the other children we visited. His Bayley performance at 13 months was strong on the MDI (117) but weak on the PDI (63). His ability to comprehend words was similar to that of our other children, but his ability to

TABLE 4.4

Means, Standard Deviations, and Pearson Product Moment Correlations of Scores on the Ordinal Scales With Comprehension and Production of Words

Deviation Score for Total Test / Variable	1	2	3	4	5	6	7	8	9	10	Mean	SD
	-.38**	-.37**	-.50^b	-.49**	.80**	.63**	.42**	.70**	.41*	.84**	1.442	2.365
1. Comp. 50 words											13.439	2.038
2. Prod. 10 words	.79**										14.151	2.527
3. Prod. 50 words	.71**	.78**									18.380	2.527
Age Scores												
4. Obj. Perman.	-.25	-.27	-.17								20.788	2.703
5. Means Ends	-.09	-.12	-.13	.38**							24.325	3.444
6. Vocal Imit.	-.49**	-.51**	-.66**	.20	.18						20.112	4.718
7. Gest. Imit.	-.04	-.05	-.34*	-.01	.20	.36**					19.902	2.053
8. Oper. Caus.	-.31*	-.37**	-.27	.32*	.61**	.36**	.04				19.666	2.903
9. Obj. Constr.	.09	.25	-.01	.04	.39**	.09	.33*	.04			17.888	1.518
10. Relate to Obj	-.36**	-.41**	-.47**	.37**	.66**	.47**	.19	.62**	.30*		22.303	2.360

*df = 49, p < .05; two-tailed. **df = 49, p < .01; two-tailed.

TABLE 4.5
Correlation Between 13 Months Bayley Scores and 20 Months Uzgiris–Hunt Scores

| | | | Correlations | |
| | | | | |
Measures	M	SD	MDI	PDI
Overall age score	21.	2.38	.28*	.501*
Deviation age score	1.4	2.34	.27*	.509**

*df = 49, p < .05. **df = 49, p < .001.

produce them was delayed. He didn't say 10 words until he was 19 months old. He also was a little late in learning to walk. It was not until almost 20 months that he could move about freely, although he sat and did other motoric things on time. His mother told us that Billy seemed to be following his father's pattern. His father had learned both to walk and talk late. His mother was not concerned about his walking, but around 18 months expressed some concern over his not talking. About a month after we gave Billy the Uzgiris and Hunt Scales, Billy's behavior changed.

As we said, he began to walk. He also rapidly added to his vocabulary. Within 2 1/2 months of his 10th word he acquired 50 words. From this point on his development looked like the rest of our children. Billy appears to have reached a temporary plateau in some aspects of his development during the first half of the second year of his life. When he began to increase his skills in these aspects, however, his progress was very rapid. This type of temporary plateau was typical of many of our children at various points over the 3–year period.

We had strong indications that Billy was doing fine in other aspects of his language and motor development. For example, his word comprehension was appropriate, and so were other motor milestones. From Billy and other children we learned that development was characterized by spurts and plateaus as well as periods of steady progress.

The final comparisons we made on these data were between our full–term and premature children. There was no difference between the groups when we compared them on their overall score. We found no difference whether or not we corrected the premature children for gestational age. Having found no difference between these groups, we then contrasted our 12 smallest premature children with the full–term babies. These 12 children had an average birthweight of 1,204 grams (range from 794 grams to 1,530 grams). This was significantly different from the rest of the premature children in the group, who weighed a mean 1,892 grams. Our 12 smallest premature or very low birthweight children (VLB) were significantly smaller than other children and, from a medical perspective, at greater risk. This group of children differed significantly from the full–term group when scores were uncorrected but performed similarly when scores were corrected. These findings are presented in Table 4.6.

In summary, the cognitive testing we did on our children during their second year of life showed that all of our babies could be considered as developing within normal limits. There was a weak but significant relation between the measures we obtained at 13 months and those taken at 19 months, even though we used different tests resting on somewhat different ways of categorizing cognitive development. Further, by 19 months of age all but our smallest premature children, those less than 1,500 grams, performed like our full-term children without correction for prematurity. Finally, we noted that our children's performance on the Uzgiris and Hunt Scales and their lexical ability were related. The strongest relations existed between lexical development and the ability to imitate and the ability to perform schemes on objects. These results must be viewed from the perspective that other aspects of cognitive development, like object permanance and means–ends, were already achieved. Other researchers (Gopnik & Meltzoff, 1986) whom we referred to earlier, found that certain words and the development of these earlier cognitions take place simultaneously. Our findings showed the interdependence of language and cognition in terms of these later developments. However, it seems logical to think that these later developments are in fact dependent on word acquisition, both comprehension and production.

The most important thing we learned from these data, we learned from Billy. He showed us so clearly that development, be it linguistic or cognitive, was not always smooth and steady but, rather, showed periods of plateaus and spurts, and that particular aspects of each of these developments might be slowed or speeded in particular children.

LEXICAL DEVELOPMENT

The mothers' diaries of their children's lexical acquisition provided us with a very rich source of data. These data are described from several perspectives. First, we discuss the childrens' rates of acquisition for the first 100 words they

TABLE 4.6
Mean Deviation Scores on Uzgiris–Hunt Scales for Full-Term and VLB Children

Variable	Group	M	SD	t
Chronological age	Full-term	1.1	2.7	2.11*
	VLB	− .9	2.6	
Gestational age	Full-term	1.1	2.7	− .34
	VLB	1.4	2.6	

*p < .05

comprehended, and the first 50 words they produced. We contrast these data with data gathered by others (Benedict, 1979; Nelson, 1973) who also used the diary procedure. Patterns found in the rate of development are described, and are associated with other aspects of development. Next, we describe some qualitative aspects of lexical development by discussing the semantic categories to which words were assigned. Finally, we contrast our full-term babies with our premature children and see how gender and socioeconomic class interacted with development.

The mean age at which the children achieved each of the milestones is presented in Table 4.7. Rates of comprehension and production were measured after the first 10 words. On the average, the children began word comprehension early. Approximately 30% of them ($N = 16$) understood 10 words before 10 months of age. Most of the children were able to understand 50 words before they could produce 10 words. There is about a 3 1/2-month lag between the time the children comprehended 10 words and produced 10 words, and almost a 5-month difference between the time they reached comparable points for 50 words. There is clear evidence here for the frequently reported claim that word comprehension preceeds production. There is also an assymetry in the rate of lexical development. Children add words to their comprehension lexicon much more rapidly than they do to their production. Further, the comprehension of the first 50 words develops more slowly than the comprehension of the second 50 words. Research on rate of acquisition of new words from 2 to 6 years suggests that it increases very rapidly over this period when so-called "fast mapping" takes place (Carey, 1978).

Other studies have used the lexical diary procedure. It is therefore interesting to compare our results to others. Table 4.8 shows the mean scores we obtained contrasted with those obtained by Benedict (1979), who followed

TABLE 4.7
Age in Months of Attainment of Comprehension and Production of Words

Variable	M	SD	Age Range ± 1 SD (Middle 68%)
Comprehension 10 words	10.7	1.80	8.9–12.5
Comprehension 50 words	13.5	2.10	11.4–15.6
Comprehension 100 words	15.8	2.40	13.4–18.2
Production 10 words	14.2	2.55	11.7–17.1
Production 50 words	18.4	2.50	15.9–20.9
Comprehension Rate Gain/Mo. 10–50 words	17.2	9.06	8.2–26.3
Comprehension Rate Gain/Mo. 10–100 words	21.7	14.58	7.1–26.3
Production Rate Gain/Mo. 10–50 words	11.6	6.27	5.3–17.8

TABLE 4.8
Comparative Data on Lexical Acquisition

		Language Indices Project	Benedict	Nelson
Comprehension	10 words	10.7	*	*
	50 words	13.5	13.50	*
	100 words	15.8	*	*
Production	10 words	14.2	*	15.1
	50 words	18.4	18.15	19.6
Comprehension rate (10–50)		17.2	*	*
Comprehension rate (10–100)		21.7	22.23	*
Production rate		11.6	9.09	11.1

*not reported

eight children, and Nelson (1973), who followed 18 children. There is remarkable similarity across the studies.

Means and standard deviations do not provide data about individual children. We therefore explored the individual children's scores for those who performed more than 1 standard deviation behind the group. These children would presumably be in the lowest 15% of children on these measures. There were three children who were below this point on each of five lexical development measures (Comprehension 10, 50, 100; Production 10 and 50). Of these three children, one was enrolled in language therapy when he was 2 1/2 years old. A second was brought in for a re-evaluation of his speech and language at his physician's request when he was a little more than 3 years old, and the third child did not perform below the group norms on any subsequent measure.

If 2 standard deviations below the mean is used as the cut-off point, none of these children is below the cut-off score on all five measures. It appears that although slow development on a simple early measure of lexical acquisition may flag children who should be monitored, this finding indicates that the late onset and mastery of a first lexicon need not be a good indication of later delay in linguistic development. This is also true from the opposite point of view. There were children who later were enrolled in therapy whose performance at this time was at or above the mean on this measure. However, delay in onset and mastery of a first lexicon, in interaction with other measures may be a good indicator. This possibility is discussed further in the last chapter.

We found that the responsiveness of the mother did not play a significant role in word acquisition. This is discussed at much greater length in chapter 6. We then wondered what other behaviors may have influenced this pattern of development. We calculated the correlations between the age the children produced a 50-word lexicon and a number of other important cognitive and linguistic variables. We found that several variables correlated significantly. The most important correlate as determined by a stepwise multiple regression was the age of comprehension of 100 words ($r = .81$), which accounted for 66% of the variance. This, of course, although it seems to make good sense, need not be the case. Rate of word production need not be related to word comprehension because they can require somewhat different abilities. However, in our study they were very highly related.

Not only were we interested in the rate of our children's lexical development, but we were also interested in more qualitative aspects. Exactly what were the children talking about? Each of the words comprehended and produced were assigned to a semantic category. The category system is described in Appendix C. The results of this analysis for all of the children are presented in Table 4.9. As can be seen in this table, the words used also fall into syntactic categories such as noun, pronoun, verb, adverb, and adjective.

A review of these data shows that the children mastered words in every

TABLE 4.9
Semantic Categories Assigned to Words in the First Lexicon

	Example	Comprehension (%)	Production (%)
Nominals		62	66
Specific	Snoopy	10	14
General		52	52
Animate	boy	2	4
Inanimate	shoe	50	47
Pronouns	he	0	1
Action Word		29	18
Social act-ion games	peek-a-boo	7	6
Events		2	★
Locatives	there	7	3
General Actions	walk	13	9
Modifiers		5	6
State	up	2	3
Attributes	dirty	1	1
Locatives	chair	2	1
Posses-sives	my	0	1
Personal–Social		4	10
Assertions	yes	1	2
Social Expressions	hi	3	8

★Not present in production by definition.

category in both their comprehension and production. Each of the children knew and used words for specific people, pets, and objects, and all used words for common objects. Object words described household items, boys, food, body parts, clothing, and vehicles. All of the children also used action words and words from the other classes. However, individual children often lacked words of a specific type.

For example, only 25% of the children used pronouns, whereas 50% used words like "yes" or "want" to assert. In general, our children understood and used words from every major semantic category. They could understand and talk about many kinds of things. Words for general nominals and action words predominated in our children's comprehension and production. Eighty-one percent of the words the children comprehended were from these two categories, and 70% of those they produced were from these two groups. There was no child whose lexicon was made up exclusively of words from these two groups.

We did observe some differences between comprehension and production. One major difference was that our children comprehended a larger number of action words than they produced. Earlier we suggested that, although there was a general trend to the overall relations between comprehension and production of words, there also might be particular differences between these two abilities. By contrast, the children produced more personal–social words than they comprehended. These same asymmetries have been noted by others (Benedict, 1979). The developmental processes that motivated these differences were not explored directly but one possibility is that the increased frequency of comprehension of action terms was related to the large number of directives and protodirectives that mothers issue to their 1-year-olds. Mothers spend much time asking their children to do things. "Clap your hands," "Get the ball," "Say night-night," are only a few of the action commands children hear daily. The frequent use of protodirectives, asking the child to do what he or she is in the process of doing, may make clear to the child the relation between an action and the word or words that code it. This is similar to the mothers' use of nominals that refer to objects in the "here" and "now." Use under these conditions clarifies relations between words and objects and events in the environment. The large number of nouns versus verbs that many researchers have found in early lexicons may be due to verbs, or actions, in relation to nouns, being understood but not expressed. Both early and later researchers concerned with the child's first words have speculated about this possibility (Menyuk, 1992). Finally, the greater production as compared to comprehension of personal– social words might be because these words are imitated rather than generated.

We also examined our diary information for any differences we could observe between individual children. In some early work, Nelson (1973) noted that there appeared to be two groups of children. One group seemed to learn an object-oriented language and the other learned a social interaction language. She called the former group referentials (R), and defined them as children whose 50-word vocabularies contained more than 25 general nominal words. She called the latter group expressives (E), and defined them as using less than 50% of their words in the general nominal category.

Within our group of children, the number of general nominals used per child ranged from 17 to 39. Rather than dividing our children using the 50% criterion, we identified a group of E children (N = 9) and a group of referential children (N = 17) using the following criterion. The R children used 60% or more general nominals, and the E children used 40% or less. To determine if there were differences in the patterns of words used by E and R children, we compared the distribution of their words into categories eliminating those words that were general nominals. Figure 4.3, shows the data.

Once the general nominals were omitted and the percentages of different word types recalculated, we found no differences between our groups. This was somewhat of a surprise because earlier researchers like Bates (1976) and Nelson (1973) not only found this type of distinction but they, and other researchers, suggested that these two "types" of language learners may either have different kinds of language learning experiences (Furrow & Nelson, 1984) or, in fact, have different neurological organizations or cognitive

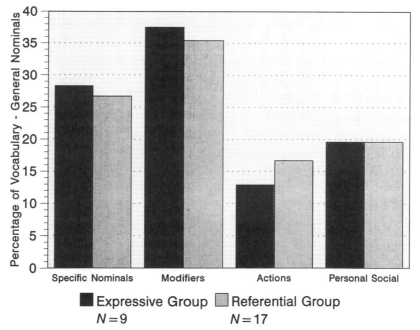

FIG. 4.3.   Distribution of word usage patterns by children classified as expressers and referrers without including their use of general nominals.

strategies for learning that will affect many aspects of their learning, not just language (Bates, O'Connell, & Shore, 1987). It has been suggested by some that E children may be those who later have language problems.

The difference between children who adopted a strategy for learning words for objects and children who adopted a strategy for learning personal-social words was examined further. To find out how these two approaches might affect acquisition, we correlated the proportion of general nominal words in the children's productive vocabularies with several other language production and comprehension measures. There was no correlation between the ages at which children comprehended or produced a 50-word lexicon and the number of R words used. There was a significant correlation between this measure and the rate at which they added words to their productive vocabularies ($r = .45$, $p < .01$), but not with the rate at which they added words to their comprehension vocabularies. Also, there was no significant correlation between R style and utterance length (MLU) measured at 22, 25, and 29 months of age, nor vocabulary comprehension measured with the Peabody at outcome. Thus, the strategy of learning a large number of names for objects appears to be related to rapid acquisition of words, but not to the final age of acquisition of a lexicon of a certain size or to the other measures of language development outlined earlier. Children whose productive word acquisition progresses rapidly seem to focus their learning efforts on the names of things. Children who are slower spread their word acquisition efforts to other areas. Because the former strategy affects rate of learning more than mastery, it is not surprising that correlations with later measures such as MLU and the Peabody are not significant.

Finally, we examined the data for differences between the lexical development of our preterm and full-term children. The mean ages for each of the comprehension measures are shown in Fig. 4.4, and for the production measures are shown in Fig. 4.5.

Some significant differences between the preterms and the full-terms were found using the corrected ages that are indicated in these figures. When the uncorrected ages for both comprehension and production are compared, our preterm children look like our full-term children. However, when our corrected ages are compared, we find that the preterm children are doing significantly better than the full-term children.

These findings raised the issue of the appropriateness of correcting scores and ages on language measures for prematurity. The use of the correction made our preterm children look better than our full-term children. To explore this issue further we contrasted the lexical diary ages we obtained from our 12 smallest preterm children (these were the babies whose birth-weights were less than 1,530 grams) with our full-term group. Table 4.10 shows our findings.

For this group of children using the correction did not affect our findings.

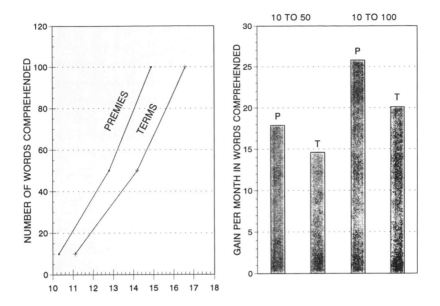

FIG. 4.4. Age and rate comparisons of premature and full-term children in early word comprehension.

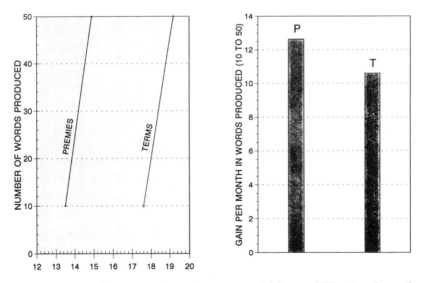

FIG. 4.5. Age and rate comparisons of premature and full-term children in early word production.

Except for the age at which the smallest children comprehended 10 words, there were no significant differences between the VLB premature children and the full-term group in the ages at which the lexical milestones were reached or in rates of acquisition.

Another method for assessing the usefulness of correction scores is to determine whether they allow you to predict subsequent development more accurately. As measures of subsequent development, we chose the scores the children obtained on the Peabody Picture Vocabulary Test, which is a vocabulary comprehension test, and the scores obtained on the vocabulary subtest of the Stanford–Binet Test of Intelligence. This subtest measures lexical production. These tests were administered to the younger children when they were 30 months and to the older children when they were 36 months. The only significant correlation we found between earlier measures of lexical development and these later tests of lexical comprehension and production was the age of production of 50 words and the Peabody scores. No other significant relations were found between the measures. This correlation is $-.39$ when corrected scores for the Peabody, and for age at which 50 words are produced is examined. It is $-.35$ when uncorrected scores are used. Both these correlations are significant ($p < .05$). The earlier the age at which a child acquires 50 productive words, the higher his or her score on the Peabody. These results raise some questions that are discussed further in the chapter.

We have now described the lexical development of our children. In summary, the children as a group mastered the comprehension of 100 words by 16 months and the production of 50 words by 18 months. Some children started to produce words when they were very young (by about 10 months), whereas others began 4 to 5 months later. Of the children who began later, there was a large group who quickly reached 50 different words. There was

TABLE 4.10

Mean Ages (in months) of Preterm and Full-Term Groups on Acquisition of Lexical Comprehension

		Preterm	
Measure	Full-Term	Corrected	Uncorrected
Comprehension 10 words	11.1 months	10.3	12.0
Comprehension 50 words	14.2 months	12.8**	14.4
Comprehension 100 words	16.6 months	14.9**	16.6
Comprehension rate 40 words	14.6 per month	20.1*	—
Comprehension rate 90 words	17.9 per month	25.77	—

*$p < .05$. **$p < .01$.

another small group who plodded along more slowly. The rate at which children progressed was most highly correlated with their lexical comprehension. This is why it was surprising that their age of acquisition of 50 productive words was related to their Peabody scores. Their rate of development did not appear to be influenced by mothers' responsiveness to vocalizations. In word comprehension and production, our premature children as a group performed as well as our full-term babies as a group. When we corrected for prematurity, our preterm babies performed better than our full-term babies. When we corrected the scores of our smallest preterm children we found that they looked no different than the full-term babies.

These early lexical scores did not, on the whole, predict later lexical performance, and only the age of production of 50 words was related to 2 1/2- or 3-year-old performance on a word comprehension test. This was true whether the scores were corrected or uncorrected. However, when all outcome language comprehension measures were examined it was found that age of comprehension of 100 words was significantly related to these outcome measures for full-term children ($r = .81$). Further, when all outcome production measures were examined it was found that age of comprehension of 100 words was significantly related to these outcome measures for both full-term ($r = .74$) and premature ($r = .71$) children. Therefore, rate of word comprehension does predict later language development in terms of the measures we used. The significance of these findings is discussed at further length in the final chapter.

TWO-WORD COMBINATION COMPREHENSION

When the children were 14 months old, we began to assess their comprehension of multiword utterances, using toys that we had given them. The testing procedure is described in chapter 2, and the protocol can be found in Appendix B. The test is divided into three parts. The first part asks the children to perform semantically predictable actions with objects as in "kiss the bunny" (PRED) where it is clear that they are the agent. The second part asks them to use others as agents, for example "make the bunny kiss" (AA). The last part asks them to perform unusual or anomalous actions like "smell the bunny" (ANOM). The degree of anomalousness had been determined by asking 20 adults to rate a list of sentences on a scale ranging from *most* (1) to *least* (5) in terms of how frequently they thought children might hear this type of request. Only sentences receiving a score of 4 or more were selected for inclusion on this part of our test.

The test was given to most of the children during monthly visits from the time they were 14 months old until they successfully completed all of the items. We began testing some of the children at a somewhat later age because

TABLE 4.11
Mean Age at Mastery of the Two-Word Comprehension Test

	Mean Age (Months)	SD	Age Range ± 1 SD
PRED	20.3	3.32	17.0–23.6
AA	21.4	2.69	18.8–24.1
ANOM	23.1	3.10	20.0–26.1
All Item	23.1	3.04	20.0–26.1

of their rate of lexical development. We describe first the performance of all the children.

Table 4.11 shows our findings. On the average, the children followed the semantically predicable requests at 20 months. About 1 month later, at 21 months, they completed the other agent–action items. They finished both the anomalous items and the test as a whole 1 1/2 months later.

We next examined differences between the performance of our preterm and full-term children. These comparisons are displayed in Table 4.12. Statistical analyses of these data reveal a consistent pattern. When we do not correct for prematurity, our full-term babies are a little earlier in completing the subtests. When we do correct for prematurity our preterms are a little earlier. However, there were no significant differences between our groups whether or not we corrected. No differences between the groups were present when we compared our term babies with our 12 low birthweight children. Children's abilities to process multiword utterances appear unaffected by prematurity when we measure their comprehension during the later part of their second year of life.

We did find a consistent and highly significant difference between the way our boys and girls performed on the test. These data are shown in Fig. 4.6 and may be easily interpreted. Our boys took longer to comply with all of our requests. It is possible that this result does not reflect a difference in competence but rather in compliance.

Examination of the data concerning the ages at which our boys and girls were able to perform items of each type confirms this impression. There were no differences between the boys and girls when we looked at the ages at

TABLE 4.12
Mean Ages (in Months) of Preterm and Full-Term Groups for Two-Word Comprehension

		Preterm	
Measure	Full-Term	Corrected	Uncorrected
PRED	21.0	19.6	21.6
AA	21.7	21.1	23.1
ANOM	23.6	22.5	24.5
All Item	23.6	22.6	24.6

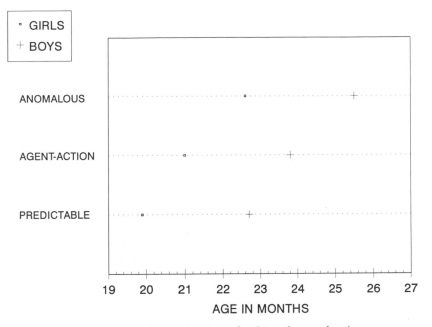

FIG. 4.6.   Age at completion of sections of multiword comprehension test.

which the children first made responses to items of each type. For example, boys and girls reponded to their first anomalous item at the same age, although it took the boys nearly 3 months longer than the girls to perform the entire group of anomalous items. This task was one of the few on which boys and girls differed to any extent.

We considered the results obtained by our children on this multiword comprehension test with language behaviors that preceded and followed it. Before we present these results, an examination of the type of knowledge the children were displaying when they performed correctly is necessary. To respond correctly on many of the items, the children needed only to comprehend the meanings of the individual words. They did not need (in most cases) to understand anything about word order. So if the children knew the meaning of the word "kiss" and the meaning of the word "flower" all they would need to do is kiss the flower. In contrast, it would be highly unlikely that we ask them "to flower the kiss." Although kissing the flower is a strange action, it does not seem to require knowledge of word order. Thus, this test, for the most part, did not measure syntax, but rather semantics. The only items on which knowledge of word order was required were the AA sentences where an agent other than themselves was required to act; that is, the child heard "bunny kiss" and needed to know that the bunny should carry out the action because it appeared before the action. That is, they had to know that the sentence did not mean "you (baby) kiss bunny." However, their performance could, to some extent, again, be based on lexical knowledge; that is, that bunnies kiss but that kisses don't bunny. The relations between multiword comprehension and other language measures are presented in Table 4.13.

An analysis of our correlational findings supports this general conclusion that the task is primarily a semantic not a syntactic one. As Table 4.13 shows, the ability to respond correctly to action requests is significantly correlated with the comprehension of 50 words, which occurred at approximately 13 1/2 months of age. Children who were doing well then continue to do well, and similarly those who took longer to develop a 50-word comprehension vocabulary also took longer to respond to the items on this test. Another look at the table suggests that comprehension and production appear to require different processes. To produce multiword utterances (listed as MLU in Table 4.13), children need to know more than the meanings of words. They need to know how to order the words in relation to the objects, people, and events they are describing. Comprehension of items on our test of two-word comprehension was not significantly related to MLU at 22 months. All together, the significant relations found at this point between early lexical abilities and later language abilities raised more questions than they resolved. These relations were re-examined at a later stage and they began to make more sense. These kinds of findings suggest that general statements concerning prediction of later language development from lexical production during the first 2 years of life need to be questioned.

SPEECH DURING THE EMERGENCE OF WORDS

The speech of the children during the emergence of words was examined acoustically. Forty children were selected for this analysis. Twenty were premature, and 20 were full-term babies. The data collection procedures are described more fully in chapter 2, which is concerned with language mea-

TABLE 4.13
Correlations of Multiword Comprehension Test With Other Linguistic Measures

	Comp. 50 Words	Prod. 50 Words	Number of Nominals	MLU 22 months
PRED	.56*	.36	.35*	.15
AA	.56*	.29	.35	.16
ANOM	.55*	.34	.36	.18
All Item	.54*	.33	.35	.17

*p < .01

sures. By way of summary, we analyzed the children's speech obtained during five consecutive home visits from the time the child first produced at least five words containing one of the target vowels. The acoustic measures consisted of pitch (frequency), time (duration), and quality (formant) measurements of the vowel.

The most interesting data that emerged from these analyses concerned measurements taken on individual children, and it is these findings that we discuss here. For each child, the age at which he or she acquired the height and backing distinctions that differentiated among the vowels was compared. Utterances with high and front vowels as targets (i as in "heat," i as in "hit," oo as in "boot," or u as in "but") were compared to those with low and back vowel targets (a as in "father" or aw as in "dog"). This was done by examining the levels of significance of paired t tests for the first formant frequency of these vowels for each child. For height, this is a primary distinction between these vowels. Development of the front vowels was compared to that of back vowels by comparing second formant frequencies in a similar manner and for the same reason. The months at which the height and backing distinctions were made (to a level of significance of $p < .01$) were noted. Although the children differed in the age at which the height and backing distinctions were acquired and the amount of time needed to achieve both distinctions, the order of acquisition was height before backing in 10 of the 40 children and backing before height in 4 children. For the remaining 26 children, the acquisition order could not be determined because their productions could not be definitively analyzed in the manner described. These data are displayed in the histogram in Fig. 4.7.

Each of the 4 children who acquired backing before height was either being seen for a speech problem at age 3, or was later scheduled for an evaluation because there was concern for the child's speech development. There were no children with diagnosed or suspected speech problems who were not isolated by this developmental reversal. This may be an early indicator of problems in speech production. The height of tongue distinction may require more articulatory control than the backing distinction. However, one would need more data on many more children to suggest that this must be the case.

SUMMARY

During the second year of life of the children in our study we examined those aspects of their development that seemed most crucial to the questions we were asking about possible differences between premature and full-term infants' development. We examined their cognitive and lexical development, and the relation between these two aspects of development. We did an analysis of their speech development as they simultaneously acquired know-

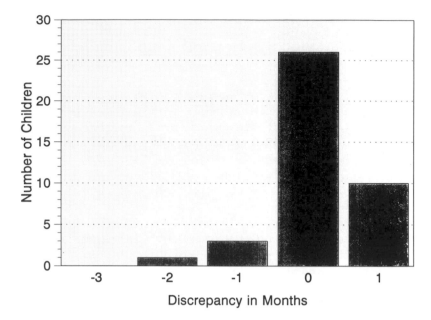

FIG. 4.7.   Delay in months between the acquisition of height and backing distinctions.

ledge of the meanings of words and how to pronounce them. Finally, we began to explore their comprehension of multiword utterances.

What we found was that most of the infants in the study were well within the range of normal on the Bayley, a frequently used measure of cognitive development in infants. Most were well above average on the mental scales of this measure and average on the motor scales. We also found in an early comparison of our premature and full-term children that the premature infants' performance on the mental scales was significantly poorer than that of the full-term infants when the chronological age of these infants was used ($p < .001$). When gestational age was used this difference disappeared.

On the Uzgiris–Hunt Scales all our children did exceedingly well. Ninety percent of them had reached at least Stage 5 on five of the six subscales, and all of them were at Stage 6 of object permanence development. Only on Vocal Imitation were more than 10% of the children functioning below Stage 5. Comparison of the children's lexical development and their performance on this cognitive measure revealed an interesting pattern. The small group of children who had not yet comprehended 100 words looked like the total group on all the scales except for Vocal Imitation and Schemes for Relating to Objects. On these, they performed more poorly. The children who had not yet produced 50 words also contrasted with the total group in this way. Only 1 of these latter 12 children could imitate either an unfamiliar word or sound pattern and only 5 played symbolically. These results might indicate that lexical development may play a crucial role in those aspects of cognitive development measured by these two particular scales.

We found that there were significant relations between the Bayley scores the children had obtained earlier and their performance on the Uzgiris–Hunt Scales. There was a stronger relation between motor scores and Uzgiris–Hunt performance than between mental scores and this performance. The fact that objects have to be manipulated on the Uzgiris–Hunt Scales might have led to this finding and one of the two children who did poorly on the scales was the child in our study who had palsy of the lower limbs.

We found that there were no differences between premature and full-term children on their overall scores on the Uzgiris–Hunt Scales, regardless of whether chronological or gestational ages were used. However, when the very low birthweight infants (average weight = 1,204 grams) were compared to the full-term infants there was a significant difference ($p < .05$) which disappeared when gestational ages were used. Except for this group, by 19 months premature children performed as well as full-term children without correction for gestational age.

Lexical development for all the children was clearly on target. A comparison of the ages at which 100 words were, on average, comprehended, and 50 produced indicated that there was a great deal of similarity between our findings and those of other studies. By about 16 months of age, 100 words are comprehended and by about 18 months, 50 words are produced. There was a significant relation between age of attainment of measures of word comprehension and of word production for individual children. Those who reached the comprehension milestone early reached the production milestone early. There were no significant differences between premature and full-term children on these measures when uncorrected age was used.

The composition of these early lexicons were also quite similar to those found in other studies. They consisted primarily of nominals (above 60%), action words (about 25%), modifers (about 5%), and personal–social words (about 8 %). Individual children had or did not have specific words within a subclass. Only 25% of the children used pronouns and 50% used words like "want" and "yes." There were some differences between the types of words comprehended and produced. The children understood more action words than they produced and produced more personal–social words than they comprehended. The reasons for these differences are probably related to the motivations of the children in comprehending and producing language. A reasonable assumption is that they had a high rate of comprehension of action words so that they could comply with their mothers' requests for action. They had a high rate of production of more personal–social words so that they could get their needs met. Thus, although there was a signifiant relation between the overall rate of development and size of comprehension and production vocabularies, there were, also, some differences between the particular words understood and produced.

It was first found by Nelson (1973) and by other researchers subsequently that children during this period of language development can be roughly divided into "expressers" and "referrers." The first group apparently learn primarily social–personal words and the second group primarily nominals. The two groups were defined by Nelson by the proportion of their use of these two types of words in their 50-word spoken vocabulary. The referrers had more than 25 general nominal words in that vocabulary. We divided our children into referrers and expressers by labeling those children whose spoken vocabulary consisted of more than 60% of general nominals as referrers and those who used less than 40% as expressers. We then made a number of comparisons between the groups. First we examined the distribution of their words into the semantic categories when general nominals were eliminated and found no differences including their use of nouns as compared to pronouns, a finding that is contrary to those of other studies. Second, we examined the correlation of proportion of use of general nominals with several other measures. There was no significant correlation between this measure and ages at which 100 words are comprehended and 50 words produced nor between this measure and MLU at 22, 25, and 29 months, nor this measure and score on the PPVT at 3 years. There was a significant correlation between this measure and the rate at which words are added to the productive vocabulary ($p < .01$). These results were somewhat surprising because a number of researchers have speculated that use of the referring strategy should lead to more rapid language development. The strategy, apparently, only simplifies the task of acquiring productive representations of new words—hence the significant effect on rate of acquisition of a productive vocabulary.

When ages of acquisition of the comprehension and production milestones by premature and full-term children are compared there are no significant differences when chronological age is used. When gestational age is used the premature infants are significantly ahead of their full-term peers in age at which 100 words are comprehended and 50 words produced. There were no significant differences between these measures of the vocabulary development of the 12 VLB infants and full-term infants. Our premature children were clearly keeping pace with the full-term children in lexical acquisition.

Our examination of the children's comprehension of multiword utterances indicated that at about 20 months they understood semantically predictable utterances, at 21 months agent–action items and at 22 to 23 months all types of items including the anomalous utterances ("tickle car"). On this measure there also were no significant differences between the premature and full-term infants. There were, however, significant differences between the boys and girls in our population. The girls were consistently earlier than the boys in completing all the items within each type of utterance. It is possible that this difference was due to difference in compliance between boys and girls since the ages at which they first began to comprehend each type did not differ.

Only a small aspect of speech development was examined as words began to emerge. The age at which each child acquired height and backing distinctions between vowels and the order in which these distinctions were acquired was determined. There were a number of children with whom no distinct order could be observed. However, It is interesting that of the 4 children who were either being seen for a speech problem at age 3, or who were later scheduled for an evaluation because there was concern for the child's speech development, all 4 acquired the backing before the height distinction. There were no children with diagnosed or suspected speech problems who were not isolated by this developmental reversal. It is possible that, because the height distinction requires more control of the tongue than does the backing distinction, this behavior marks a difference in articulatory ability. This is highly speculative and we discuss the relation of speech development to other aspects of language development in the next chapter.

SOME IMPLICATIONS FOR ASSESSMENT

The linguistic and cognitive behaviors of the infants in our study indicated that certain measures might be used to determine those children who should be carefully followed. Clearly, cognitive and linguistic measures are related to each other. There was a relation between the ability of the children in our study to repeat words and to engage in symbolic play on the Uzgiris–Hunt Scale and the age at which 100 words were comprehended and 50 produced. There seems to be a great deal of similarity across studies in the average age at which 50 words are produced. Therefore, age at which 100 words are comprehended (approximately 16 months) and age at which 50 words are produced (approximately 18 months) seems to be important early measures of language development. Use of the test referred to in chapter 2 might be the best procedure for obtaining this measure. Other studies that have looked at word production as a predictor of later language development are discussed in the final chapter.

CHAPTER 5

The Development of Expertise: The Third Year

Ellen was the younger of two children in the family. When we first started visiting with her family, Ellen's older sister Amy was 2 years old. It took us a while to get to know Ellen because Amy, who was quite talkative, outgoing, and able, was always around. Ellen's mother would sometimes express concern that Ellen did not get as much time alone as she might need. She also felt that Ellen was developing more slowly than Amy had developed. From our perspective, Ellen was doing just fine, although she may have learned to do things later than her sibling. Both girls were wonderful by any standards, and their language development was quite rapid.

When we arrived for our last visit, Amy, Ellen, and their mother were busy preparing to act out a play. They had recently seen the movie, *Annie,* most likely for the third time. Amy had just put on her Annie dress, and Ellen was dressed up too. The play began.

Ellen: Down to the basement with you and all the spiders.
(She pretends to kick her mother with her small foot and her mom backs away slowly.)

Mom: Down to the basement with me. (Said in a tiny voice.)
(Ellen pushes her mom into the next room)

Ellen: Down to the basement with you, you rotten orphan. We gotta do what Miss Hannigan says.
(Pretending to be in the basement. Ellen now assumes the role of Molly.)

Mom: Are you scared Molly? Are you in the basement now with all the spiders? Is it scary?

Ellen: Yeah, but I like spiders. Spiders aren't so bad. They can't really hurt me very much.

Amy: Oh yes they can. Spiders can eat you up.

This little episode indicates that Ellen was clearly on her way. She had mastered many of the structural aspects of the language system, and knew multiple ways to use the system. Although many children of Ellen's age may not be as adept as Ellen at language structures, by 3 years old most are able to form both simple and complex sentences, and to use them in a variety of interpersonal situations.

The year between 2 and 3 is an exciting and sometimes trying one for parent and child. The child not only begins to free him or herself from the initial physical dependencies of the early years, but frees him or herself from previous reliance on non-verbal behavior to get what is wanted. Even during the second year of life, mothers spend their time changing diapers, washing and dressing, carrying and feeding their babies. Babies spend time pointing and reaching toward what they want, vocalizing and saying a few words at a time. The majority of their message is carried by single-word, two-word utterances, and phrases combined with actions. In the third year, words, or more properly multiword utterances, replace much of the action part of speech. Children can now say what they want to do, and what they don't want to do. One way to look at the terrible 2s is that it is the child's way of demonstrating the power that he or she has found in words.

There are many new aspects to the child's acquisition of language during this third year of life. One aspect is that the child begins to combine words together in longer and longer utterances that demonstrate progressive mastery over the adult language system. Very rapidly the child moves from making two-word utterances like "more milk" and "open door," to saying things like, "Spiders aren't so bad. They can't really hurt me very much." Little direct teaching can be pointed to as the basis for this language growth.

Another aspect is that children are able to use language to accomplish more and more things. They can use words not only to get things and to describe them, but they also use words to engage in long sequences of imaginary play around a central theme. They can act out and/or tell stories, and can be speaker and listener in a conversation. They can even be themselves and someone else in a play. They can use words to say "no" and, occasionally, even "yes," and use words to reason and to begin to solve problems.

A final aspect of language growth during the third year is that the child, having developed more complex language forms to fulfill more varied functions, now increases her efforts to use language to learn. This means that the child will acquire new knowledge more rapidly as he or she can now learn through words. Parents and others will begin to tell the child as much as they show him or her.

The child, using the language skills mastered during the first 2 years, has a great deal more to learn, both about the world and about language itself. There are myriad details still to be acquired, and many different levels of knowing still to be explored. The third year can be said to mark the beginning of a transition from "learning to talk," to "learning through talk," a task for which the child is now well prepared.

In this chapter, the cognitive development of the children in the study is described first. Then, the varying aspects of language development that were measured are discussed. These aspects include speech development, syntactic development in terms of sentence length and structure and morphological development, lexical or vocabulary development, and conversational development, or how the children in the study participated in conversation. Findings concerning children who appeared to be having problems with particular aspects is discussed in terms of how these problems related to outcome measures. In the final chapter these outcome measures for all our children are presented. This is a comparatively lengthy chapter because language development during the third year of life is filled with dramatic changes.

COGNITIVE DEVELOPMENT

The children's cognitive development was assessed twice during Year 3. All of them were given the Bayley Scales of Infant Development at 28 months of age, and these data were compared to Bayley performance at 13 months. We also gave the children the McCarthy Scales of Children's Abilities (1970) when they exited from the study so that we might have a final measure of cognitive ability. Here we discuss our findings on both of these tests and contrast the results to earlier measures of cognitive performance. We discuss the children's test performance both corrected and uncorrected for prematurity but, as we show, there is little that convinces us to use corrected cognitive scores when children are over a year old.

Measures of Cognitive Development

Bayley Scales of Infant Development. Table 5.1 displays the children's performance on the Bayley Scales at 28 months. As can be seen, the children are doing very well on the mental portion, the average child being more than 1 standard deviation above the mean for the more general population. The children are also doing fine on the motor portion, but on this portion of the test the group looks more average.

We next compared the full-term and premature infants at 28 months of age. The data are described in Table 5.2. Inspection of the data reveals the

TABLE 5.1
Bayley Mean Scores at 28 Months

Scale	N	M	SD	Minimum	Maximum
MDICA	53	121.3	13.09	84	145
MDIGA	53	124.4	13.77	90	145
PDICA	53	104.4	19.36	50	150
PDIGA	53	107.4	20.35	50	150

TABLE 5.2
28-Month Bayley Means Scores for Full-Term and Premature Children

Scale	Full-Term Children		Premature Children	
	M	SD	M	SD
MDICA	123.2	12.52	119.2	13.58
PDICA	109.3	18.30	99.2	19.83*
MDIGA	123.2	12.52	125.6	15.61
PDIGA	109.3	18.30	105.4	22.47

$*t = 1.93$, $df = 51$, $p < .058$.

same pattern we have seen in earlier cognitive data. The premature children do less well than the full-term children, but not significantly so. There is a weak statistical difference on the psychomotor portion as measured by the PDI when the data are not corrected for prematurity. There is no difference on the MDI whether or not the data are adjusted. When the 12 low birth-weight premies are compared to the full-term children, the same pattern is revealed. The only statistically significant difference is between the full-term and premature infants on the PDI when the uncorrected score is used ($t = 2.10$, $df = 37$, $p < .04$). It should be noted, however, that the scores for even these very low birthweight children are well within the normal range. These children's MDI scores were mean = 119.3, standard deviation = 16.05, and PDI scores were mean = 95.0, standard deviation = 22.50. In summary, our Bayley Scales data show that our premature children, including those who were very small at birth, look no different from our full-term children when they are 28 months old. Further, the perceptual and cognitive skills of the group of children we followed are more than 1 standard deviation above the mean of the sample on which the test was standardized. This high score persists whether or not we correct for prematurity, and whether or not we include the scores achieved by our very low birthweight children.

Given how well our children were performing at 28 months, we wondered if this represented a significant change in their performance from 13 months of age. Figure 5.1 shows the amount of change from 13 to 28 months when corrected and uncorrected PDI and MDI scores were used. Inspection of the figure reveals that the greater shift occurs in the MDI scores over the

15-month period. The MDI score when corrected for prematurity yields a statistically significant gain ($t = 3.49$, $df = 100$, $p < .001$), and the same is true when the uncorrected values are used ($t = 2.25$, $df = 100$, $p < .05$.) The children's PDI scores change but only the PDI uncorrected score changes significantly ($t = 2.44$, $df = 100$, $p < .05$). This means that over time our children were performing better and better on this standard test.

McCarthy Scales of Children's Abilities.   As stated previously, all of the children were given the McCarthy when they exited from the study. The older group of children were tested at 36 months and the younger group at 30 months. The McCarthy Scales yield a measure of General Cognitive ability (GCI) that is obtained by combining scores achieved on the Verbal, Perceptual Performance, and Quantitative Scales. Table 5.3 describes our results. These data add support to the conclusions we reached using the Bayley Scales. Our children are performing consistently above the mean. All of the children performed at higher levels than 1 standard deviation below the mean on the McCarthy, and the average for the group was more than 1 standard deviation above the mean.

We next explored the influence of prematurity on McCarthy scores. The tests revealed no significant differences between the groups. These results are

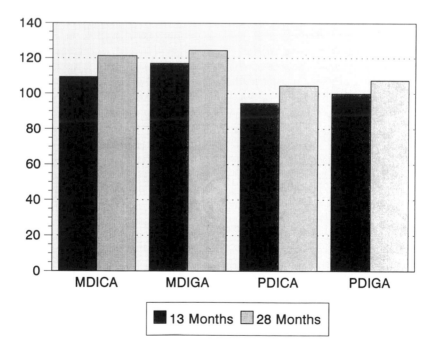

FIG. 5.1.   Comparison of Bayley scores at 13 and 28 months.

TABLE 5.3
McCarthy Mean Scores for All and for Full-Term and Premature Children

Scale	All Children					Full-Term		Premature	
	N	M	SD	Minimum	Maximum	M	SD	M	SD
GCICA	53	120.2	14.29	88	150	123.1	13.08	117.2	15.11
GCIGA	53	122.9	13.49	95	150	123.1	13.08	122.8	14.16

also shown in Table 5.3. Using the uncorrected scores we found a significant difference between the 12 low birthweight children and the full-term children ($t = 2.31$, $df = 37$, $p < .05$). This difference disappeared when the scores were corrected. A look at the average scores obtained from these 12 very small babies, however, shows that even these children as a group performed well above average. Their mean uncorrected score was 112.42 with a standard deviation of 13.85.

Predicting Cognitive Development

A question we asked was what was the relation between earlier cognitive scores and later ones. This question is frequently asked about premature children. The hope is that if a relationship is obtained, researchers and educators might then determine those children with whom early intervention is required. The correlations of the earlier cognitive measures with our later cognitive measures, the McCarthy scores (corrected and uncorrected), are shown in Table 5.4. All of the statistically significant correlations are marked. In terms of prediction, Columns 1 and 2 in this table are of most interest. If we are interested in predicting a corrected McCarthy score, inspection of the data reveals that it makes no difference if corrected or uncorrected Bayley scores

TABLE 5.4
Correlations of the Bayley and the McCarthy Tests

Variable	1	2	3	4	5	6	7	8	9	M	SD
GCICA										119.96	14.53
GCIGA	.94**									122.83	13.75
MDICA 13	.38**	.31*								109.12	21.22
MDIGA 13	.29*	.31*	.90**							116.70	20.71
PDICA 13	.38**	.31*	.55**	.52**						94.67	19.13
PDIGA 13	.32*	.34*	.43**	.53**	.94***					100.09	20.81
MDICA 28	.56**	.59**	.35**	.31*	.30*	.30*				121.31	13.05
MDIGA 28	.49**	.58**	.24	.31*	.26	.35*	.96**			124.51	13.82
PDICA 28	.50**	.42**	.25	.14	.53**	.46**	.55**	.47**		104.00	19.8
PDIGA 28	.46**	.42**	.17	.14	.51**	.50**	.55**	.53**	.98***	107.09	20.67

$*df = 49$, $r < .05$. $**df = 49$, $r < .01$. $***df = 49$, $r < .001$.

are used. If our interest is in predicting the uncorrected McCarthy score there appears to be a difference in which score should be used. For purposes of describing level of cognitive functioning the uncorrected score may be a better indicator, since at some point in the child's life 8 to 12 weeks of prematurity can no longer make a difference. Inspection of the data in column one suggests that no matter which measure is used, the uncorrected score is a better predictor of McCarthy performance than the corrected score.

When we compared the differences between corrected and uncorrected Bayley scores with the McCarthy, there was no difference in our ability to predict from the corrected or uncorrected scores at 13 months. However, a significant difference did exist in this comparison at 28 months. (MDI: $t = 2.94$, $df = 48$, $p < .01$; PDI: $t = 3.28$, $df = 48$, $p < .01$). If prediction is the goal then the uncorrected scores are more predictive of later cognitive performance, and should be used for this purpose.

To determine if there were differences between children with above average cognitive outcomes and those with below average (for the group) cognitive outcomes, we contrasted children whose GCICA scores were at least as deviant as 1 standard deviation above and below the mean. We did this for both the corrected and uncorrected scores to determine if correcting interfered with or facilitated our ability to detect children with markedly different outcomes at a young age.

Table 5.5 shows the comparisons. At 13 months, the only score that differentiated the groups was the MDICA. At 28 months all but the MDIGA score differentiated the group. It seems that the uncorrected MDI score at 13 months and the MDI and PDI uncorrected scores at 28 months were the

TABLE 5.5

Comparison of the Children 1 Standard Deviation Above and Below McCarthy GCI Mean Scores

	Above Average Outcome	Below Average Outcome
Bayley: 13 months		
MDICA	128.8	101.2*($t = 2.55$)
MDIGA	132.6	112.6
PDICA	109.4	85.7
PDIGA	111.8	92.1
Bayley: 28 months		
MDICA	131.0	111.7*($t = 2.35$)
MDIGA	132.4	115.7
PDICA	119.6	86.9*($t = 2.70$)
PDIGA	120.4	90.1*($t = 2.32$)
Uzgiris and Hunt: 19 Months		
EDACA	2.7	.57
EDAGA	2.2	−.70

*$df = 13$, $p < .05$

measures that could be best used to predict children's later cognitive scores and was the measure that could best be used to detect children with good and below average cognitive outcomes as measured by the tests we used.

SPEECH DEVELOPMENT

In the previous chapters we described the early development of speech in our children. In this section, we describe later sound acquisition and its relation to the earlier measures and to outcome. We describe how our children performed on each of the following measures of their speech:

1. Closed syllables (CLO): proportion of closed syllables to syllables that could be closed;
2. Articulation score (ART): number of initial and final sounds that reached criterion frequency; that is, appeared in a minimal number of different instances;
3. Phonetic ability (TOT): total number of sounds produced out of a possible 43;
4. Initial matches (IMAT): proportion of initial sounds mastered to those attempted;
5. Final matches (FMAT): proportion of final sounds mastered to those attempted; and
6. Total matches: proportion of total sounds matched to those attempted.

We also measured two other aspects of language development that might be considered to be some what related to speech development. They were :

7. Average percentage correct of each of 14 morphemes, and
8. Score on the Peabody Picture Vocabulary Test.

Acquisition of bound morphemes requires knowledge of both what the morpheme represents (e.g., past or present tense, plural, or possession) and how to realize or phoneticize the morpheme (e.g., past tense after a + voice sound = /d/ , as in play/d/; or plural after a -voice sound = /s/, as in bat/s/). Vocabulary identification requires both lexical/semantic knowledge and perception of the phonological representation of the word. Thus, the Peabody Picture Vocabulary test measures recognition of both the phonological and semantic features of words.

The first six of these measures were taken at 21, 29, and 35 months. Measure 7 was taken at 25 and 29 months and Measure 8 at 35 months. In addition, Measures 4 through 6 were cumulated over time and converted into an index by multiplying the number of matches by the cumulative number of matches, that is, IMAT x CIMA (initial matches times cumulative initial matches) = IIM, FMAT x CFMA = IFM, TMAT x CTMA = ITM. This was done to avoid having the children lose credit for an early match not later found because of the random sampling that occurs in collections of language samples. In summary, we used eleven different measures to examine our children's abilities to say the sounds in words.

The overall questions addressed in the analyses of our babies' speech were as follows:

1. Are there differences in any of the measures of phonological production or lexical development between premature and full-term infants at any of the ages sampled?
2. Are there any such differences between infants who are categorized as high risk as compared to those categorized as low risk regardless of gestational age at birth?
3. Are there any measures of early phonological and lexical development that are significantly correlated with such measures at a later age?
4. Are there significant correlations among the later measures? and
5. Are there early signs of sound production difficulties in children who, at a later age, develop speech problems?

These questions deal with our ability to predict later speech from earlier in different ways. Questions 1 and 2 examine whether the birth state of the infant is a good predictor of sound and word production. Questions 3 and 4 ask whether early language behaviors predict later language behaviors, and whether later measures relate. The final question requires that we look back and see whether those children who turn out to have some form of difficulty show signs of this difficulty early on.

The first two questions just posed can be answered quite simply. T tests comparing each of the variables showed that there were no significant differences between prematurely born and full-term babies in any of the speech measures used at any of the ages sampled. This was true whether or not we corrected for prematurity. This was the case although findings in other studies have pointed to premature infants' motoric difficulties. These difficulties could have led to differences in the articulation abilities of premature and full-term children but no such differences were found. This was also true even when only the 12 infants who had the lowest birthweights were compared to the rest of the population.

Early and Later Measures

In an earlier chapter, we discussed several measures of the children's speech. We described the relation between the proportion of syllabic utterances at 12

months, the age at which 50 different words were produced and the proportion of words produced per utterance at 16 months. In this chapter, we
examine the relation of these measures to the children's ability to use the same
sounds that adults use when producing words. For example, if the target
word is "TV" and the child says "TB," the child has matched the "T" but not
the "V."

There was a significant correlation between proportion of syllabic to noise
productions at 12 months and the proportion by which children achieved
final matches and over all matches at 29 months ($r = .42, p < .004$). There
were significant negative correlations between the age at which 50 different
words were produced and total matches (ITM) at 29 months ($r = -.30, p <
.04$) and 35 months ($r = -.36, p < .09$). That is, children who were
producing 50 different words earlier were also more accurate in producing
consonantal segments at 29 months and continued to be more accurate at 35
months. There are significant correlations between proportion of words
produced per utterances at 16 months and total (ITM) and final matches
(IFM) at 29 months ($r = .45, p < .002$ and $r = .26, p < .09$, respectively).

The examination of the correlations between early and later speech behaviors seems to indicate that some significant relations exist. It is possible that
others we did not look for could be found within the data collected. What is
surprising, and encouraging, is to find any at all in a population of essentially
normal children who exhibit a great deal of variation in patterns of language
development. Further, the correlations we found seem to make sense.

The correlation between structured vocalizations at 12 months and final
matches at 29 months may be evidence of the child's ability to work on the
overall shape of a word; that is, to keep the whole in mind. Because syllable
final consonants are often later acquisitions than syllable initial consonants it
seems logical that those children who are early in more frequently articulating
CV syllables are also early in matching the final consonants in words. Thus,
there may be a developmental chain between early CV production, the early
production of words and the realization of final consonant sounds in words.

In turn, the significant relation between proportion of words per utterances at 16 months and total and final matches at 29 months fits well with the
notion that there is a sequence in the development of sound production that
begins with the shaping of vocalizations into CV syllables. When this is done
early words appear earlier proportionately more frequently, more different
words appear earlier and the production of sounds, especially the final
consonants in single syllable words, is mastered earlier. The significant
relation between age at which 50 different words are produced and total
matches at 29 and 35 months extends the chain a bit further. It appears that if
you are good at approximating word formation early you will likely turn out
to be good at correctly producing target phones in words early and continue
to be better at it at least until 35 months of life.

Although the picture just painted appears to be generally accurate we did not find the converse. That is, we did not find that bad beginnings lead to bad endings. Most of the children in the study ended up producing the speech sounds just fine. Thus, at this point, it is not clear to what degree deviance in the first step of the chain, proportion of structured vocalizations to all vocalizations produced at 12 months, might lead to bad endings. Those few children (3 in all) who ended up with clear articulation problems (as well as language problems) are discussed later.

Relations Among Later Measures

There was no way in which we could specifically trace the development of phonological mastery per se from 12 to 35 months because 12-month-old babies are not in the business of matching segments. However, we could do this tracing from age 22 months on when most of our children were seriously into the business of saying words (and, in fact, some were producing sentences).

Relations among all of the later measures (listed previously) were examined at 22, 29, and 35 months in most instances. There was one measure, percent mastery of 14 morphemes, that was examined at 25 as well as at 29 months. The questions asked about these measures were: Is each of the measures correlated with itself over a 12-month period (i.e., from 22 to 35 months)? and Are the phonological measures correlated with the lexical measures? The answers to these questions were dependent on the ages looked at and the particular measure being examined. Table 5.6 presents the correlations among all the match measures used that showed significant correlations.

As can be seen in the table, match measures are highly correlated with each other between the ages of 22 and 29 months, even more highly correlated between 29 and 35 months and less so between 22 and 35 months. These data indicate that, in general, the ability to match phone targets is consistent over

TABLE 5.6
Correlations Among Match Measures

	IFM22	ITM22	IFM29	ITM29	FM35	ITM35
			Categories			
IFM22		.80	.65	.70	.63	.46*
ITM22			.58	.76	.59	.43*
IFM29				.86	.82	.83
ITM29					.76	.84
IFM35						.88

Note. See text for explanation of Categories.
*All measures, except those with an asterisk, are significant at the $p < .01$ level and above.

the 1-year period that marks the beginning of very rapid lexical and syntactic development. Children who are good at producing matches of segments in words at 22 months continue to be good at 35 months.

The correlations between initial matches and other measures are not included in Table 5.6. Although it was the case that there were significant correlations between Indices of Initial Matches and other match measures throughout this developmental period, these correlations did not present a consistent developmental picture. We do find that the ability to match final consonants in single syllable words appears to be an early sign of an overall and persistent ability to reach sound targets. However, being less able to reach final targets is not, necessarily, a sign of trouble. Certainly, it was not a sign that predicted difficulty when the children exited from the study.

Table 5.7 presents the correlations among the later sound measures discussed previously and the match measures themselves. It will be remembered that these included the proportion of syllables closed (CLO), the number of initial and final sounds that reached criterion frequency (ART) and the total number of sounds out of 43 possible that were produced (TOT). All of the measures in the table are significant at $p < .05$ or greater.

The ability to close syllables appears to be most consistently related to the ability to match throughout the developmental period of 22 to 35 months. The other measures, ART and TOT, are partially related to match measures, depending on the ages being compared. The first finding makes sense because the ability to close syllables indicates that the child is working on the whole syllable and is being successful, in particular, in producing the final consonant in the syllable.

That the ART scores are more related to match scores over this period than TOT scores also makes sense. The ART score, very likely, represents a child's more frequent attempts to realize a range of phones. The TOT score simply represents an attempt at a number of target phones.

TABLE 5.7
Correlations Among Phonological Measures

	IFM22	ITM22	IFM29	ITM29	IFM35	ITM35
			Categories			
CLO22	.80	.77	.68	.69	.63	.53
CLO29	.56	.54	.54	.65	.57	.55
CLO35	.55	.50	.68	.71	.82	.80
ART22	.79	.88	.52	.70	.52	.55
ART29	.50	.60	.50	.68	.47	.53
ART35				.44	.46	.44
TOT22	.64	.81	.46	.67		
TOT29	.46	.49	.51	.65	.50	.56

Note. See text for explanation of categories.

In addition to examining relations among phonological measures, we considered the relation between them and measures of lexical development as well. Significant correlations were found between the IFM and ITM at 29 months and the percentage of the 14 morphological markers achieved at 25 and 29 months ($r = .61$ and $.60$, respectively, $p < .01$ in both instances). There was also a significant relation between these match scores at 29 months and level of performance on the Peabody Picture Vocabulary Test at 35 months ($r = .43$ and $.33$, respectively, $p < .01$ and $p < .03$).

It again makes good sense that children who are achieving target phones more frequently, and, in particular, final syllable phones, should be earlier acquirers of morphological markers because such markers are, with greatest frequency, at the ends of words. It is interesting to find that the better articulators are also more advanced in lexical comprehension. This relation may simply be a more developmentally advanced analog of the significant relation found during earlier months between structured vocalizations and the age at which 50 different words are acquired; that is, phonological and lexical development may be significantly related. In order to acquire a lexicon the child must store information about the phonological composition of the words as well as their meanings so that different instances of the word can be recognized.

Children With Speech Problems

There were three children in the group who were recommended for or were receiving therapy for articulation problems by the end of the study. These children were not remarkably higher on the risk index than children not recommended for such therapy. Also, they were not particularly smaller babies than others in the population. In fact, one of the three was full-term.

They had significantly lower percentages of structured vocalizations at 12 months, but other children in the population without articulation problems had also. In like fashion, they were as a group, older when they produced 50 different words as compared to the average age for the entire population. That is, the mean for the subgroup was 21 months as compared to 18 months for the population. However, one of the children in the group produced 50 different words at 17.3 months, well within the average for the population. Finally, they also had lower percentages of words per utterances than the average for the population at 16 months, but, also again, other children who did not develop articulation problems were lower than the average on this behavior as well. In summary, these children's early productive speech behavior did not remarkably differentiate them from the rest of the population. There might, however, have been early differences in speech perception that went undetected. Our findings about the significant relation between early measures of language comprehension and later measures of both language comprehension and production lend some support to this possibility.

By the time these children reached 22 months there were continued differences between them and the average for the population on some of the later phonological behaviors. These data are presented in Table 5.8.

In this table the average scores for the measures CLO, TOT, IIM, IFM, and ITM are given for the population as a whole and for the subgroup of three children with articulation problems at 22 and 29 months. The degree to which the group deviated from the average is also indicated in terms of number of standard deviations. Data are not presented for 35 months because two of the three children in the articulation problem group were in the younger cohort and exited the study at 30 months. As the scores in Table 5.8 indicate, the three children in the articulation problem group are 1 or 2 standard deviations below the average on all the phonological scores examined. They are remarkably below the average in TOT and IFM at 22 months. The ability to match final segments again appears as a possibly important characteristic of phonological behavior to distinguish between those children who are getting on well in phonological development and those who are doing less well.

The picture becomes less clear when one examines comparisons at 29 months. At this time, although there continue to be substantial differences between the two groups of children, they have become less marked. One might assume that the inverse would be the case; that is, as the language produced becomes more complex, the difficulty in matching target segments should increase. Another possibility, however, is that, indeed, these children are getting better control of their speech in time but still lag behind their peers and, therefore, are marked as being deviant. This and one other possibility will be discussed next.

The overall findings with this small group of children do not point to

TABLE 5.8
Scores of Children With Articulation Problems

Categories	Score of Average	Score of Subgroup	Deviation
CLO22	5.8	1.7	-1 SD
TOT22	2.7	.3	-2 SD
IIM22	47.5	6.0	-1 SD
IFM22	21.8	.8	-2 SD
ITM22	65.3	5.9	-2 SD
CLO29	7.1	6.5	-1 SD
TOT29	3.7	2.8	-1 SD
IIM29	92.5	56.0	-1 SD
IFM29	44.8	38.5	-1 SD
ITM29	134.7	93.7	-1 SD

Note.   See text for explanation of categories.

clear–cut signs of prospective phonological difficulty up ahead. Thus, even when the outcome information and background information are available, we still have difficulty in determining those early speech production factors that may be related to outcome.

A review of our findings suggests that there may be a link between some early phonological and lexical behaviors and later ones. The early ability to shape vocalizations into syllabic structures and words is a precursor to a later ability to map sound segments accurately onto words. In particular, a child's ability to map final segments onto words correctly appears to be a strong indicator of speech and lexical development.

As to factors other than early speech and lexical behaviors predicting later speech and lexical behaviors, it was stated previously that there were no differences between premature and full–term infants on any of the measures used in the study. It was stated further that there were no significant differences between high–risk infants and others in the population. This was certainly true of comparisons on each of the measures discussed. However, comparison of the extremely low birthweight infants with full–term infants indicates that there is a significant difference between the two groups in the age at which a short speech discrimination task is completed. Further, the age at which this task is completed is significantly correlated with ITM scores at 29 months ($r = .33, p < .03$). Thus, the hypothesis that speech perception difficulties might lead to articulation problems is further supported by these data.

In addition to the information just given, a regression analysis was carried out to determine which factors among a set of likely word production, word comprehension, and state factors might account for the variance in later phonological behaviors. It was found that one factor, when considered alone, accounted for 33% of the variance. This factor was the age at which the short discrimination task was completed. The age at which 50 different words are produced accounted for 30% of the variance, and risk scores for 28%. Three factors in combination with each other, age at which 10 and 50 words are produced and risk scores accounted for 30% of the observed variance. Thus, although risk does not lead to specific significant differences in aspects of the phonological and lexical behaviors examined, it does play a sizeable role, after all, in accounting for later phonological behavior. It should be noted that rate of lexical production, an early behavior that was significantly correlated with later phonological behaviors, does so as well.

Risk characteristics, it should be remembered, include not only low birth-weight, but, also respiratory distress, intraventricular hemorrhaging, and reported otitis media. All three of the children who were receiving or who had been recommended for articulation therapy had reported early incidence of otitis media and two had tubes placed. As stated previously, the possibility of early and persistent otitis media as a cause of speech and language development problems has been discussed at great length (e.g., Menyuk, 1980,

1992). As we also discussed, children who were both rapid and slow in development had frequent episodes of otitis. The data in this study were not collected in a manner to allow examination of the possibility that otitis media alone, rather than in conjunction with other risk factors might be the cause of this risk factor being the significant one in accounting for variance. This, again, is an area for further research, but certain of the findings of this study strongly point to the possibility of risk factors affecting speech discrimination; that is, the finding of a significant difference between high-risk infants and other infants in age of completion of a speech discrimination task and the significant relation of the latter to ITM at 29 months.

As a final comment, it is surprising that the differences between match, CLO, and TOT scores of the articulation problem children as compared to those without such problems did not increase. A possible explanation is that maturational expectations might increase, and, thus, mark these children as doing poorly when in fact they are getting a little better. Another possibility is that their problems do increase as the language to be acquired becomes more complex. However, these problems become more submerged or compensated for by phonological realization strategies the children have developed. Their phonological problems may only manifest themselves when phonological knowledge is put to a stringent test, as in reading acquisition.

MEAN LENGTH OF UTTERANCE

The measure most often used to assess children's level of language development during the third year of life is average MLU. We calculated the average length of our children's utterances when they were 22, 25, 29, and 35 months old. Figure 5.2 summarizes our findings.

This a frequently used measure, thus we were able to compare the MLUs of the children we studied with those studied by others. As the basis for this comparison we used data reported by Miller and Chapman (1981) that were collected on 123 children. Figure 5.3 contrasts our group of children with theirs. Inspection of these data reveals that the two groups of children look remarkably similar initially although they grow somewhat further apart with age. At 3 years old, our children's average utterance length is about three-fourths of a word longer than theirs.

We next compared our full-term children with our chilidren born prematurely. There were no differences between the groups. For example, at 22 months, full-term children's average utterance length was 1.5 and premature children's also 1.5. At 35 months full-term children's average utterance length was 3.8 and premature children's 3.7 Further, there were no differences when we contrasted our full-term children with our 12 low birth-weight babies.

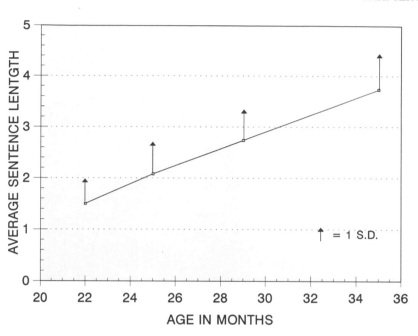

FIG. 5.2.   Increases in average sentence length with age.

We also examined these results to determine if there were any differences between the children on the basis of gender or socioeconomic status (SES). Although we found that our results were not affected by SES, we did find a difference between the average sentence length of our boys and girls. These results are reported in Fig. 5.4.

The fact that there is a consistent and significant difference between the boys and the girls at each of the age levels suggests that the difference is not the result of chance. Further, as we show later, this gender difference continues to appear on multiple measures during the third year of life. It seems from our data that there is support for the notion that girls develop some aspects of language more rapidly than boys. It is difficult to determine if there is a biological or environmental explanation for the difference because we did not measure differences in parental input to boys and girls. It may be that both factors contribute to the difference. What we did find was that all of the children in our study who were in trouble were boys. This finding is a general one. There are usually greater numbers of boys than girls in populations that have difficulties with aspects of language.

VOCABULARY DEVELOPMENT

We measured lexical diversity in our children during the second year of life by determining the number of different words used and the total number of

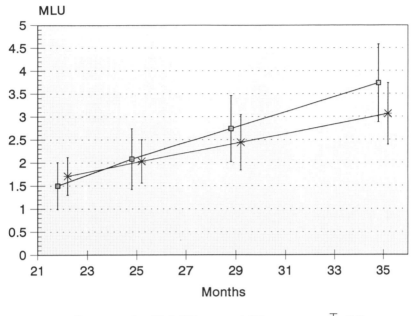

FIG. 5.3. MLU and standard deviation for our children contrasted with Miller and Chapman.

words used in a sample of 50 consecutive utterances. Table 5.9 displays the data. We found that the ratio of the number of different words used to the number of total words (TTR) revealed less about our babies' developing semantic ability than was revealed by the number of different words or the number of total words. The TTR did not change with age. This is consistent with the findings of Templin (1957), whose data on children ages 3 to 8 years showed a consistent TTR of approximately .45 throughout this period.

When we compared the children born prematurely with the full-term children on this measure we found no differences. We also found no differ-

TABLE 5.9
Average Number of Different Words to Total Words

Age (in months)	Different Words		Total Words		TTR (Different Words/ Total Words)
	M	SD	M	SD	
22	32.3	11.03	73.0	14.77	.44
25	43.9	15.33	103.4	30.53	.42
29	50.9	15.50	131.8	30.00	.39
35	75.4	14.93	181.4	44.31	.42

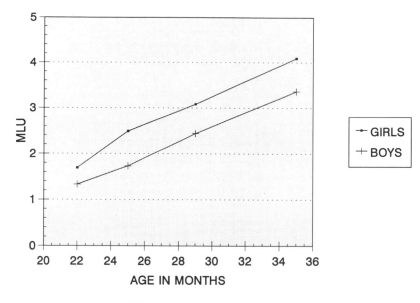

FIG. 5.4.   MLUs in young children.

ences for gender or SES. Although this might indicate that input to boys and girls is not different in this aspect we were surprised by the finding that there were no significant differences due to SES.

Next we were interested in determining the relation between the rate of development of a first lexicon and lexical diversity. In other words, would children who showed early comprehension and production of a first lexicon show greater lexical diversity during the third year of life. Table 5.10 summarizes our findings. There is a strong positive correlation between diversity at 22 months and diversity at 35 months. Those infants who have a more diverse vocabulary at 22 months continue to have a more diverse

TABLE 5.10
Correlations of First Lexicon Acquisition and Lexical Diversity

Variable	1 Prod 50	2 Comp 100	3 Div. 22	4 Div. 25	5 Div. 29	M Lexical Score	SD Diversity
PROD 50							
COMP 100	.78**						
Divers. 22	.62**	.42**				32.3	11.03
Divers. 25	.58**	.38*	.66**			43.9	15.33
Divers. 29	.52**	.33*	.37*	.58**		50.9	15.50
Divers. 35	.24	.17	.33*	.59**	.54**	75.4	14.93

$*df = 41, p < .05.$ $**df = 41, p < .01.$

vocabulary at 35 months. There is a strong positive correlation between the age at which our children produced 50 words and lexical diversity at 22, 25, and 29 months of age. There are similar correlations between the age at which our children comprehended 100 words and lexical diversity at these months. There is not a significant relation between these measures and lexical diversity at 35 months. This suggests that although age of acquisition of a first lexicon is a good predictor of lexical diversity for the following year, it tells little about what happens 1 1/2 years later in this aspect of vocabulary development. This is consistent with a pattern reported by Menyuk (1979). After reviewing existing data on prediction, Menyuk found that the ability to predict later language behavior from earlier behaviors was very possible within 6-month increments but not, usually, for longer periods of time. Therefore, she suggested that we look for logical linkages rather than direct ones that would allow for prediction over this early developmental period.

USE OF LANGUAGE

Most of our children had acquired quite a lot of language by the time they were 2 years old. We were interested in how they used this language when interacting with others. We classified each of 100 consecutive utterances according to how it functioned within mother–child interactions. Where percentages were small they were combined into the category "Other." This category included utterances that request permission, performatives, and utterances that were unclassifiable. Table 5.11 presents the proportion of use of different types of conversational acts as the children matured.

As Table 5.11 shows, there is a remarkably stable pattern across time. From the time the children were 2 years old they most often used language to make

TABLE 5.11
Distribution of Children's Conversational Acts to Their Mothers

Category	Month 25		Month 29		Month 35	
	M (%)	SD	M (%)	SD	M (%)	SD
Descriptions	14.4	9.7	15.4	8.4	13.2	4.9
Statements	29.0	15.0	35.7	13.6	43.7	13.8
Requests for info.	7.8	7.0	11.4	8.4	10.8	6.9
Requests for action	8.0	7.6	8.0	6.8	7.0	4.0
Organization Devices	14.4	7.3	13.1	7.4	12.8	8.0
Labels	13.8	10.5	7.6	8.6	7.1	8.4
Repetition	6.5	4.5	5.0	4.2	3.0	2.2
Other	6.1	3.4	3.8	2.8	2.4	2.3

statements and their use of this category increased significantly as they grew older. Descriptions, organizational devices, and labels were used with medium frequency when the children were 2, although labels decreased significantly when the children were 2 1/2. Requests for information and action and repetitions were used with low frequency. The use of repetition declined significantly from 25 to 35 months.

It is interesting to compare the differences between how the mothers and the children used language when they talked to each other. Figure 5.5 summarizes the pattern that emerged at 25 months, and Fig. 5.6 summarizes the pattern at 29 months. There is consistency in the 25- and 29-month patterns. The mothers primarily used language to request information from their children, and the children responded with statements and descriptions. The disproportionately high use of the requesting function by the mothers reflect both social and language differences between adults and children. Adults quite naturally assume the dominant role by eliciting responses from the children. If we use the frequency of organizational devices as an indication of commitment to maintaining interaction, we find that once the conversation is started both mother and baby appear to be working equally to keep the conversation going when the babies reach 25 months. This indicates how rapidly infants get on to the requirements of conversational interaction. In summary, the mother takes the lead, and the child follows.

In terms of the parameters that we have measured, it is probable that adult and child patterns come to approximate each other. This approximation most

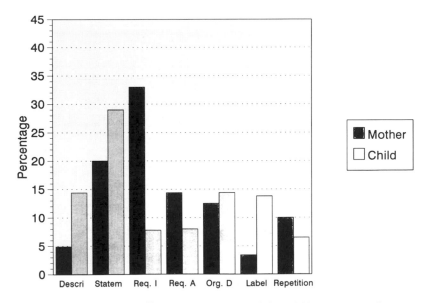

FIG. 5.5.   Functions of language in mothers and their children at 25 months.

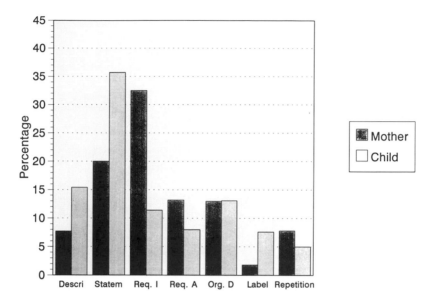

FIG. 5.6.   Functions of language in mothers and their children at 29 months.

likely results more from linguistic rather than social changes because turn-taking is a behavior that infants are capable of. They are simply not capable, very early on, of producing the language of requests. Because linguistic maturation primarily motivates the change it may occur when the child is around 5 years old and has firm control of many aspects of the language. However, social and linguistic maturation continues and children's conversational participation changes in many other parameters than the ones we measured until they reach adulthood (Dorval & Eckerman, 1984).

One final observation relates to the use of the labeling function. It seems that mothers must be requesting labels for objects, and their children complying with the request. Both at 25 and 29 months the children are providing labels four times more often than their parents. This is very different from what was seen when the child was 2 years old and mothers engaged more frequently in telling their children the names of people and objects.

Conversational Role

Another way to explore the use of language by the children is to look at the conversational roles that their utterances play. Looking at the utterances in this manner reveals additional data to support the idea that, interactionally, mothers take the initiative and attempt to maximize the child's ability to make conversational contributions. Some children appear to have an easier time providing responses than others, as some mothers have an easier time providing support for answering. Elizabeth, 25 months old, and her mother seem to be enjoying reading together, and naming pictures. Book reading is an occupation that is very frequent among mothers and their children in middle-class families.

> (Mom reading book with Elizabeth)
> Mom: Who's that? (Mom points)
> Elizabeth: Big Bird.
> Mom: Right. What's he eating? We ate that the other day and you loved it. Do you remember?
> Elizabeth: Apple.
> Mom: No, what's this right here? Water.
> Elizabeth: Melon.
> Mom: What? Right, melon. Very good.

Steven, 25 months old, and his mother seem to be having problems and unlike Elizabeth's mother Steve's mother seems determined to get Steve to do it her way. She also offers him less help than Elizabeth's mother provided.

> (Mom brings in two books-)
> Mom: You got two books, three books.
>   (Opens book and points.)
>   Steve, who's this?
> Steve: Mickey.
> Mom: No who's that?
> Steve: Duck.
> Mom: Steve you are so embarrassing.
> Steve: Mickey. Duck.
> Mom: Who's that? No, it's not a duck..Who's that? Think. Who's that?
> Steve: Duck.
>   (Finally, indesperation.)
> Mom: Say Goofy.
> Steve: Goofy.
> Mom: That' s right.

Now that Steve's mother feels she's won the naming game and told him the "right" answer, she returns to the same picture and requests again.

> Mom: Who's that?
> Steve: Goofy.

Mom: That's right.

Steve: Duckie.

More: What?

Steve: Duckie.
     (Child walks away.)

Mom: Steve come here and we'll read the story.

The mother's role may be contrasted with that of a tennis teacher who attempts to place the ball in just the right place so that the new player can hit it back perfectly. The difference is that the tennis teacher purposefully places the shot to allow the student to take the swing. Mother attempts to place her shot properly so that she and the child can communicate with one another. Sometimes the shot is better placed than at other times as these two conversations indicate.

Table 5.12 describes the distribution of the children's utterances according to the role they played in the conversation.

As the table indicates, there is a relatively consistent pattern over time. The roles used most frequently by the child are Gives and Responds to Mom. The high frequency with which Gives are used shows that much of what the child says when he or she is 2 is not said in answer to mother nor does the child expect a response. The child may be attempting to be "in charge." An example from Katie (25 months old) may prove helpful.

(Mom walks into the room carrying paper and crayons.)

Katie: I wanna write. On the paper.
     (Mom hands her a crayon. They draw side by side.)

Katie: What you write on there?

Mom: It's a face.

Katie: I write on these. On my fingers.

TABLE 5.12
Distribution of the Conversational Role of Children's Utterances

Category	Month 25		Month 29		Month 35	
	M (%)	SD	M (%)	SD	M (%)	SD
Elicits	16.2	9.0	18.5	11.1	17.0	6.2
Continues	3.0	4.1	4.2	5.8	3.5	3.2
Responds to self	0	0	.1	.4	.2	.6
Responds to mom	23.5	14.7	26.8	11.5	22.5	14.8
Acknowledges	7.5	5.0	6.6	4.9	5.1	3.7
Other	8.3	7.6	5.1	3.8	3.4	2.9

Mom: There's room on the paper.

Katie: (Turning the paper over.). I turn this over. I gonna write a face.
(Katie drawing)

Katie: I write a nose. Here my eyes.

The data further reveal, however, that 2-year-olds are also quite capable of eliciting responses from others. Approximately one move in five is an attempt to get something accomplished. The reputation of 2-year-olds, as presenting unique problems for parents, is probably tied to the children's ever expanding language skills. Not only can 2-year-olds say "No" often, but they can give quite elaborate orders of what they want done, when, where and how.

Jack: Mom build a tower. (Trying to add a third block to a stack of two.)

Mom: I'm tired Jack. (Sitting on the couch.)

Jack: Build it.

Mom: I wanna do something else for awhile.

Jack: Build it! I wanna tower!

Mom: You can build it.

Jack: I need help. Mom, build it.

A conversational move that is still difficult for the 2-year-old is a Continue. A Continue is a move that responds to the previous utterance and serves to elicit a future response. This type of move is very hard for children because it is more dependent on what is said than what is done. Children during the early months of this year both give and respond to orders based on the nonverbal context more often than to those based on the verbal context. To continue a conversation, that is, to remain on the topic and add to it so as to evoke another response, requires more language sophistication than the 2-year-old has achieved. Inspection of the data in Table 5.12 shows that the children at 35 months were using this move less than 5% of the time. Many children did not use it at all. This does not mean that parent and child did not maintain a topic beyond two utterances, but rather that topic maintenance was achieved in other ways.

Figures 5.7 and 5.8 contrast the children's use of conversational roles with that of their parents. The differences between children and adults are quite obvious, and stable over this time period. In this aspect of language, many social and linguistic changes will need to occur before the discourse pattern is altered to reflect a more equal relationship.

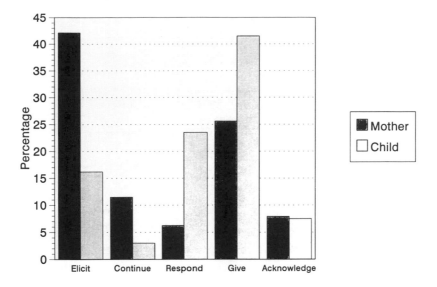

FIG. 5.7. Distribution of conversational roles between mothers and their children at 25 months.

SENTENCE COMPREHENSION

In the previous chapter we noted that children could comprehend multiword utterances before they could produce them. By the time our children were 2 years old they showed us that they understood anomalous sentences like "kiss the truck," and shortly thereafter most of them began to combine words together into two-word utterances. When the children were 27 months old, we assessed their comprehension again. We were interested in answering several questions. First, we wanted to know how comprehension of two-word utterances that were strongly related to the individual meanings of words was related to comprehension of longer units that were more dependent on children's understanding word order. Second, we were interested in confirming our findings that our premature children performed no differently than our full-term babies in language comprehension. Third, we wanted to determine if the gender difference we found in comprehension at 2 continued to persist. Finally, we were interested in examining the relation between this measure and the standardized comprehension measures that we gave the children at the end of the study.

Table 5.13 describes the 14 test items and reports the percentage of correct, incorrect, and noncontingent responses. Noncontingent responses included task refusals. These data reveal some interesting things about our children's comprehension. First, the children appear to understand quite a lot about language, but they clearly have more to learn. Although they easily under-

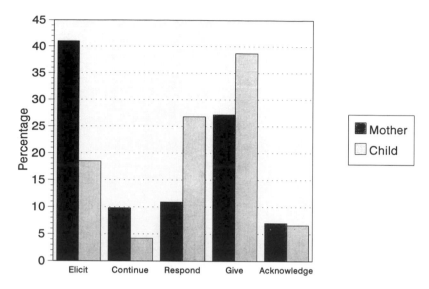

FIG. 5.8.   Distribution of conversational roles between mothers and their children at 29 months.

stand sentences like, "Doll eat the cheerio," difficulty arises with complex sentences that require them to understand more than agent + action + object relations as in "Doll push the truck on the box." Children appear to know that dolls, like people, can perform actions. They further understand that trucks can also do things. Immovable objects like houses, however, cannot do things. Houses can neither push dolls nor eat them. At the beginning of the third year of life children's ability to understand sentences appears to have more to do with the notion of what they consider capable of performing actions, or animacy, than what they perceive as the normal course of events. For example, approximately 75% of the children showed us the doll eating the house, whereas only 40% showed us the house eating the doll.

The length of the sentence they were asked to comprehend played only a minor role in their performance. For example, the children had more trouble understanding little than big, in two sentences of equal length. They also had no more difficulty understanding "Doll push big truck" than they did "Doll push truck." Thus, the content of the sentence and its structure had more to do with comprehension than length, at least within the lengths of the sentences presented to the children.

As a group the children achieved a mean score of 53.1% correct on the test, with a range of 14.3% to 100%. The standard deviation for the group was 25.1. The full-term children performed no differently than the premature children. The mean score for the terms was 54.2% $(SD = 23.5)$ and for the premature children was 51.9% $(SD = 27.07)$. There was also no statistically

TABLE 5.13
Types of Responses to Noncontingent Requests by Children at 27 Months

Items	% Correct	% Incorrect	% Noncontingent
Doll eat cheerio.	92.5	5.6	1.8
Truck run over doll.	77.4	15.0	7.5
Doll push house.	66.0	22.6	11.3
House push doll.	32.0	58.5	9.4
Truck push doll.	67.9	26.4	5.7
Doll push truck.	71.7	24.5	3.8
Doll eat house.	73.6	13.2	13.2
House eat doll.	39.6	41.5	18.9
Big doll push truck.	58.3	27.0	14.6
Doll push big truck.	70.8	12.5	16.7
Little truck push doll.	43.8	35.4	20.8
Truck push little doll.	39.6	33.3	27.1
Doll on the box push the truck.	15.5	51.1	33.3
Doll push the truck on the box.	20.0	48.9	31.1

significant difference when we contrasted the high-risk, low birthweight infants with the full-term babies, although the low birthweight babies average score was only 39.3%. Whatever average group differences there are are hidden by the variability in both groups. These findings are consistent with those we obtained on the two-word comprehension test completed by most children 6 months earlier. At that time, there were no statistically significant differences between the groups and there continued to be no such differences.

We next compared the relation between the way our children performed on the Sentence Comprehension test and their performance on the Multi-word Comprehension test. The correlation between these two measures was .49 ($df = 51$, $p < .01$). Children who were able to demonstrate their understanding of anomalous sentences early were the same children who performed well on this later test.

On the earlier comprehension measure we found that our boys and girls differed in their performance. We suggested that the differences might be attributed more to compliance than to a genuine difference in comprehension ability. This interpretation of the data is supported by our findings on the Multiword test. Here our boys and girls performed similarly. The girls achieved a mean score of 53.57% ($SD = 27.65$) and the boys a mean score of 52.65% ($SD = 22.95$). This lends further support to our conclusion that the earlier difference we found was due to noncompliance on the part of the boys rather than noncomprehension.

Our final interest in this measure concerned its ability to predict the children's comprehension at the end of the study. The children's comprehension at exit was measured by administering a standardized battery of tests. The battery was described in detail in Chapter 2. To derive a comprehension score for each child, the difference in the child's age equivalent score on the Peabody, the Northwestern Syntax Screening Test (NSST), and the Sequenced Inventory of Communication Development (SICD) were each subtracted from the child's chronological age. The three difference scores were then averaged to obtain a single measure reflecting comprehension ability. The children's scores on this exit measure (RECLAC) were then correlated with their percentage scores on the sentence comprehension measure. The relation between the two scores as reflected by the correlation was statistically significant ($r = .49$, $dr = 53$, $p < .01$). Children who do well on the sentence comprehension measure tended to do well on standardized testing at the end of the study.

SENTENCE PRODUCTION

We examined sentence production in two ways. We examined the use of different syntactic classes and phrases in their sentences and the different sentence types they were using. The results of the structural analysis are described first.

Structural Analysis

To assess the structures in the sentences our children were producing at 2, 2 1/2, and 3 years of age, we analyzed 100 consecutive multimorpheme utterances taken from the 25-, 29-, and 35- month tape samples. Not too surprisingly, 20% of the children did not produce enough multimorpheme utterances at 25 months to allow us to perform the analysis. The specific procedures we used to do the analysis resulted from some modifications we made to the procedures described in Tyack and Gottslaben (1974). Essentially, we assigned each of the utterances to 1 of 16 categories. These categories, with examples are shown here:

Catagories	Examples
N	a ball, balls
Modifier + N	little ball, this side
V	take out, go around
V +	have it, open it
N + V	it cook, I paint
N + (cop) +N	what that?, that Oscar
V + Mod + N	got mother goose record, ride sissy car
N + V + N	I get a Oscar, I see Oscar
Modal + V + N	wanna go on floor, gonna put it on

N + V + N + N + A	Momma drive car home, Mommy see book on chair
N + is + N/Adj.	this is snoopy, It's delicious
N + Modal + V	I wanna see, I gonna get up
N + Modal + V + A/N	I wanna go on floor, I hafta eat lunch
N/be + N + A	I'm on the floor, they're both circle
Compound and	I'm trying to stand up
Complex	Go get me juice

Figures 5.9, 5.10, and 5.11 summarize our findings at each of three age intervals. At 25 months these children's MLU averaged 2 morphemes, at 29 months it was 2.74 and at 35 months it was 3.73. Inspection of these figures shows the great amount of variation in the types of constructions used by the children. Even at 25 months the group as a whole was using constructions from each of the categories. Further, many of the sentences were fully formed, and an occasional sentence was compound or complex. At 25 months, 72% of the multimorpheme utterances contained a verb, and this increased in frequency to 85% by the time the children were 35 months. Although as a group the children frequently omitted the verb "to be" (copula), they even more frequently used it. In fact there were only three children who omitted the "is" completely at 25 months of age. Similarly,

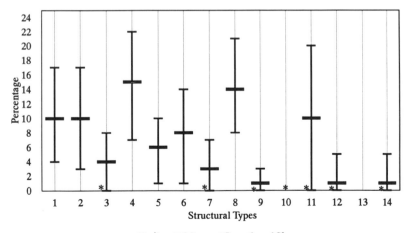

I s.d.   ⊞ Mean   * Less than 1%

FIG. 5.9. Means and standard deviations for structural types at 25 months. Structural types: 1 = N; 2 = Modifier + N; 3 = V; 4 = V + N; 5 = N + V; 6 = N + Cop 0 + N; 7 = V + Mod + N; 8 = N + V + N; 9 = Modal + V + N; 10 = N + V + N + N + Adv; 11 = N + is + N/Adj; 12 = N + Modal + V; 13 = N = be + N + A; 14 = Compound + Complex.

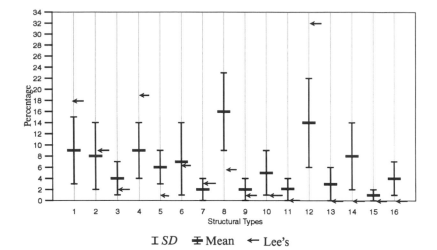

FIG. 5.10. Means and standard deviations in use for structural types at 29 months compared to Lee's use of these structures at his age. Structural types: 1 = N; 2 = Modifier + N; 3 = V; 4 = V + N; 5 = N + V; 6 = N + Cop 0 + N; 7 = V + Mod + N; 8 = N + V + N; 9 = V + N + N; 10 = Modal + V + N; 11 = N + V + N + N; 12 = N + is + N/Adj; 13 = N + Modal + V; 14 = Modal + V + N; 15 = N + am/are + N; 16 = Compound + Complex.

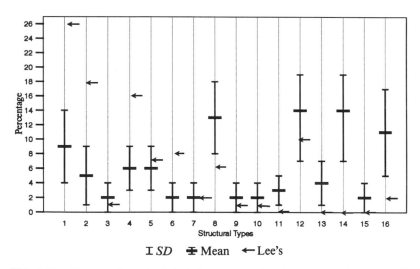

FIG. 5.11. Means and standard deviations in use of various structural types at 35 months compared to Lee's use of these structures at his age. Structural types: 1 = N; 2 = Mod + N; 3 = V; 4 = V + N; 5 = N + V; 6 = N + Cop 0 + N; 7 = V + Mod + N; 8 = N + V + N; 9 = V + N + N; 10 = Modal + V + N; 11 = N + V + N + N; 12 = N + is + N/Adj; 13 = N + Modal + V; 14 = N + Modal + V + N; 15 = N + am/are + N; 16 = Compound + Complex.

122

every child produced at least one complex sentence by the time he or she reached 35 months. In summary, what appears to characterize the utterances produced by the 2-year-old is the ability to use many different construction types, most of which contained each of the major categories of N + V + N.

What does a child who is having difficulty look like? To answer this question we contrasted the constructions used by Lee at 29 and 35 months with the group profiles. These data are displayed in Figs. 5.10 and 5.11 by superimposing an "X" to indicate Lee's percentage of use of these structures. We did not contrast him with the rest of the children at 25 months because he did not produce enough multimorpheme utterances to allow for a meaningful analysis. At 29 months, Lee is producing more constructions without verbs than his peers, 34% as contrasted with 25%. Interestingly, he shows frequent use of the verb "to be," which he says in 32% of his utterances. A look at his actual sentences shows that he most frequently produces utterances like "This is Snoopy" and "There's a book."

Further, Lee only used one sentence that contained a modal construction. The sample taken at 35 months reveals an even more deviant pattern. In this corpus, 52% of the utterances lack a verb, and 78% contain only two of the three major parts that make up a fully formed utterance. There is still an absence of modal constructions, because this sample, like the previous one, contained only one modal verb. Lee's multiword sentence production is markedly different from that of his peers. He seems to be using a different strategy for acquisition of sentence structures. This strategy appears to be one of memorization of short chunks in the sentence frame. Further comparisons support this notion.

Table 5.14 lists the categories that occurred more than 10% of the time in the 25-month samples of the group as a whole, and contrasts the frequency of use of these categories by Lee when he was 29 months old. Inspection of Table 5.14 reveals that Lee at 29 months is overusing the categories that most frequently occurred in our children's samples at 25 months. For example, he uses N constructions and Modifier + N constructions more than the 25-month-old children. Interestingly, he uses V + N constructions like the other children, but uses N + V + N constructions less frequently. This behavior suggests that it takes a great deal of effort on his part to move from labeling (Ns and Mod + Ns) to talking about relations between objects and events, that is, as suggested previously he does not chunk together all items within a sentence frame. For Lee, his next step will probably be to use the verb in longer and more complex utterances.

Table 5.15 contrasts Lee's use of the categories most frequently used by other children with his use of these constructions. For the purposes of discussion, the other general usage of these categories at 25 months is also included in the table. Table 5.15 further describes how Lee's underutilization of the verb makes his language different from his age-matched peers. He uses

TABLE 5.14
Lee's Use of the Most Frequently Used Categories at 29 Months Compared to Other
Children's Use at 25 Months

Construction Types	Children's Use at 25 Months	Lee's Use at 29 months
N	10	26
Modifier + N	10	18
V + N	15	16
N + V + N	15	6
N + Cop + N	10	10
Totals	60%	76%

TABLE 5.15
Lee's Use of the Most Frequently Used Categories at 35 Months Compared to Other
Children's Use of These Categories

Construction Types	Children's Use at 25 Months	Children's Use at 35 Months	Lee's Use at 35 Months
N + V + N	15	13	6
N + Cop + N	10	14	10
N + Modal + V + N	6	14	0
Compound & Complex	2	11	1
Totals	33%	52%	16%

no N + Modal + V + N construction and offers only one compound or complex sentence. It is likely that the more frequent use of the verb in longer constructions will make Lee's profile more closely approximate his peers. His use of modal constructions should increase shortly thereafter. In summary, Lee at 35-months-old does not appear to use constructions with the same frequency of use as his younger peers, who show greater use of the verb. This nonuse of the verb suggests that Lee is using a different language learning strategy than his peers, one that does not take the verb as a central focus of the sentence. In turn, his use of this strategy suggests that he does not chunk the sentence as a whole but only takes a piece of it at a time. If this is the case then intervention with Lee might be based on getting him to chunk appropriately by using prosodic cues such as rising then falling intonation within clauses and pause between clauses. In chapter 6 we discuss some recent research that indicates that infants, during the first year of life, are sensitive to such cues.

Sentence Type Development

Another way in which we analyzed our children's language ability was to look at their sentence type development. First, we measured the percentage of sentences considered gramatically correct by adult conversational usage. The percentage of sentences used that might be considered grammatically correct grew from 22% at 21 months to 36% at 29 months. By 35 months of age, our children were, on the average, using 46% grammatically correct sentences. This does not mean that their grammar was remarkably different from adult grammar at this age. Rather, the children were using many single words and phrases that most likely were conversationally highly appropriate. Grammatical correctness in conversation is a poor measure of children's syntactic competence.

As stated, the sentences that the children used were analyzed according to type: declaratives, yes–no questions, Wh-questions, imperatives, and indicators. Table 5.16 shows the percentage of occurrence of each of the different categories. The majority of sentences at each age point were declaratives (e.g., "It has tape on it."), but all of the children produced utterances of each type at each age. The percentages of declaratives and questions increased during the children's third year of life, and imperatives (e.g., "Turn the screw."), and indicatives (e.g., "That's Snoopy.") decreased with age.

Once children are able to talk in sentences, their sentence structure quickly becomes more complex. During the third year, most of the children began to use more sophisticated sentence structures. By 35 months of age, all of the children but two had produced two different compound or complex sentences in a 100-utterance corpus. Further, all but two children had demonstrated mastery of at least one complex sentence type. One of the children who showed no such mastery was Lee, who we described earlier. The second case was a child who was often slow in beginning to learn new things, but once started would catch-up quickly to his peers. Table 5.17 describes each of the complex sentence types we analysed in our children's speech, gives examples of each construction type, and reports the percentage of children using each construction type at 25, 29, and 35 months of age.

A final characteristic of structural development that we measured was our children's ability to talk about the past and to refer to the future. We considered this an important characteristic of language development to evaluate for two reasons. Acquisition of morphological markers of time reveals

TABLE 5.16
Percentage of Occurrence of Each Sentence Type

Sentence Types	Month 25		Month 29		Month 35	
	M	SD	M	SD	M	SD
Declaratives	47.3	2.46	56.9	1.75	66.7	1.37
Yes–No Questions	0.6	.15	1.3	.29	4.1	2.43
Wh- Questions	7.6	8.78	12.4	1.19	7.5	6.06
Imperatives	37.4	2.37	24.6	1.72	17.2	1.31
Indicatives	6.9	1.14	5.0	5.66	4.4	3.79

TABLE 5.17
Percentage of Children Demonstrating Mastery[a] of Complex Sentence Types[b]

Type	Example	Percentage Mastery at		
		25 mos.	29 mos.	35 mos.
Simple infinitive clauses with equivalent clauses	I need to talk to this. I forgot to turn on the light.	2.4	19.0	36.3
Full propositional complements	I think I make the other circle. I'm sorry you can'tgo to the movies.	2.4	9.5	22.7
Simple noninfinitive Wh- clauses	See if we can find another one. Look what he's doing.	4.8	14.3	63.6
Infinitive clauses with different subjects	I want Mommy read it. I want Gabsy comeover my house.	—	4.7	18.1
Relative clauses	That's a boy holding a kitty. I wanna blow bubbles that you brought.	—	4.8	13.6
Gerund clauses	Stop watching me dance. I like switching on the light.	—	2.4	—
Unmarked infinitve clauses	She let me put ice cubes i n my cup, Can you help me put my feet in the trapeze?	—	9.5	—
Wh- infinitive clauses	I don't know how to open it. I'll show you where to put the horse.	—	—	—
Double embeddings	I wanna go find a tub. I hope I can find where it is.	—	—	27.2

[a]Child uses two different exemplars in 100 utterance corpus.
[b]Sentence types as defined and discussed by Miller (1981).

the child's growing linguistic independence from the here and now. It is a mark of the child's increasing conceptual competence. Although early language development requires a significant amount of contextual support for both production and comprehension, later acquisition and use is not as dependent on the immediate context. Acquisition of morphological markers of time also indicates increasing linguistic competence. The child must learn to separate endings from stems of words and to apply these endings under appropriate circumstances.

As children become increasingly adept at talking about yesterday and tomorrow, they learn to use the specific forms that adults use to describe the past and the future. For example, they begin to use "ed," the word "yesterday," and the modal "will." Table 5.18 shows our children's movement from talking predominantly about the present to their ability to use words and endings that describe other times. An inspection of the data reveals that even at 3 years of age, the children are still primarily talking about the present, that is, the things they can see and touch and the things that they can do. They choose to talk about what just happened or what will happen, and hardly ever talk about last week or next month. This does not mean that they cannot do so but, rather, that the focus of their attention at this age is on the here and now.

Looking at the use of tense markings by individual children, we see that half of the children on whom we had this information (16 of 39 of the children) used only the present tense at 25 months of age, whereas at 35 months no child used this tense exclusively. At all ages, the remote past and the remote future were used by almost no children. All of the children were able to talk about not-present actions. However, it is unclear whether they used these tenses with the same meaning as adults.

Becky told us all about her trip to California. She had gone to visit her grandmother 2 weeks before our visit. "The day after Sunday I flied to California. After the night I flied the airplane. Not today after Sunday, I see my grandma."

MORPHOLOGICAL MARKERS

Shortly after our children began combining words into sentences, they began using word endings. For example, they put an "s" on the ends of words to refer to multiple objects, or they used an "ed" to indicate the past. All of our children began to use endings like this by the time they reached the age of 3. In a very real sense, they began to apply rules to the use of words, like the

TABLE 5.18
Percentage Usage of Tense Markers at Various Ages

Tense Marker	Month 25 (%)	Month 29 (%)	Month 35 (%)
Present time	94.0	91.1	82.9
Immediate past	2.6	3.5	4.9
Immediate future	1.8	4.0	6.0
Remote past	1.1	1.3	3.6
Remote future	0.5	0.1	2.0

rules adults use. For example, when more than one object is under consideration, they put an "s" on the end of the word to talk about more than one object.

Children in this stage of acquisition are said to be demonstrating their ability to make linguistic generalizations. They appear to have formulated a rule about language and are using the rule to create new exemplars. This same phenomenon was noted by Berko-Gleason (1958) many years ago when she demonstrated that children could systematically add endings to nonsense words incorporated into sentences. Showing them a nonsense shape, Berko told the children, "This is a wug. Now there are two of them. There are two ___?" Another sample follows: "This is a boy who knows how to *glitch*. He is glitching. He did the same thing yesterday. Yesterday he ___?" The children responded "wugs" to the former question and *"glitched"* to the latter, revealing an understanding of these markers of plural and past in the language.

We measured our children's production of 14 morphemes that begin to emerge at 2 years of age. Although other morphemes could have been studied, we selected those studied in many previous investigations to be able to compare our results with those of others. Table 5.19 summarizes our findings for ages 25, 29, and 35 months. For each morpheme, the mean percentage correct is displayed. For a child to receive a score on a particular morpheme, there would need to be two contexts identified in which the use of the morpheme was obligatory regardless of whether it was used correctly or incorrectly. By example, if the child said, "I see two book," the presence of the word "two" makes the plural ending on "book" obligatory. Such an instance would count as an obligatory context. Because these data are based on 100 utterances, many children did not use the morphemes or appropriate contexts two times and therefore could not receive a score.

Inspection of the tables reveals some interesting findings concerning the acquisition of morphology. First, the process of acquisiton is gradual, with mastery (arbitrarily established at 90% correct use) not reached until after 3 years of age. Second, although some children use a few of the earlier developing morphemes at age 2, most children did not begin to use the morphemes correctly until age 2 1/2. This is not unexpected, because most children just begin to put words together at 2 years. Third, the variation across the sample of children is great at 25 months, decreases by 29 months, and decreases again by 35 months. This suggests the pattern of acquisition that we discussed previously. Some children begin to develop an aspect of language early, and progress toward mastery quite quickly. Another group begins to develop later, but they too move rapidly toward mastery. A third group of children develops slowly, and reaches mastery much later. They appear neither to acquire these markers early, nor to apply them across a wide range of examples.

Table 5.20 shows the percentage of children who used each morpheme

TABLE 5.19
Morphology–Mean Percentage Correct

Marker	25 Months		29 Months		35 Months	
	M	SD	M	SD	M	SD
Plural	61.6	44.2	75.6	36.8	87.0	28.7
On	59.2	45.8	66.8	42.4	73.9	41.7
In	52.0	47.7	79.2	32.7	87.0	29.2
Articles	45.0	32.2	66.2	27.0	84.7	14.6
Progressive	43.2	38.3	62.1	37.9	77.5	31.5
Copula	42.9	36.5	68.8	29.0	87.8	13.8
Possessive	28.5	39.2	27.1	40.9	19.4	31.5
Irregular Past	22.9	35.3	34.2	38.5	71.9	30.0
Contracted Copula	20.8	35.1	45.6	37.5	73.4	31.3
Regular 3rd	20.4	33.5	45.5	43.0	51.8	42.8
Contracted Aux	14.6	26.0	46.8	39.2	70.6	33.1
Irregular 3rd	11.11	29.2	24.8	40.2	32.6	44.9
Regular Past	10.5	24.9	21.4	36.8	34.9	45.4
Uncontracted Aux	0.7	5.0	3.9	14.5	31.1	43.8

correctly at least two times in 100 utterances. These findings are similar to those previously described. At 25 months, the majority of children used only a few morphemes. By 35 months, only a few morphemes were omitted. At 25 months the children used an average of 3.8 morphemes correctly (range 0–10); at 29 months, they used 6.5 correctly (range 0–12); at 35 months, they used 8.8 morphemes correctly (range 3–13). Although many children showed no mastery at 25 months, only the slowest developing children showed no mastery at 35 months.

When we compared our preterm children to our full-term babies on these measures, we found no significant differences. This was true for each of the morphemes, even at the earliest age level. We also found no significant differences when we contrasted full-term children with our low birthweight infants.

Summary

During the third year of the children in our study we examined their cognitive development and how this related to their earlier cognitive development. We measured many aspects of their language development. In this section of the chapter we summarize the findings.

The results of the Bayley indicated that our children were 1 standard deviation above the average in mental development and average in terms of motor development. This was also true of the premature children, even when the very low birthweight children were included in the analysis. The differ-

TABLE 5.20

Percentage of Children Demonstrating Correct Morpheme Use in Two Obligatory Contexts

	Percentage of Children		
	Month 25	Month 29	Month35
Plural	62.7	76.7	90.9
On	60.5	65.1	77.3
In	53.5	81.3	90.9
Articles	28.0	65.1	81.8
Progressive	34.9	58.1	81.8
Copula	37.2	70.0	90.9
Possessive	25.6	27.9	18.2
Irregular Past	16.3	37.2	72.7
Contracted Copula	16.3	37.2	72.7
Regular 3rd	14.0	16.3	50.0
Contracted Aux	7.0	41.8	68.2
Irregular 3rd	9.3	23.3	36.4
Regular Past	9.3	16.3	36.4
Uncontracted Aux	0.0	2.3	31.8

ence in motor development is an interesting finding and is reflected on other measures. There seems to be evidence of an initial lag in motor development in the premature population but subsequent, significant catch-up over the 15-month period that divided the times in which the early and later Bayleys were given. On the McCarthy Scales of Cognitive Development, given as the children exited the study, they were performing consistently above the mean. The average for the group was more than 1 standard deviation above the mean on these scales. Thus, the children in our study, both premature and full-term, were progressing well in terms of cognitive development.

The pattern of speech development in the children indicated a mutually dependent sequence. Those children who produced structured vocalizations (syllabic productions) proportionately more early and with greater frequency in the first year of life, were then early lexical acquirers, then achieved early mastery of articulation, and, finally, were above the average of the group in lexical comprehension. However, our measure of speech sound discrimination accounted best for variance in articulation mastery. These findings indicate that speech sound production is basically dependent on speech sound discrimination but that the course of development of articulation then follows its own path, and is highly dependent on motoric development. Comparative delays in articulation mastery might be accounted for by delays in motor development. However, those few children in our study who had articulation problems that required intervention were not all among those who were delayed. They were children who had had frequent bouts of otitis media and had needed intubation. This suggests that hearing problems that lead to speech sound discrimination problems might lead to severe articulation problems.

Our children's vocabularies grew substantially over the third year. There were no significant differences in amount and diversity of vocabulary among the children that were due to prematurity, gender, or SES. There were significant correlations between the age at which they comprehended 100 words and produced 50 words and later lexical diversity up to 29 months. Those who were fast vocabulary acquirers at an earlier age continued to be fast vocabulary acquirers up to this later age. This relation was not found at 35 months indicating that early fast acquirers need not continue to be so over the third and fourth year of life.

The children's comprehension and production of sentences changed dramatically over this third year. MLU grew steadily over this period, as did structural diversity in terms of the categories represented in utterances and in terms of sentence types. There were no significant differences between premature and full-term children in these measures and no differences due to SES. However, boys were significantly slower in developing longer sentences than girls. In this study boys were slower than girlls in language development but only in some aspects and during some periods of development. The one child, a full-term boy, in the study with outstanding difficulties in this aspect of language development produced utterances that were primarily composed of noun phrases, nouns and modifiers plus noun. It was as if he was stuck at the stage during which language is produced to label.

The children continued to have some difficulty in comprehending lengthier utterances, those that contained subject, verb and object plus prepositional phrase. They also used the animacy of the subjects to decide whether an action could be carried out. The amount of processing required and the animacy of subjects were the two factors that played an important role in correct performance on the sentence comprehension task we devised. However, it should be kept in mind that sentence comprehension was assessed at 27 months, at the beginning of the third year of life. The VLB infants tended to do less well on this task but not significantly so. Performance on this task was significantly related to outcome comprehension measures.

As with sentence structures there were no significant differences in the children's development of morphological markers due to prematurity. Surprisingly there were also no significant differences in this aspect of development due to SES. Other studies have found differences in vocabulary and morphological development due to SES, and we did not. There are at least two factors that might account for this. The children were not old enough and had not developed sufficient knowledge of these aspects of language to show differences, and none of the children in our study were in poverty stricken families.

Not only did the children's structural knowledge of language grow during this period but, also, their use of language. In much of the first half of the third year of life children primarily use language to respond to their mothers' requests for action and information. Mothers take the lead and their children follow. Many of the children's responses are noncontingent. That is, they do not follow the topic of the conversation. During the second half of this year changes occur in these two aspects. Children introduce topics more often and maintain them. They talk about events in the immediate past and future. They also become more contingent in their responses. Language, rather than action alone, is being used to obtain goals.

The development of language during the third year is very exciting. The child goes from being able to say a few words about a small number of things, to being able to carry on a rich and interesting conversation. Many of our findings are very similar to those reported on in other studies of language development from age 2 to 3 (Bloom, 1991; Schlesinger, 1982). Because half of the children in the study were born prematurely, many of them with very stormy early histories, it was reassuring to us that most of the children developed language in a manner that was very similar to full-term children in other studies.

SOME IMPLICATIONS FOR ASSESSMENT

The frequency of occurrence of otitis media seemed to be related to a number of measures of speech development we obtained. In turn, there were a number of measures of language development during this period that were predictive of later language measures. These measures might be quite useful in determining those children who are at risk for later language delay.

The test of speech sound discrimination, presented in Appendix F, that was given periodically to the children was significantly related to the measures of articulation mastery that we took. Therefore, early measures of speech sound discrimination might be helpful in predicting those children who might have speech articulation problems. We found that our measures of the development of MLU were very consistent with those found in other studies. Therefore, a marked departure from the MLU found at various months over this year might indicate a child at risk. Even more dramatic was the finding that the child who was truly having great difficulty in language development was unable to produce utterances that contained a verb phrase as well as a noun phrase. This inability to use both verbs as well as nouns seems to indicate a child with a language impairment. Finally, it was found that there were significant differances in the age at which the VLB babies and full-term babies in our population could complete the sentence comprehension task. The two-word comprehension task is presented in Appendix B and the three-part task in Appendix E. The measures just cited could be used not only as signposts of language problems but, perhaps could be the basis for language intervention.

CHAPTER 6

Mother–Child Communication Interaction

This chapter focuses on the types of communicative interactions that take place between the mothers and, in a few instances, other caregivers , and their infants over the first 2 1/2 or 3 years of life. The possible role of these interactions on the children's language development is also discussed. We begin by briefly discussing what the literature has said about the role of this interaction, and the possible importance of some very recent findings about mothers' speech during Year 1. We then discuss our findings and indicate what we think is important about them in terms of understanding the effect of communicative interaction on language development. We conclude by discussing how what we found might be translated into intervention suggestions.

OTHER RESEARCH ON THE EFFECT OF INPUT ON LANGUAGE DEVELOPMENT

For some time, investigators have pursued the question of the effect of mothers' language on their infants' language development. Three primary positions were taken on the question. One position was that what mothers and others do as they communicatively interact with infants is totally unrelated to the content of the child's language development. This position was labeled the *innatist* position because it suggested that the content and course of language development was the result of the biological endowment of the human infant alone. Input played no role in development except for providing the information that the child needed to acquire language. Language evolved over the course of development as a function of that biological endowment. A second position was that mothers' and other people's language behavior to their infants essentially shaped the content and course of the child's language development. This position was labeled the *behaviorist* position because from this position it is only the environment that determines the course of development. The infant him or herself has little to do with the process. These two positions may be considered the extreme positions.

The third position was that mothers both adapt their behaviors to the content and rate of development of their infants' language, and, also, show the way in terms of some behaviors. It is possible that the infants' level of language development gives rise to a set of behaviors that was once called "motherese" and is now labeled *child-directed speech* (speech addressed to infants as compared to children older than 2 years and to adults). These behaviors appear to be elicited by the lack of communicative competence on the part of the infant, the wish on the part of caregivers to interact conversationally with the child, and their desire, also, to acculturate the child, to have him or her become a member of society as a him or her. The first two factors that are said to elicit child-directed speech appear to produce universal behaviors on the part of caregivers. The last factor, logically, produces culturally variable behaviors on the part of caregivers. In other words, mothers throughout the world want their children to become members of their society, not of some strange one.

With this third position the question is not: Is it nature or nurture that plays the most important role in language development? Rather, the question becomes: What behaviors on the part of caregivers during which periods of development make it easier or harder for the infant to engage in the language acquisition process, and what behaviors on the part of the infant make it easier or harder for caregivers to help them engage? For those concerned with the language development of infants at risk for possible language delay, the answers to these questions are very important cues to possibly needed interventions.

How Mothers Talk to Infants in the Beginning

The research reviewed here is primarily concerned with the first important problem that the infant has in acquiring the language of the community, to determine what the boundaries are for the words, clauses, and phrases in the language. This is also our first important problem when we, as adults, learn a second language. It is a problem because when people talk they do not pause at the ends of word or phrases or clauses that are inside a sentence. Even when moms talk to their infants, the speech they produce is continuous; they do not pause between words.

Previous research on communicative interaction between mothers and their children in primarily middle–class familities in this country had found that child–directed speech had a number of characteristics. They are listed as follow:

1. Simplification of syntax and lexicon;
2. Using clear articulation;
3. Reducing the rate of speaking;
4. Talking about the here and now;
5. Ending sentences with rising intonation and using a great deal of contrastive stress;
6. Leaving space for response and contingent response; and
7. Repeating words, phrases, and sentences.

For a long time, research was carried out to examine what effect mothers' simplification of their language to the infant had on their child's acquisition of the grammar of the language. The question asked was whether mothers talking in simpler sentences helped their children acquire the sentence structures and the sentence types that were discussed in chapter 5. To answer this question, researchers looked at the relation between mothers' amount of simplification and the rate at which their children acquired syntax. Overall, little effect of mothers' special input was found on the child's acquisition of syntax (Gleitman, Newport, & Gleitman, 1984).

The focus of research then shifted to the effect of this input on lexical and discourse development. It was found that mothers who more frequently talk about objects and events in the here and now and who are contingent (focus on what the infant just said) in their responses to the words produced by their children have infants who are more rapid in their lexical development (Cross, 1977). Infants whose mothers encourage them to participate in conversation by allowing them sufficient time to respond and who acknowledge their response by praise or further extension of the topic have children who more rapidly initiate conversation (Menyuk, 1988). Much current research on the effect of input on language development has begun to concentrate on the effect of this input on the acquisition of phonology, the segments and suprasegments of the language. Simultaneously, researchers have been re-examining mothers' speech input from the point of view of determining how they speak and how the manner of their speaking might play a role not only in acquisition of phonology, but, also, syntax and lexicon (Menyuk, 1992).

Even in early studies, although some researchers concentrated on the words and sentences that mothers used with their language learning infants, others concentrated on the way in which these words were produced. Early research indicated that mothers spoke more slowly to their children under 2 years old than to older children and adults, articulated more clearly to their word-acquiring children (Bernstein-Ratner, 1984; Moslin, 1979), and from their earliest interactions with the baby spoke with exaggerated and varied stress and intonation patterns (Fernald, 1984). Why mothers did this was argued about, but regardless of why mothers speak the way they do, the question then arose as to whether or not this speech style could in any way help their children in the language-learning task.

Perhaps clearly produced speech might help children to learn to articulate more clearly. However, there is no evidence that this, in fact, does help the infant to learn to articulate more clearly. Like syntactic development, mastery of speech production seems to be influenced largely by the infants' increasing perceptual and productive linguistic competences. In some sense, the inverse seems to occur. It is not the mothers who appear to lead the children to more clear articulation but, rather, the children who do the leading. At the point at which children are beginning to produce recognizable words, mothers start to slow their speech to them and stress content words.

Slower speech, louder speech, and prosodically exaggerated speech may not teach the child how to articulate the sounds in the language but another possibility is that these behaviors might help children to segment the stream of speech into words; that is, these cues might help infants to learn the lexicon of the language. This possibility is currently being explored.

Another question that is being asked about the effect on language acquisition of how mothers talk is concerned with segments larger than words. The question is: Could infants use the exaggerated intonation patterns used by their mothers to help them segment the stream of speech into phrases and clauses? English-speaking mothers have been found to end their clauses with rising intonational contours with significantly greater frequency when speaking to infants than when speaking to adults . Mothers speaking other romance and germanic languages have been found to do the same thing. Worldwide, in certain cultures, it has been found that pitch is raised when speaking to infants. Given these data, it is possible that the exaggerated rising intonational contour is a cue to sentence or clause boundary in addition to the pause that usually occurs at these boundaries. Other data point to lengthening of the final vowel in the last word of the clause, rather than rising intonation, as a clue to the boundary.

Additionally, possibly universal cues to clause boundaries have been found in a recent study of mothers speaking to their 8- and 14-month-old infants (Fisher & Tokura, 1992). Apparently, mothers speaking both American English and Japanese pause at the completion of a clause, shift fundamental frequency, and increase the duration of the vowel in the lexical item at the boundary. Cues to phrase boundaries might be similar, although the data are not currently available. In addition to possible prosodic cues, it has been found that mothers repeat a great deal when speaking to their infants, and these frequent repetitions are often at phrasal not necessarily clausal boundaries . For example, mothers say things like "Put the blocks in the box, in the box, put the blocks, the blocks, in the box, put them in the box." The interaction of prosodic and repetition cues might make the task of phrase determination easier.

Use of these cues at clause and phrase boundaries on the part of mothers is said to be due to their intention that the baby take his or her turn in the conversation. This is why pause, lengthening, and rising intonation are said to occur at the end of clauses when it is the baby's turn. Two generalizations might be made about these findings. The first is that mothers' speech to infants contains cues to crucial boundaries in continuous speech. The second is that more than one cue to both clausal and phrasal boundaries is contained in the speech they hear, and this probably helps the infant to access both types of segments. This is probably also true about word boundaries. There the cues might be the internal one of exaggerated stress on strong syllables including increase in loudness and duration of vowels, and the external one of talking about the here and now or pointing. Table 6.1 summarizes the cues to boundaries that have been found in caregivers' speech to their infants.

How Infants Respond to Input

Suprasegmental or prosodic features are those that are said to be most salient to, and learned first by the baby. Much of this claim is based on the observation that long before infants recognize lexical items they not only discriminate between but also recognize the communicative intent in words and phrases spoken with different prosodic features, even when there are no facial cues. Infants react negatively to neutral words and phrases produced angrily, and react positively to the same words and phrases when they are spoken happily. So, very early on, babies attend to these acoustic signals.

TABLE 6.1
Cues to Boundaries in Caregivers' Speech

Segment	Cues
Word	Stress
	Lengthening of vowel
	Precision of articulation
	Repetition
	Talking about here and now
Phrases	Shortening to two syllables
	Repetition
	Intonation shift?
	Lengthening final vowel?
Clause	Marked pause
	Intonation shift
	Lengthening final vowel
	Repetition

We now know a great deal more about the speech perception of infants than we did when these claims were first made. For some time now we have known that infants who are only a few weeks old are capable of speech sound discrimination; that is, they can discriminate between two syllables that begin with different segments in the language (e.g., /pa/ vs. /ba/), and they can do this regardless of whether the sounds are or are not from the language they are exposed to. At the same early period of development, they discriminate among syllables with rising, falling, and steady intonational contours. Thus, there appear to be no age differences between the infants' abilities to discriminate between segmental or suprasegmental feature differences within and across syllables. The difference in discrimination for these two sets of features at this early age is that the segmental differences are treated as acoustic differences, whereas the suprasegmental differences that convey the intent of the message (I am angry at you or I am happy with you) are treated as both acoustic differences and communicative differences. It is not until they are approximately 1 year old that infants treat different words spoken by their caregivers as conveying different meanings.

Mothers make special use of prosodic features (they exaggerate intonation, stress, and pause). These cues, which may help infants to segment continuous speech, are present in the speech addressed to them. However, there have, as yet, been few studies that have examined the question of whether or not these cues are of benefit to the baby. The results of those few studies do suggest that the cues to segmentation that have been discussed are used to determine morpheme (word), phrase, and clause boundaries. As already stated, such segmentation is a first step in the analyses required in phonological, lexical, conversation, and syntax acquisition.

To find out whether the baby is sensitive to these cues, particular types of experiments have been carried out. The infant is seated in the mother's lap in the center of an enclosure. Lights and a speaker are on the walls to the left and right of the baby. Stimulus samples are presented either visually by pictures or objects and auditorily through speakers on each wall. After a pretrial phase during which the infant becomes familiar with the set up and learns to expect that different pictures or speech stimuli will come from the left or the right, the target stimuli are presented. In these experiments the stimuli vary in a number of ways. The most important way in which they vary is that the speech is either speech that has been addressed to an infant or to an adult. Another important way in which the speech varies is that it is either spoken by females or males. Continuous speech is varied in the two ways described earlier. It is spoken to babies or adults and spoken by either males or females. Another way in which it is varied is that it either contains pauses at appropriate boundaries or pauses that are inserted within segments. Thus, for example, infants hear sentences spoken by males or females talking to infants or to adults, that are appropriately segmented ("The big boy . . . ran into the house . . . ") or such speech inappropriately segmented ("The big . . . boy ran . . . into the . . . house").

A study examined recognition of words by infants 12 to 18 months under some of the varying conditions just described (Fernald & McRoberts, 1992). Because screens to the right or left of the infant depict the objects referred to, the experiment measured recognition by measuring the direction of looking by the infant. The varying conditions of input were either presenting lexical items from the speech of females or males addressed to infants or to adults. It was found that 12-month-olds recognized items from the speech of females addressed to infants significantly better than items addressed to adults. This tended to be the case with males' speech to infants but it was not significant. By the time the infants were 18 months old they were slightly, not significantly, better in recognizing lexical items from speech addressed to adults. These data indicate that lexical items that are produced by females when they speak to infants is more accurately identified by 1-year-old children than when these same lexical items are produced by other speakers and in other conditions. They also indicate that infants become more attuned to the regular, not special, production of lexical items over the second year of life. They recognize words no matter who produces them.

There are lots of questions that need to be answered. It is not clear that what the babies do is because of their greater attention to females' speech or to the clarification provided in that speech, or whether the baby is actually recognizing the word it attends to, or is in the process of learning the word. We also do not know what characteristics of speech were important for recognition. However, we know from the data obtained in other studies that slowed, clearly articulated, and stressed speech might be the important cues. The data obtained in this study are preliminary, but despite these very valid questions the data suggest that segmenting words from speech might be made easier by the prosodic cues provided in mothers' speech. Further, if proven to be the case, then there might be better insight into the problems of children who, for varying reasons, cannot hear and/or code what they hear accurately.

Additional data from this study indicated that there were word position as well as prosodic effects on recognition of lexical items. This probably means that exaggerated stress cues were used for recognition of the words. Mothers, in speaking to infants, put additional stress on syllables that would be naturally stressed in connected speech and these occur in certain positions in an utterance. In summary, although many questions remain about how the infant uses the information, there is evidence to indicate that the prosody of speech input to the infant might make the lexical acquisition task easier.

One footnote is required. In a recent study of mothers' speech to infants it was found that there was a great deal of variability across mothers in terms of the clarity of their speech to their infants as measured by adults' perceptions of the sentences they produced as they read a story and nonsense sentences

(Silber, 1992). Furthermore, there was a great deal of variability in how clarity was achieved by different speakers. For example, the mother found to be the clearest speaker among the four mothers in the study was also the most rapid speaker. Because no acoustic measures were made of the speech input it is hard to know what characteristics made the speech clear to adults. The researcher hypothesized that perhaps precise articulatory movements accounted for the results. These findings of variability make it difficult to determine what speech movements and acoustic consequences would lead to easier lexical accessing, and, therefore, make acquisition possible. Another factor might make mothers' speech clearer to their infants. The data from a series of studies of syllable and word identification by adult listeners suggest that there is much greater accuracy in identification when the items to be identified are all spoken by one speaker as compared to a mixture of speakers (Pisoni, 1992). It is possible that there are both across-the-board characteristics, and particulars of an individual mothers' speech to her infant that make lexical accessing easier. Thus, 1-year-olds recognize lexical items spoken to them by females significantly better than lexical items produced by males or spoken by adults to other adults. But infants may become accustomed to a particular input from a particular mother, and learn how to use the special input given them to access lexical items even better and earlier. The effect of speaker variability on infant speech perception supports this notion (Jusczyk, Pisoni, & Mullenix, 1992). Environmental cues or mothers talking about the here and now would make this task even easier. There are obviously a great many questions that remain to be answered before final conclusions can be reached about the role of the prosodic aspects of speech input in lexical acquisition. But the data collected so far point to possibilities for early diagnosis of problems and also, even more importantly, for intervention if it turns out that prosodic cues in mothers' speech are so crucial early on.

In studies examining the effect of prosodic cues on sensitivity to clausal boundaries on the part of infants, stimuli are presented that are from the speech of females to infants or to adults and are appropriately segmented or are not. The four types of stimuli, speech addressed to children or adults and appropriately and inappropriately segmented, contain an equal number of pauses of equal duration. Two types of stimuli are presented simultaneously, one type on one side and the other on the other. A head turn to one side or the other triggers a type of stimuli. The percentage of head turns to one side or other out of the total number of head turns is measured. The results are quite interesting. Infants significantly prefer infant-directed speech that is appropriately segmented to all other types of stimuli (Kemler-Nelson, Hirsh-Pasek, Jusczyk, & Cassidy, 1989). Thus, it is only with female-produced speech addressed to infants that one can observe the language-processing behaviors that we think are crucial to lexical and syntactic acquisition.

Clearly, this speech contains information for the young infant that other speech does not.

Other research found that infants' preferential looking behaviors indicate that they are sensitive to cues that mark morpheme, and phrase as well as clause boundaries. Although the research is quite preliminary, it is important to note that, apparently, infants are sensitive to cues that correspond to clausal units at approximately 4 to 6 months of age, to those cues that correspond to phrase units at approximately 9 months, and to those that correspond to word units at 11 months (Hirsh-Pasek, 1989). The finding that the sequence of segmentation is clause first and then phrase and then word coincides with other findings. The first unit of segmentation, the clause, conveys the intent of the utterance, as was discussed. The ability to discriminate among sequences that convey different intents is said to appear in the early months of life, approximately at 3 months. Word recognition, and, thereby, lexical acquisition, begins approximately at the end of the first year of life .

Research on both segmental discrimination and sensitivity to boundary cues point to the first year of life as being crucial to the development of the perception of both segments and suprasegments in the infants language. More recent research on speech discrimination has determined that language-specific speech perception occurs early on in this first year. It had been found that at some point in development the infant no longer discriminates between all possible speech sound segments with comparable ease, but, rather, has greater difficulty with the speech sound contrasts outside the native language. Initially this point in development was put at approximately 10 months of age (Werker & Lalonde, 1988). That critical time has now been moved to 6 months, at least for vowels (Kuhl, 1990). In like fashion, language-specific sensivity to clausal boundaries has been found (Jusczyk & Kemler-Nelson, 1992). Infants in an American English environment, who are between 4 and 5 months old, look significantly longer toward the speaker with appropriately segmented American English speech as compared to such Japanese speech. Previous research had found that 4- to 5-month-old infants in an English-speaking environment are sensitive to clauselike speech chunks for both Polish and English samples, whereas at 6 months they are sensitive to clause boundaries for English alone. Thus, both segment and suprasegment discrimination appear to develop from the general to the specific. Additional research indicates that, as in lexical acquisition, this sensitivity to boundary cues is present when the speech heard is from females speaking to infants but not to speech in general.

These data indicate that not only does the speech of mothers provide cues to segmentation but that infants are probably using these cues very early in life to segment continuous speech. The term *probably* is used because much more research needs to be carried out before these very preliminary findings can be substantiated. However, the ability to segment during the first year of life seems to be limited to the ability to segment speech that is familiar, that is, speech of females (preferably mother) addressing infants in their native language. This particularity suggests that there needs to be consistency in input for this segmentation ability to work the "right" way, that is, to segment in the appropriate way for the target language. Apparently, once the heuristic, or learning strategy, has been found to work, it can be applied to other input data. The finding that conditions for significant recognition of lexical items shifts from particular conditions at 12 months (speech of females addressed to infants) to more general ones (a tendency for better recognition of lexical items from adult-addressed speech) at 18 months indicates that this might be the case. There are no data as yet on when this might occur for phrase and clause boundaries. In addition, the environment provides other cues to segmentation, outside of prosodic ones, to the language-learning child. Mothers talk about the here and now and probably use gesture to indicate what they are referring to. They frequently repeat words and phrases in their utterances. The particularity of input or consistency apparently required by the child is balanced by the child's obvious ability to make rapid generalizations from the particular to the general. This indicates that a great deal of hypothesis testing must be taking place at a very early age. Table 6.2 summarizes the findings, thus far, concerning infants' responses to the cues in caregivers' speech.

As stated earlier, these findings are very exciting because they point to new possibilities for early assessment of language processing and, also, possible intervention techniques if problems are found. In the chapter 3 we discussed the order of acquisition of a vowel distinction (front–back) before another (high–low) that seemed to distinguish between children who did and did not turn out to have articulation problems. Research on early discrimination of native language vowels may be important for early determination of difficulties in speech processing. In chapter 5 we discussed a child who was very delayed in syntactic development because, apparently, he was not chunking

TABLE 6.2
Age at Which Infants Perceive Cues to Various Segments

Segment	Age	Response
Clause	4–5 months	Listen longer to appropriately segmented language addressed to infants
	5–9 months	Prefer appropriately segmented native language addressed to infants
Phrase	9 months	Prefer appropriately segmented native language addressed to infants
Word	12 months	Recognize words spoken by female to infants
	18 months	Recognize words addressed to adults

the input data appropriately. Response of babies to appropriately and nonappropriately segmented speech may be an early indication of diffculties in processing connected speech. This is why the results of these very preliminary studies are exciting and important.

In summary, recent research indicates that what mothers do to their speech when talking to their infants is used by their infants to acquire very important basic information about language. Mothers do not seem to be particularly aware of what it is that they do to their speech. This is substantial evidence that the mother does not shape language acquisition nor does the child learn language alone. This evidence also indicates how important it is that the infant have good perception of speech in order to acquire this basic information. Some of the children in our study had frequent episodes of otitis media. Some of the children had speech problems. One had serious language problems. Although we did not measure their perception of speech boundaries during the second half of the first year of life, this appears to be something that should be done in future studies of at-risk infants.

INTERACTION IN OUR STUDY

Development of Syllabic Utterances

In our discussion of early language development we described finding a relation between early development of syllabic or structured vocalizations and the age at which the children developed a 50-word productive vocabulary. Having found this relation, we wondered about mother's influence on the acquisition of syllabic vocalizations. Specifically, we were interested in determining if the mothers of the children in each of the three groups described, EFD, LFD, and SD responded more or less often to their children's syllablelike utterances. To do this, we calculated the percentage of syllables that were responded to by each of our mothers. Figure 3.3 showed the mean percentage of mother responsiveness to syllabic utterances for each group at each time interval.

Examination of the overall patterns of difference showed that the mothers of EFD children appear to be more responsive than the mothers of LFD children, who are more responsive than mothers of SD children. To understand these differences better we contrasted the mothers of the EFDs with the mothers of the LFDs and SDs when the three groups had approximately equivalent amounts of structure. Table 6.3 displays our findings.

Here we see that mothers of the EFDs are less responsive than the mothers of the LFDs, who are somewhat less responsive than the mothers of the SDs when their children have equal amounts of structure. These data suggest that the more rapid develoment of the EFDs cannot be accounted for by mother

TABLE 6.3
Average Mother Responsiveness Score When Children Show Equal Amounts of Structure

Group	Month	Mean Structure Score	Mean Responsiveness Score
EFD	12	27.1	38.8
LFD	16	26.1	50.2
SD	19	27.4	54.6

responsiveness scores. In fact, the data suggest that mothers of children who are developing a lexicon more slowly are working harder than the mothers of more verbal children. This finding that mothers of children who they perceive to be more at risk work harder at eliciting responses was referred to in chapter 1 when mothers' amount of interaction with premature as compared to full-term infants was discussed. This finding also points to the fact that their infants can make it easier or harder for mothers to provide appropriate conditions for learning and practicing language.

Early Turn-Taking

In previous chapters, our account of the child's language development was described as if it took place in isolation. A great deal of the child's vocalizing takes place in an interactional context. The adult with whom the child speaks is motivated to understand the child, to try to make sense of the communication, and to keep the communication going. Parents will respond to all kinds of behaviors, and will attempt to relate them to the topic. The exchange described here is typical of the lengths to which a mother will go to interpret behavior and maintain the conversation.

> Barry: (Begins to crawl across the floor. A doll lies in his path.)
>
> Mom: Oh you want the doll. (Mom picks it up and holds it out to Barry).
>
> Barry: (He stops crawling, sits next to his mother, takes the doll, vocalizes).
>
> Mom: Good, you want to play.
>
> Barry: (Flings the doll down.)
>
> Mom: Oh, you don ' t want it. Well would you like to play with this. (Hands him a large hour-glass shaped rattle.)
>
> Barry: (Reaches for it and flings it away.) Vocalizes. (Smiles.)
>
> Mom: You think I'm going to play your favorite game of give and throw.

Barry may or may not have intended his vocalizations and behaviors to be taken the way in which his mother interpreted them. He may not even have intended for them to be taken as communicative behaviors at all. For example, he may have been on his way to the kitchen to find his bottle and not have been interested in playing at all. At this young age, it is impossible to determine the child's original intent, for we cannot ask him or her. Those interested in studying this aspect of development are mostly left to interpret the child's intent from the available cues. A possible way of determining whether the baby intends to communicate was suggested in a study (Golinkoff, 1986) of mother–infant interaction at mealtime. This study examined the baby's persistence of vocalization to apparent noncomprehension on the part of mother as a way of determining intention. Using this criterion, the study found that at an age long before recognizeable words were being consistently used, infants give evidence of intending to communicate by repeating their vocalizations over a number of turns. Our resolution of this problem was to count behaviors as communicating if the mother responded to them as if they were communicative.

Four different possibilities can occur when an adult and a child with limited language skills are within sight and sound of one another. The first possibility is that the child takes a turn and means for that turn to be taken as part of a communicative interaction. The mother reads the turn as communicative and responds. In this case, there is a communicative exchange.

A second possibility also results in a communicative exchange and this is where the mother attributes communicative intent to one of the child's possibly noncommunicative behaviors and uses it as the basis for the communicative exchange. A third condition is where the child intends his or her turn to be taken as communicative and the mother makes no response. This is a case of communication failure. A final condition is where the child does not intend his or her behavior to be communicative and the mother does not respond to it. Babies vocalize and mothers do not attend and both are content. Therefore, this is not a communication failure. Babies do spend time talking to themselves.

There are differential probabilities associated with interactional sequences. Parents are usually able to signal their intent at having their move count as a conversational turn. They are not always successful in getting a response. Children, on the other hand, are less able to signal their intent, and very often it is the adult's response that determines which moves are conversational. The following examples may prove useful:

(Rachael, age 12 months, is sitting with a tissue on her head.)

Mom: Can we put it on my head?

Rachael: (Removes tissue.)

Mom: Put it on mommy's head.

Rachael: (Touches mom's head with tissue.)

Mom: (Fixes the tissue.)

In this example, the mother's intent is quite clear. Rachael's response to the intent also seems clear. She understands her mother's request and with a little help she follows it. Michael's behavior in the next sequence, however, is a little more difficult to interpret, as far as his intent to communicate is concerned.

(Michael age 12 months is playing with some blocks and a bottle.)

Michael: (Tries to put a block in the bottle.)

Mom: No, won't go that way. Try it another way.

Michael: (Does something and the block goes in.)

Mom: That's it.

Another sequence between Michael and his mother is even harder to interpret.

Michael: (sniffs)

Michael: (sniffs)

Michael: (sniffs)

Mom: What is that noise, Michael?

From the perspective of the development of communication, these examples show how adults continually read intent into their children's behavior. As the child grows, his or her nonverbal and vocal behaviors change to verbal behaviors and the child's intentions become more clear.

We examined the turn-taking skills of our babies and their mothers during the last third of the child's first year of life. We were interested in determining (a) the amount of communicative interaction during this period, (b) the effect of this interaction on later aspects of language development, and (c) the differences if any between the interactions of our full-term and premature children and their parents.

Because we were no more able (probably less so) than the mothers in our study to determine if a child meant his or her move to be taken as a conversational turn, we counted as a conversational move those behaviors and/or vocalizations that were responded to by the mothers. If there was uptake by the mother the turn was counted as an interactional move. For example, in the sniffing sequence, Michael would have been credited with three interactional moves and his mother would have been credited with one. Together they composed a single sequence. We treated the mothers' moves in the same way. If the mother took a turn or repeated turns and the baby made no response, the turns were considered noninteractional.

The samples from which we coded these data were each 25 minutes long.

TABLE 6.4
Average Number of Turns and Proportional Contributions of Mother and Baby

	Ages		
	8 Months	10 Months	12 Months
Mean number of Turns	524.4	454.1	558.7
(in 30 minutes)	(141.87)	(166.37)	(157.45)
Proportion of baby	1.0	1.1	.8
turns to mom turns	(.819)	(1.03)	(.33)

*Standard deviation shown in parentheses

If the baby cried during this 25 minute period, we timed the cry sequence and added that amount of time to the noncry interaction.

On the average, we scored 524 turns at 8 months, 454 turns at 10 months, and 558 turns at 12 months. The variation in the number of turns taken by the dyads was great. The smallest number of turns was 194. This occurred during a 10-month visit where one of our mothers washed lettuce in the kitchen as she interacted with her baby. The largest number of turns was 582 and this occurred during a 12-month visit. At 8 and 10 months of age the turns were distributed equally between mother and child, whereas at 12 months, the babies took approximately three turns for every four turns taken by their mothers. Developmental changes are occurring both in the frequency of the mothers' attempts to elicit a turn from the children and in the frequency of their taking a turn. Table 6.4 summarizes the data.

We next looked at the proportion of interactive turns to the total number of turns. This proportion, called an *interaction score,* represents the proportion of communicative interaction taking place when mother and baby were within sound and mostly within sight of each other. Table 6.5 describes what we found.

Mothers and their children engaged in conversational exchanges approximately 50% of the time, and the proportion of interactional turns increased as the children got older. There was a significant change in the average proportion of interaction from 8 to 12 months ($t = 5.93, p < .0001$). Looking at the maximum and minimum scores reveals great diversity among our dyads, but in no instances lack of communication nor total success. The issue of how little communication typically goes on when a mother and child are

TABLE 6.5
Proportion of Interaction at 8, 10, and 12 months

Ages	M	SD	Minimum	Maximum
At 8 months	.47	.14	.22	.69
At 10 months	.50	.15	.15	.79
At 12 months	.61	.12	.35	.83

alone in a room together cannot be answered by these data. The presence of researchers and recording equipment must have suggested to our mothers that some interaction was appropriate. However, the maximum score may indicate just how intense interaction can get during these early months of life.

The relative contributions of mother and child to the interaction were also explored. Within each interactive sequence we calculated the contribution of the mothers relative to the contribution of their children. The higher this score, the greater mother's contribution to the exchange. At 8 months this proportion was 1.54, at 10 months it was 1. 54, and at 12 months it was 1.49. Over the 4-month period, the proportional contribution did not change. The mothers, on the average, took three turns for every two turns taken by the baby. When these data are compared to the data in Table 6.5, we see a similar pattern. Mothers make more total moves at these early ages, and, within successful exchanges, they are more active.

Our perspective on turn-taking is that a conversational move is defined by its getting a response. If mother asks the child to do something or say something 20 times and the child does not respond, then there has been no exchange. Similarly, if the child takes a verbal or nonverbal turn and the mother does not respond, there is no exchange. To determine the amount of responding by our mothers, we calculated the proportion of baby turns that were incorporated in sequences to the total number of baby turns. The total number of baby turns includes turns where there was no response. These data are described in Table 6.6 for the same 4-month period.

These data show that uptake increases as the child gets older. There is a significant increase from 8 to 12 months ($t = 4.59, p < .0004$) and a similar significant increase from 10 to 12 months ($t = 3.59, p < .0009$). How much of this increase is attributable to the child's increasing competence in making his or her intent to communicate known cannot be determined. When two adults or when an adult and an older child are engaged in a conversation, very few turns go unacknowledged. (Parents of teenagers may be able to cite obvious exceptions, as when there are chores to be done, etc.)

We next questioned the relation between these results and other aspects of acquisition. Specifically, we looked at the correlations between the child's interaction score or response score with ages at which our babies comprehended and produced their first 50 words. We found no meaningful pattern

TABLE 6.6
Proportion of Mother Response From 8 to 12 Months

Ages	M	SD	Minimum	Maximum
At 8 Months	.51	.21	.14	1.00
At 10 Months	.54	.20	.08	.94
At 12 Months	.65	.16	.35	.93

in our analyses. That is, we sometimes achieved a weak positive correlation for one-time interval but not for another. For example, the interaction score and the child's comprehension of a 50-word lexicon were significantly and negatively correlated at 10 months ($r = -.328, p < .05$) but not significantly correlated at 8 or 12 months. It appears that parents and their children move toward greater amounts of communicative interaction, but that neither the amount of this interaction nor mother responsiveness, as measured by the response score, has much to do with the rate at which children acquire words. It may have more to do with commuicative interaction per se than with acquisition of particular aspects of language. That is, infants who are given more opportunities to interact may learn to interact more frequently and earlier but not, necessarily, learn more words earlier.

A final concern we had with turn-taking during these months when, for the most part, no recognizeable words were being produced, was to examine potential differences between mothers of premature and full-term infants. Given the differences in the early histories of these two groups of children, we wondered if the communicative interaction would differ. Quite simply it did not. Mothers of premature children interacted with their children as much as mothers of full-term children, and they were neither more nor less responsive. We found this result very interesting, for our premature children included children who had different medical histories from our full-term children. One child was diagnosed as having cerebral palsy when he was 1-year-old, another had been placed on a respiratory monitor after two episodes during which the child had stopped breathing, and a third was on seizure medication. The interaction data generated by these children and their mothers were not different from the data obtained from the other dyads.

Although other researchers have found differences in interaction between premature and full-term infants and their parents, our data did not show these differences. There are at least three possible reasons for this. Perhaps no difference was found because, on the whole, the premature children in our study were developing at the same rate as the full-term children. When a child was slow in lexical development the mother worked harder to elicit responses. Another is that our measures might have been too gross to reveal differences (others have used microanalysis procedures and collected intensive samples of videotape data). A third possibility is that our use of a large sample of children followed longitudinally, revealed tremendous variation in dyadic interaction. This magnitude of variation would keep any one child or group of children from looking too different.

Directives

Our measures of turn-taking examined the structure of communicative interaction and did not deal very much with the content. We did select one aspect of communicative interaction for in-depth exploration. This aspect was mothers' directive-giving behavior. We selected the directive as our basis for study for several reasons. Directives have often been discussed in the literature as having both positive (Barnes, Gutfreund, Satterly, & Wells, 1983) and negative (McDonald & Pien, 1982) consequences. They are, apparently, used with much greater frequency by mothers of developmentally delayed children than by mothers of normally developing children (Buium, Rynders, & Turnure, 1974). We felt that the directives mothers give to their children might offer insight into what mothers believe about their children's ability to respond, and also into the child's ability to respond. Mothers would help their children to fulfill their conversational obligations by asking them to perform directives within what the mother perceived as her child's level of ability. They ask their children to do what they think their children can do or can almost do. Twelve-month-olds are asked "to throw the ball," rather than "to answer the phone." Usually, they are asked to throw the ball only when they are about to throw it anyway.

As we described in chapter 2, we made 30-minute videotapes of our babies playing with their mothers at 12, 22, and 29 months of age. From these tapes, we coded all of the mothers' requests for action. Each action request was considered an episode that contained one or more subacts. We defined an episode as a unit of interaction consisting of one or more verbal directives, all accompanying gestures, and repetitions, and the child's subsequent response. In this section, we discuss what we found our parents and their children doing at 12 months of age.

Our mothers gave their children lots of orders. During 30 minutes of interaction, mothers on the average made 32 requests ($SD = 18.33$), or 1 per minute. The least number of directives given by a mother was 2 and the most was 83. Table 6.7 shows the percentages of the different types of directive. This distribution shows our mothers' tendency to ask their children to do things that their children were capable of doing.

Almost 33% of the directives, the protodirectives, required no new response from the child. The directive was given while the child or the mother was doing the activity. Children were asked to "play peek-a-boo" while they

TABLE 6.7
Percentage of Different Types of Mothers' Directives to Children

Type	M	SD	Minimum	Maximum
Protodirectives	30.1	15.4	0	60.0
Baby doing	12.0	10.3	0	51.5
Mother prompts	3.8	5.3	0	22.7
Mother doing	14.3	10.9	0	48.0
In-focus directives	59.1	14.2	30.4	85.0
Out-of-focus directives	10.6	9.9	0	50.0

were already playing peek-a-boo, or "turn the page" as the mother was turning the page. Another 60% were requests for the children to perform actions within their visual field or focus of attention. Only 10% of the actions children were asked to perform had no available contextual support; they were out of focus. Mothers appeared to be asking children to do the kinds of things the children could do.

It is no wonder that parents frequently say that their very young children understand everything. If the children are asked to do what they are, in fact, doing then of course they look like they understand everything. To examine how well our children did respond to their mothers' directives, we calculated the percentage of appropriate responding to in- and out-of-focus directives. The babies responded to in-focus directives 47.9% of the time ($SD = 18.4$), whereas they responded to out-of-focus directives 21% of the time ($SD = 32$). These data indicate several things. The first is obvious; babies respond to in-focus directives twice as often as to out-of-focus directives. Given the marked difference in standard deviation of the percent of responses in these two situations, they also indicate that babies are much more random in their behavior to out-of-focus directives. Finally, they indicate that babies early on rely heavily on context when attending what mothers say to them.

For a better understanding of how mothers make requests for action, we divided our children into good and poor comprehenders. The basis for categorizing them into the two groups was the number of words their mothers reported that they understood. Good comprehenders ($N = 12$) were children who understood 50 words at the time of the audiotaping, and poor comprehenders ($N = 8$) understood 10 or fewer words. We next compared the amount of appropriate responding made by the two groups to the in- and out-of-focus directives. We found that good comprehenders, by our definition, responded 48.9% of the time to in-focus, and responded 53.2% of the time to out-of-focus directives. Poor comprehenders responded 53.2% of the time to in-focus and 17.9% of the time to out-of-focus directives. Poor comprehenders seemed to be relying more on context than good comprehenders.

There were no significant differences between the groups in their ability to respond. This at first may appear quite surprising when we consider that the poor comprehenders were reported by their mothers to understand 10 words or fewer. We therefore examined the other kinds of things that mothers could do when giving a directive that might help their children follow the request. Mothers seldom gave directives once. The average number of subacts in a directive was 2.3. This means that the mothers either repeated their requests exactly or changed the form of the request while maintaining the intent. In addition, every request was accompanied by at least one gesture and, on the average, at least one of the requests was accompanied by rising intonation. It is likely that some combination of these cues allowed the children to respond correctly. The children could not have done so from the words alone because half of them could not understand even single-word utterances. The mothers of poorer comprehenders may have been providing many more nonverbal cues. This could account for a nonsignificant difference between the two groups of children in their overall amount of responding. If this is the case, mothers' frequent use of nonverbal cues and in-focus directives may be very critical interactional devices for children who are slow in lexical acquisition. The possibility is certainly worth further exploration.

Interaction During Year 2

How mothers talk to their babies before, during, and after their children acquire a first lexicon may play a role in this aspect of language development. We analyzed 100 consecutive mother utterances to their children during the home visits we made when the children were 8, 12, 16, and 22 months old. At 8 months of age, none of our babies had produced words, whereas at 22 months all but a few of the slowest had produced 50 words. Most were beginning to combine words together. After describing how mothers talk, we attempt to isolate aspects of child-directed speech that we think may facilitate the process.

The first aspect we explored was what mothers talk about to their young ones. Table 6.8 describes the distribution of mothers' utterances according to the functions they served. Where percentages were small, they were combined into a category labeled "Other." This category included such things as performatives, requests for permission, and utterances where the function was unclear. A pattern emerges as we look at these data.

At all ages, mothers are doing lots of different things when they talk to their children. Approximately 25% of their contributions are requests for information. This is true even before the baby can provide verbal answers. One interpretation of this is that mothers are working hard to elicit responses

TABLE 6.8
Distribution of Mothers' Conversational Acts to Their Children

Category	Month 8 %	Month 12 %	Month 16 %	Month 22 %
Descriptions	5.3	6.0	7.1	6.2
Statements	18.8	12.8	14.2	14.9
Request information	27.4	25.4	27.8	31.2
Request action	14.0	20.8	21.6	17.8
Organizing device	21.3	19.0	15.9	13.2
Labels	.8	4.8	4.2	2.9
Repetition	.4	1.1	2.5	8.7
Elicit imitation	2.3	8.7	5.7	4.2

from their children. Another is that they are simply trying to keep the conversation going by requesting information even though they know they won't get an answer. Mothers also make many requests for action. This probably means that they simply want a response from their children. Other than these behaviors, three changes in the pattern become apparent over time. The first is that mothers use fewer organizational devices over time. This means that they need to devote fewer and fewer utterances to maintaining conversation. A second is that parents begin to label objects for their children with some regularity during the period of time that their children are developing initial vocabulary. The third is that the use of repetition increases significantly from 16 to 22 months of age. All of the children are giving their mothers more to repeat. (This analysis did not attempt to determine the function of repeated utterances.) All of the other functions served by mothers' speech remained relatively stable over this period.

The next aspect of mothers' talk we examined was the conversational role played by their utterances over the 14-month period. These are described in Table 6.9.

Again, a clear pattern emerges. Mothers spend most of their time attempting to elicit responses from their children, be they action or verbal responses. Utterances described as Gives decrease over time and this is expected. As the child becomes more and more verbal and begins to respond, there is less and less use of moves that do not require uptake. However, Gives never disappear. Analyses of mothers' speech to our babies when they were 2 to 2 1/2 show that Gives constitute 25% of all moves. Conversational moves that allow for maintaining topic increase with age. Continues, which are moves that both respond to a previous utterance and expect a response increased from 0% at 8 months to almost 6% at 22 months. Two other moves that increase with time are Acknowledgments and Responses to the child's

TABLE 6.9
Distribution of the Conversational Role of Mothers' Utterances

| Category | Age in Months | | | |
	8	12	16	22
Elicits	45.1%	48.7%	51.2%	47.8%
Continue	0	.2%	1.2%	5.7%
Responds to self	.3%	.7%	.4%	.6%
Responds to baby	.1%	.5%	1.1%	5.9%
Gives	37.3%	36.1%	28.8%	24.6%
Acknowledges	.1%	.8%	2.4%	6.5%
Continues to vocalization	2.2%	1.05	.7%	.6%
Responds to vocalization	1.4%	1.5%	1.6%	.8%
Acknow vocalization	2.5%	1.9%	1.4%	.4%
Other	11.0%	8.6%	11.2%	7.1%

conversational turns. The increase in moves that Continue, Acknowledge, and Respond to baby persist into the Year 3.

Other aspects on which we classified our mothers were some of the structural and referential aspects of their speech. These are described in Table 6.10.

A look at Table 6.10 shows that mothers' speech does not change very much in terms of its structural characteristics. The one exception is the gradual increase in MLU. Even with this increase, mothers' utterances are short, and characterized by simple forms of the verb. Most sentences are simple and contain a simple proposition. The utterance is most often about people or objects present in the environment, and is about ongoing present action.

The final characteristic of mothers' speech that we investigated was the frequency of initiation and repetition. Utterances that contained neither of these characteristics were considered new. Table 6.11 describes what we found.

One of the most frequent occurrences in mothers' speech to children at this stage was their use of repetition and paraphrase. Mothers said something and then repeated it. This repetition helped maintain the verbal interaction while not damaging the content. Over the 14-month period the mothers' use of repetition declined, as the children became increasingly able to deal with new content. Whereas self-repetition decreased, imitations of what the child said and expansions of the child's utterances increased. Apparently, what was occurring was that mothers could use the child's utterances to maintain the conversation rather than doing all of the work themselves.

Interaction During Year 3

During this third year we focused on a comparison of the use of language by the children and their mothers when they talked to each other because most

TABLE 6.10
Structural and Referential Aspects of Mothers' Speech

Structured	Age in Months			
Characteristics	8	12	16	22
Mean length of utterance	3.38	3.42	3.74	4.15
NP ratio	1.39	1.45	1.49	1.46
VP ratio	.37	.31	.31	.35
Propositions per utterance	1.18	1.19	1.20	1.19
Percent of complex sent.	11%	12%	13%	16%
Referential characteristics				
Other time ratio	.07	.05	.08	.09
Absent people object ratio	.01	.01	.01	.02

TABLE 6.11
Mothers' Proportional Uses of Imitation and Repetition by Child's Age

	Age in Months			
	8	12	16	22
Category	%	%	%	%
New content	78.8	77.9	77.7	73.0
Partial repetition of self	3.3	2.7	3.2	1.7
Exact repetition of self	9.1	8.2	5.5	3.4
Expansion of self	2.8	2.4	2.5	2.6
Paraphrase self	4.6	5.5	6.3	5.8
Partial imitation	0	0	0	.2
Exact imitation	.8	2.2	2.0	5.1
Expand baby	.4	.4	1.1	5.5
Paraphrase baby	0	0	.1	.8

dyads were doing a great deal of this by 25 months. The question we asked was whether the mothers and children were getting closer in their use of language, and the answer is "no." The pattern that emerged at 25 months, and the pattern at 29 months were very similar. The mothers primarily used language to request information from their children, and the children responded with statements and descriptions.

The disproportionately high use of the requesting function by the mothers may reflect both social and language differences between adults and children. Adults quite naturally assume the dominant role by eliciting responses from the children. If we use the frequency of Organizational Devices as an indication of commitment to maintaining interaction, it appears that once the conversation is started both mother and baby appear to be working equally to keep the conversation going. But it is the mother who most often gets the conversation going even during the third year. The mother continues to take the lead in this sense, and the child follows. However, the important difference is that in the third year of life the child is doing a very good job of following. Also, as is discussed later, it is equally important for the mother to follow as well as lead.

In terms of the parameters that we have measured, it is probable that adult and child patterns come to approximate each other. This approximation most likely results more from linguistic rather than social changes because turn-taking is a behavior that infants are capable of. They are simply not capable, very early on, of producing the language of requests. Because linguistic maturation primarily motivates the change it may occur when the child is around 3 to 4 years of age and has firm control of many aspects of the language. However, as stated previously, social and linguistic maturation continues, and children's conversational participation changes in many other parameters than the ones we measured until they reach adulthood.

One final observation relates to the use of the labeling function. It seems that mothers must be requesting labels for objects, and their children complying with the request. Both at 25 and 29 months the children are providing labels four times more often than their parents. However, this is very different from what was seen when the child was 2 years old and mothers engaged more frequently in telling their children the names of people and objects. Now their children are telling them.

Summary

In summary, there are several characteristics of mothers' speech to their children that make it different from adult-to-adult talk. It is shorter, less complex, and more grounded in the present. It is also more repetitive and there is a strong tendency on the mother's part to attempt to elicit responses and maintain interaction. The speech produced by mothers over the first 2 years contains cues that the baby appears to use to carve out the important units in continuous speech: the clause or sentence, the phrase, and the word. All of these characteristics are probably motivated by the mother's need to interact.

The child's learning of language, apparently, is assisted by these interactions. Although the interactions may be crucial for the learning of language, at least in the sense of exposing the child to the language, mothers are not obviously motivated to engage in interactions to teach language, nor do children learn language only as a result of the interactions. Nevertheless, it is likely that within the interaction there are aspects of mothers' speech that may be facilitative of the child's linguistic growth. Such an aspect may be the mothers' use of special prosody in child-directed speech. Although much of what is learned is clearly determined by the characteristics of the learner, differences in input appear responsible for variations in the rate of development of some aspects of the infant's language knowledge.

THE EFFECT OF INTERACTION ON LANGUAGE DEVELOPMENT

To investigate which aspects of input were crucial for language development, we performed a series of investigations. The basic design of these studies was to equate the children for level of linguistic development at some point in time and to analyze the kinds of input mothers made to these children at that point. We then measured how much the children's language changed from this time to some later point in time, and tried to identify the aspects of mothers' speech that were related to the change in the children. When we performed this series of analyses, we found that the children's rate of development was not affected by the structured aspects of mothers' speech. That is, characteristics like sentence length, sentence complexity, type of sentence, and so on, made little difference in children's rate and quality of development. We corroborated previous findings. What appeared to affect the children were pragmatic, discourse, and conversational aspects of input. We also found that which particular variables affected children changed somewhat over time. This makes good sense in light of what we have suggested. Pragmatic, discourse, and conversational aspects of caregiver input should be sensitive to the child's ability to participate in interaction.

We built statistical models at various developmental points. Using these models, we attempted to predict the exit behavior of our ten most rapidly developing children and our 10 slowest developing children from mothers' speech at 16, 22, and 25 months of age. Table 6.12 describes our ability to predict. Using how the mothers talked to their children at 16 months, we were able to classify 75% of the children correctly. Using our 22-month-old model, we classified 70%, and using the 25-month-old model, we classified 90%. These data suggest that mothers are quite sensitive to their children's rate of development. Further, these data, like the data on word comprehension and production, indicate that mothers are quite realistic about this development.

The range of different mothers' behaviors that accounted for variance in gain scores over time among the children changed at the various points in

TABLE 6.12
Classification by Discrimination Function Analysis of 10 Highest
Scoring and 10 Lowest Scoring Children at Exit

		16 Months Prior Classification	
Assigned Classification	High	9	1
	Low	4	6
		Correctly Classified 75%	

		22 Months Prior Classification	
Assigned Classification	High	6	4
	Low	2	8
		Correctly Classified 70%	

		25 Months Prior Classification	
Assigned Classification	High	10	0
	Low	2	8
		Correctly Classified 90%	

TABLE 6.13

A Model of Mother Input I: Mothers' Discourse and Conversational Characteristics at 12
Months in Relation to Children's Residual Gain Scores From 12 to 16 Months

	F	Prob > F
Complete model	15.74	.0001
Absent ratio	2.68	.110
Conversational acknowledge	27.34	.0001
Request action	5.07	.030
Elicited imitation	5.94	.019

development. As Table 6.13 indicates, the amount of mothers' repetition and expansion of herself as well as amont of response and acknowledgment of baby, when baby is 16 months, accounts for variance in the child's gain scores at 22 months. Although amount of repetition of self when the baby is 22 months old continues to be an important factor in gain scores from 22 to 25 months other factors are also playing an important role. Continuing the conversation and paraphrase and partial repetition of baby are now significantly contributing to gain scores. These results are shown in Table 6.14.

By the time the babies are 25 months old the mothers' behaviors that account for most variance in gain scores at 29 months are expansion and repetition of baby as well as acknowledgment. When the babies are 29 months amount of elicitation of imitation of baby, requesting action from baby and paraphrasing baby as well as response to baby account for the most variance in gain scores at 35 months. These data are shown in Tables 6.15 and 6.16.

What seems to be happening in time is a shift from use of mothers' own utterances to expand upon to use of the infants utterances to, finally, elicitation of verbal behavior. This seems to represent the mothers' knowledge that more can be given to and asked of the baby in terms of conversation, and this has a positive effect on gain scores. However, although this is happening, mothers simultaneously spend a great deal of time acknowledging the infants contributions, and responding to them. This also makes a significant contri-

TABLE 6.14

A Model of Mother Input II: Mothers' Discourse and Conversational Characteristics at 16
Months in Relation to Children's Residual Gain Scores From 16 to 22 Months

	F	Prob > F
Complete model	14.19	.0001
Conversational acknowledge	7.93	.008
Expand self	6.17	.030
Label	5.11	.030
Paraphrase self	3.80	.059
Respond to baby	9.50	.004

TABLE 6.15

A Model of Mother Input III: Mothers' Discourse and Conversational Characteristics at 22
Months in Relation to Children's Residual Gain Scores From 22 to 25 Months

	F	$Prob > F$
Complete model	4.95	.001
Continue	6.66	.015
Exact repetition self	6.31	.017
Paraphrase baby	7.97	.008
Partial repetition	11.83	.002
Respond of vocalization	4.46	.043

TABLE 6.16

A Model of Mother Input IV: Mothers' Discourse and Conversational Characteristics at 25
Months in Relation to Children's Residual Gain Scores From 25 to 29 Months

	F	$Prob > F$
Complete model	5.50	.002
Conversational acknowledge	5.48	.0266
Expand baby	8.56	.006
Expand self	5.76	.023
Partial repetition	4.07	.050

bution to the gain scores achieved throughout this period. Acknowledging and responding seem to us to be important affective factors as well as contributions to keep the conversation going. These figures indicate, again, that it is not the structural aspects of mothers' speech that influence rate of development. Rather, particular discourse or conversational devices appear to have the greatest effect.

A look at the range of characteristics at the different age levels that allowed us to make these predictions revealed an important overall principle to us. Mothers who were good conversational partners had children who developed more rapidly. Mothers who had more difficulty conversing had children who developed more slowly. The kinds of things that mother did that made her a good conversational partner were, in general, to follow the child's lead by expanding on his verbal and nonverbal contributions; to make his or her conversational contributions fit by acknowledging and responding to them; to provide responses rather than demand them.

Notice that all require input from the child. Thus, a child who provides little material to expand or to fit into the conversation or to acknowledge or respond to creates problems for the mother. However, perhaps the most important contribution is to set the stage for the child to make his or her conversational contribution, without limiting his or her turn so that he or she cannot make any move at all. Thus, modeling as well as support may be required sometimes and by some children The example that follows is taken

TABLE 6.17
A Model of Mother Input V: Mothers' Discourse and Conversational Characteristics at 29
Months in Relation to Children's Residual Gain Scores From 29 to 35 Months

	F	Prob > F
Complete model	5.46	.005
Elicit imitation	6.80	.018
Paraphrase baby	5.74	.028
Request action	13.92	.002
Responds to baby	5.42	.033

from 16-month-old Rosa. Rosa has played with her duck many times before, and has said the word "duck" on other occasions.

Rosa: (takes a duck out of the box.)

Mom: What's that? Duck?

Is that your duck?
  (Mom reaches for the duck, squeezes it and moves it toward Rosa.)
  What's the duck say, quack, quack, quack, quack, quack?

Rosa: Duck.

Mom: Duck.

In this example, Rosa's mother follows Rosa and keeps going until Rosa can take her turn. She quickly gives Rosa the needed information and, when Rosa makes her move, her mom is right there with an acknowledgment.

Now contrast this interchange with one between Jeff and his mother.

Jeff: (picks up doll from the floor.)

Mom: Oh what a cute little dolly.
  Say doll.
  Say doll.
  Say baby.

Jeff: (turns the doll down.)

Mom: No go nice. You make nice.

Jeff's mother also followed his lead by using his actions on the doll to establish the topic. But rather than focusing his interests on the doll and what the doll could do, she attempted to draw from the child a specific verbal response. He not only made no response to his mother, but quickly gave up the doll as well.

The development of language in the child is the result of the communicative interaction between the child and important others in the environment. When important others are good conversational partners, the child's language skills develop more rapidly. When important others are not as good conversationalists, the child's rate of acquisition can be slowed. Aspects of interaction that appear to make a difference include:

1. setting up the child to take conversational turns through question asking, and other techniques designed to draw the child into a conversation;
2. attending to what the child is attending to either as the basis for starting a conversation or continuing one;
3. acknowledging the child's conversational turns;
4. taking verbal and nonverbal turns whose function is merely to keep the conversation going and on the topic (uh-huh, I see!, yeah); and
5. taking account of the amount of information the child has and needs in order to take his or her turn.

What is most important about these aspects of communication is that all adults engage in them to a greater or lesser degree, and consequently most children have no trouble learning to communicate.

SOME IMPLICATIONS FOR INTERVENTION

The results of our study suggest that the caregiver's sensitivity to the child's ability to participate in the communication interaction plays a crucial role in the success or failure of the interaction. This seems particularly important in those cases where the child provides very little material for the caregiver to work with, and still is in great need of opportunities for communication. There are some general principles that seem to be important for all interactions between infant and caregiver and others that are particularly important for the very slowly developing child.

The general principles seem to be:

1. Talk about the here and now when communicating with infants.
2. Follow the child's lead by expanding first on nonverbal and then verbal contributions.
3. make the child's contributions fit by first acknowledging them and then
4. by responding to them.
5. With the child who provides little material, modeling is appropriate to set the stage. With this child responses should be provided rather than demanded.

The examples provided in this chapter of more or less successful communicative interactions make clear what is meant by these suggestions.

CHAPTER 7

Summary and Implications

We have primarily discussed normal patterns of language development over the first 3 years of life. We have compared full-term and premature infants, discussed how mothers (and, on occasion, other caregivers) talk to their children during these 3 years, and some patterns of language development among children who turn out to have some difficulties in developing language. In this last chapter, we first present the results we obtained from the outcome measures we used when the younger group of children was 30 months and the older group of children was 35 to 36 months. We then summarize our findings in each of the areas of language development we examined. We end by presenting some of the findings we obtained with some of the premature children in a follow-up study of their language development.and that of other premature children. We conclude by discussing what we think are the implications of our findings for researchers, clinicians, and teachers of young children. We also discuss what our longitudinal study told us about assessing the language development of young children and about the ability to predict outcomes in language development from these assessments. We expect these kinds of information may be helpful in terms of thinking about normal language development and about measures for determining children at risk for language development problems. Finally, we present some suggestions for intervention that we think our study indicates.

OUTCOME MEASURES

When our older babies reached 36 months of age and our younger babies reached 30 months of age, their language was assessed by a certified speech pathologist at a large metropolitan hospital. They were tested using a battery of standardized assessment measures frequently used to evaluate children of this age. The person who tested them was naive concerning the developmental status and history of most of the children. She had visited with about six of them before they were 1-year-old. The tests they received are summarized in Table 7.1, and are grouped according to whether they measured receptive or expressive development.

For all of the tests, the results are reported as the number of months the child performed above or below his or her chronological age. For the premature children, their actual birth date was used to calculate test scores because, as stated earlier in this volume, correcting for prematurity after 1 year of age inflates the child's performance. Figure 7.1 describes our results for children born at term, and for those born prematurely. It also summarizes our findings for the group as a whole. At 3 years of age, the full-term and the premature children were both doing very well. On every measure, the children performed several months beyond what could be expected for their chronological age. When we averaged all of the tests of receptive language together (RECLAC), the full-term children were 6.6 months ($SD = 6.12$) above expected age level, and the premature children were 7.3 months ($SD = 6.74$) above. On the tests of language production (EXPLAC), the full-term children averaged 7.5 months ($SD = 4.46$) above expected age level, and the premature. children averaged 5.3 months ($SD = 5.99$) ahead. Thus, at the end of our study, our children as a group were about 6 months above expected age level. In addition, there was only one test on which the premature and full-term children differed to a significant statistical degree, and that was an expressive measure. Differences between full-term and premature infants appeared early on the Bayley motor measures. Therefore, this finding is

TABLE 7.1
Outcome Measures of Language

	30-Month Battery	36-Month Battery
Receptive	Sequenced Inventory of Communicative Development (SICDR)	Sequenced Inventory of Communicative Development (SICDR)
	Peabody Picture Vocabulary Test (PPVT)	Peabody Picture Vocabulary Test (PPVT) Northwestern Syntax Screening Test (NSST)
Expressive	Sequenced Inventory of Communicative Development (SICDE)	Sequenced Inventory of Communicative Development (SICDE)
	Developmental Sentence Scoring (DSS) Reynell (REYN)	Developmental Sentence Scoring (DSS)

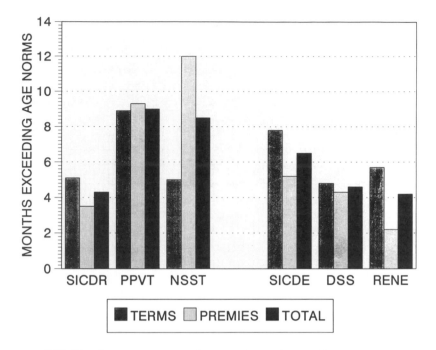

FIG. 7.1.   Average outcome performance, in months exceeding age norms.

interesting but its importance is not clear because measures of outcome at 3 years did not put these infants into a risk category. They were only less ahead on this measure as compared to other measures, and less ahead than their full-term peers.

The outcome measures we took on our 12 VLB infants were equally positive. Table 7.2 illustrates the results. Only those tests that we gave to all 12 children are included in the table. Inspection of the data shows how well our VLB children performed. They were all comfortably within the normal range. There was a statistically significant difference between the VLB and the full-term children on both the SICD receptive and expressive portions, but even our smallest babies were clearly doing fine as compared to test norms by the time they reached 3 years of age.

There were 4 children who scored more than 1 standard deviation below the average on both the receptive language comprehension and language production outcome measures. One of these children was Lee, the full-term child described in chapter 5. The other 3 children were all premature. Among them were our smallest baby (794 grams birthweight), and the child with cerebral palsy. None of these 4 children had test scores that were a year or more behind their chronological age, and only 1 of the 4 children was in

TABLE 7.2
Average Performance on Language Outcome Measures for Full-Term and Low
Birthweight Children (in Months Above Age Norms)

Test	Full-Term Children		Low Birthweight Children	
	Mean	SD	Mean	SD
Language comprehension				
SICDR	5.1	4.33	1.7*	5.48
PPVT	8.9	7.75	8.8	6.19
Language production				
SICDE	7.8	3.20	4.3*	6.08
DSS	4.8	9.12	2.2	10.63

*$df = 37; p < .05.$

therapy. Our children, including those who were developing more slowly, were progressing within the normal range. In most cases, it was difficult to discern those who were born at risk from those whose early months were more tranquil.

Most of the children in the study were 6 months ahead of developmental norms on the exit tests used. This was surprising given the fact that half the children were born prematurely and were considered to be at risk for developmental delays. The results of testing the children on exit measures indicated that there were no significant differences between premature and full-term children in either language comprehension or production. There were some differences between full-term and VLB children on some of these measures, although the VLB children were performing well within the normal range. In general, there was a tendency for the VLB children to be a little behind the rest of the children, both full-term and premature, on a number of language measures.

It is possible that these findings, which depart to some extent from other studies of premature infants, were the result of a combination of factors. The first factor is the overall health of the sample population, Once all the premature children (except our cerebral palsied child) had passed through the early months of life, they and their full-term peers had no obvious and lasting health problems outside of those encountered by all developing children. This is clearly not the case for all premature infants, among whom birth defects occur at a significantly greater rate than among full-term infants.

The second factor may be the study itself. That is, the home visitors may have carried out an intervention by the fact of their home visits. These visits may have lent support, without interference, to the mothers. This support may have implicitly focused the mothers' attention on their children's language development accomplishments. These factors may account for the performance above age expectations on tests of language comprehension and production by both premature and full-term infants.

The evidence about the effect of home visits on premature and full-term children's intellectual and communicative development has been discussed at length in a recent volume on the topic (Behrman, 1993). Several studies examined the effectiveness of various types of programs for children who are born into poverty and average families. Our children fell into the latter category. The concensus of opinion appears to be that home visits are necessary but not sufficient to guarantee good outcomes in these areas, and that programs that target one or a few domains of functioning, as ours did, are not likely to have a lasting beneficial effect. Therefore, the possibility of our unconsciously carrying out an effective intervention for communication development seems unlikely. However, a home visit study focused only on moving slow talkers into greater use of language by increasing their motivation to speak found short-term effects on language production at 3 years (Whitehurst et al., 1991). We also present data here on language performance at 3 years.

Prediction

A major interest of ours in following these children was to determine a series of measures that could predict which children would be at risk for problems in language development at age 3. Very few of our children had such problems. However, we were still interested in measures that accounted for variance in outcome scores. Such measures could be useful in other studies of at-risk children To answer this question, we began with an analysis of our risk variables. The results of stepwise linear regression analyses on language comprehension (RECLAC) and language production (EXPLAC) are shown in Table 7.3. Both single correlations and overall multiple correlations are described.

The table illustrates that, for premature children, a combination of biological and environmental factors predict language comprehension and production, whereas environmental factors alone predict language outcome in full-term babies. These data are consistent with the findings of Siegel (1982), who used a similar procedure for analyzing data. Thus, variation in language outcome measures could be accounted for by presence of RDS and 1- and 5-minute Apgars, as well as some environmental measures, in our premature children. However, such factors did not result in language disorder. This suggests that language development cannot be detrimentally affected by the biological insults that the particular premature infants in our study suffered pre- and postnatally.

Although the risk scores allowed us to predict with reasonable accuracy,

TABLE 7.3
Stepwise Regression Between Risk Variables and Language Outcome Scores

| Language Measure | Preterm Children | | | Full-Term Children | |
	Multiple r	Single r		Multiple r	Single r
Language comprehension					
Mother's education	.48	.48	Gender	.45	.45
Gender	.55	.34	Father's education	.52	.17
RDS	.60	.23	Smoking	.58	.18
SES	.62	.45	Father's age	.59	.13
Mother's age	.64	.20			
Language production					
Apgar 1 minute	.39	.39	Mother's education	.50	.50
Gender	.54	.31	Father's age	.56	.42
Mother's education	.58	.33	Gender	.59	.26
Apgar 5 minute	.59	.20	Father's education	.63	.31

we were interested in determining the strength of some of our early language measures for predicting later language outcome. We were particularly interested in determining if any of our easily administered measures were predictive. Our special interest in these measures lay in the possibility that they might present an efficient and effective means for investigators, clinicians and teachers of children at risk to follow children about whom there were concerns.

To perform this analysis, we selected the variables we measured using the parents' lexical diaries of their children, along with the variables of the multiword comprehension test. Our results are described in Table 7.4. Using variables derived from both these measures, we obtained correlations of .72–.85 with subsequent language development. These variables were more highly correlated with outcome than the risk variables. It therefore appears reasonable to suggest that language behaviors that emerge during the second year—that is, the ability to say words and the ability to follow simple directions—can be used to predict language performance at least to age 3. As is discussed in the Epilogue section of this chapter, some of these measures predict even later language behavior.

NORMAL PATTERNS OF LANGUAGE DEVELOPMENT

To begin, it is important that we found that language development is not different in premature children solely because of prematurity. Among our premature children, there were some who were behind their full-term peers

TABLE 7.4
Stepwise Regression Between Language Variables and Language Outcome Scores

Language Measure	Pre-term Children			Full-term Children	
	Multiple r	Single r		Multipl r	Single r
Language comprehension					
Comprehension of predictable sentences	.71	.71	Comprehension of predictable sentences	.72	.72
Production rate	.80	.62	Comprehension rate	.80	.41
Sentence comprehension at 22 months	.81	.55	Comprehension 100 words	.81	.48
Comprehension test completion	.82	.65	Comprehension test completion	.83	.57
			Sentence comprehension at 22 months	.85	.51
Language production					
Comprehension test completion	.66	.66	Sentence comprehension at 25 months	.63	.63
Comprehension of predictable sentences	.69	.65	Comprehension of 100 words	.74	.54
Comprehension of 100 words	.71	.48	Sentence comprehension at 22 months	.76	.44
Sentence comprehension at 25 months	.72	.51			

in development during the first 18 months of life. At this point, they caught up with their peers, both premature and full-term. This was also true of some of our full-term babies. That is, slow development at the beginning of life is not limited to premature children, nor is fast development limited to full-term infants.

For the most part, both premature and full-term babies showed sudden spurts and plateaus in individual measures of language development. This indicates that rate of development can vary within infants as well as across infants. Only in more extreme instances do we see consistent patterns of development, either fast or slow. For example, EFDs, LFDs, and SDs of lexicon were consistently members of their respective groups throughout the study. However, spurts and plateaus vary for different aspects of language development as well as for language growth as a whole. For example, some children were very quick at learning new vocabulary during 1 or 2 months and slow at learning how to put the words into sentences during the next few months. What we find is that rate of development varies overall, and also that the rate of development of particular aspects of language varies. Further, spurts and plateaus in development of an aspect of language occur from month to month.

In addition to variation within children, there is a great deal of variability among children. Different children are working on the same aspects of language at different times. This variation among children was not predictive of bad outcomes. Because a large majority of the children in our study were performing normally or better on standard tests of language at age 30 or 36 months, it is clear that taking somewhat different paths through the language development garden may not lead to difficulty. Despite individual variation within children, which is the rule rather than the exception, some general developmental trends emerge in each aspect of language across our population of 53 children. There are two topics, then, that we discuss under the headings of normal patterns of development. The first topic is our findings on general trends and variations in aspects of language development. The second is some comparisons between premature and full-term infants on these aspects of development.

General Trends and Variations

Under this heading we discuss the four main aspects of development that we studied: engaging in conversation, acquiring the speech sounds of the language, acquiring words and cognitive development, and comprehension and production of words in sentences. In each of these aspects, we discuss general developmental trends and how our findings relate to the findings of other studies of language development in children of the same ages as those we followed.

Engaging in Conversation.   One of the behaviors that occurs very early in life is taking a turn in a conversation. Many of the studies of early language development have found that infants participate in "proto-conversations" at about 3 to 4 months old. That is, babies respond with eye contact, smiles, and vocalizations when their caregivers talk to them. This ability to take a turn in conversational interaction seems to be given by nature to all normally developing babies, and one can see this turn-taking behavior in other animal babies as they interact with their mothers. When babies take a turn, caregivers are encouraged to continue the conversation. This, in turn, can be of help to the babies in their language development.

We considered just how big a help it is as we examined the effects of mothers' talk to their children. We found that all of our babies participated in turn-taking, although there were substantial differences in the frequency with which they did this, and in how long they carried on a conversation. In general, mothers and infants engaged in conversationsal exchanges about 50% of the time during any observation over the developmental period of 8 to 12 months. At least while we were present, mothers engaged their children in conversational interaction very frequently as their infants achieved some developmental maturity. This finding is quite similar to that of other studies, both earlier and later ones (e.g., Hoff-Ginsburg, 1991; Lewis & Freedle, 1972). Also, generally, mothers take more turns that their infants in these early conversations; they take three turns to every two turns of the baby. Mothers do this to keep the conversation going when the baby is still too young to be an equal conversation partner. The proportion of successful turns (when an elicitation gets a response) increases with time over the period from 8 to 12 months, largely due to the fact that the infant's uptake increases over this time period.

One generalization then that can be made about normal patterns of language development is that conversational turn-taking is an early behavior that occurs with all caregiver–infant pairs. The behavior takes up a large proportion of all infant–caregiver interactions in the period from 8 to 12 months. During this developmental period, mothers (and other caregivers) take the responsibility of providing the larger share of the elicitations. However, the infants' responses to elicitations increase during this time, increasing the proportion of successful turn.

As said previously, there was a large amount of variation among the baby–mother pairs in the amount of turn-taking in which they engaged. The smallest number of turns that we observed during any visit over the period from 8 to 12 month was 194, and the largest number was 582. This is quite a difference but, as we discuss later, differences in frequency and duration of turn-taking apparently make no difference in comprehension and production of language as measured by standard tests at approximately 3 years of age.

Acquiring the Speech Sounds of the Language. Both cry and noncry vocalizations occur during early infancy. The noncry vocalizations that do occur early are not what one can call true babbling. They are more general soundmaking, rather than speech-soundmaking. We measured both the acoustic characteristics of early cry in our very young infants and the frequency of crying in our older infants. We found that the boys and girls differed in the pitch characteristics of their cry, even at an early age. We also found that babies cried very little during the later months of the first year of life. By the time they were 12 months of age, cry made up only 10% of their vocalizations.

True babbling increased over the second half of the first year of life. So-called syllabic utterances (those that contain both a vowel and a consonant as in "dada" and "mama") increased in proportion to all utterances during the period from 8 to 12 months. Babies produced these babbled utterances at the rate of about six times per minute. This was true both of boys and girls. This situation suggests that, in general, babbling is a frequent occurrence during this period of development while babies are awake.

There were a group of babies we called the EFDs because they shifted over to producing more speech sound utterances than general sound utterances at an earlier age than did the group of babies we called LFDs and the group we called SDs. The EFD group continued to be early in all aspects of speech development that we measured: matching sound targets in general, and matching final sounds in single syllable words earlier than the other children. With some few exceptions, all the children in the study were successfully producing the speech sounds of their language quite accurately at the time the study ended. However, these patterns of being early and fast, late and fast, or slow in speech sound development persisted over the entire period of the study. These sound development patterns were also related to the rate at which vocabulary was acquired, which is the next topic discussed.

In addition to these group characteristics, there was a large amount of individual variation in the ages at which speech sound discrimination and speech sound production were accomplished. On the speech sound discrimination task we gave the children, the age range for successful completion was from 20 to 32 months, a difference of almost 1 year. At 22 months, one child achieved a speech sound match score of 12.1, whereas 18 children received no score at all. By 29 months, the range of total match scores was 5 to 25; at 35 months, when a ceiling in match scores was being reached, the range was 9 to 26. Clearly, the range included all children who later turned out to have some articulation problems. However, not all children who had a score of 0 at 22 months turned out to have articulation problems. As well, those who did turn out to have some problems did not always have the lowest match scores in each period measured. Therefore, the range of normal development in terms of speech sound discrimination and articulation mastery seems to be fairly wide, and children who will turn out to have articulation problems cannot be identified early as a result of simply being slower in speech sound discrimination or production. However, there was a significant relation between speech discrimination scores and later articulation and word production.

Acquiring Words and Cognitive Development.   Most of the children developed words at the same rate and at the same ages that other studies have found. Our children talked about the things that children of other studies have been found to talk about first and then later. There seems to be great universality among normally developing children in acquisition of words and topics of discourse during this very early age period.

We know that word comprehension occurs before word production. In general, the children understood about 50 words before they produced 10 words. More specifically, there was a lag of 3 1/2 months between compre-

hension and production of 10 words, and a lag of 5 months between comprehension and production of 50 words. In general, acquisition of early
vocabulary took place at a slower rate than acquisition of later vocabulary.
There was no gender difference in the rate at which girls and boys comprehended new words after 10 words were acquired. There was a gender
difference in the age at which boys and girls produced new words. Boys were
1.2 months behind the girls in 10 word production, and 1.5 months behind
the girls in 50 word production.

There seems to be an interdependence, which we find logical, between
vocabulary development and some measures of cognitive development. On
the Uzgiris–Hunt test, the two measures that correlated with the rate of
vocabulary acquisition were the ability to imitate verbally and the ability to
act on objects. In other words, symbolic play and verbal imitative competence are related to vocabulary acquisition.

In addition to these general developmental trends, the age at which 10
words were comprehended ranged from 8.9 to 12.5 months. The age at
which 50 words were comprehended ranged from 11.4 to 16 months. The
age at which 100 words were comprehended ranged from 13.4 to 18.2
months. In general, then, the differences among children in word comprehension stayed pretty steady over the period of acquiring 10 to 100 word
comprehension. The age at which 10 words were produced ranged from 14.8
to 16.6 months, and the age at which 50 words were produced ranged from
14.8 to 22.7 months. Differences increase during this developmental period
among children in the ages at which words are produced. However, both the
the slower as well as the faster variations are well within the normal range for
word acquisition. Therefore, these differences in rate do not signal any
difference in outcome measures in any significant way.

Of course, over the entire developmental period studied, there is an
increase in the number of different words to total words produced. The
average number of different words produced in a 100–utterance corpus at 22
months is 32.3 words, and at 35 months is 75.4 words. There is no significant
difference between boys and girls on this measure.

In summary, there are differences among children in the rate of vocabulary
acquisition. These differences, on the whole, are not related to gender and
may be interrelated with certain aspects of cognitive development. The
differences in observed rate of acquisition were well within the range of
normal as indicated by the results of other studies and by our outcome
measures.

In the recent literature there has been a great deal of discussion of what has
been termed the *vocabulary spurt* that occurs at about 18 months, after 50
words are acquired. Two patterns of early lexical development have been
pointed to, the first consisting primarily of noun acquisition and the second of
other parts of speech or phrases (the expresser–referrer distinction discussed

earlier). This difference has been discussed in terms of possible biological or cognitive processing differences (Bates, Bretherton, & Snyder, 1988; Bates, O'Connell, & Shore, 1987). If that is the case, then our findings and those of others suggest not simply two patterns of development but, rather, individual patterns of lexical development that all fall within the range of what can be considered normal (Lieven, Pine, & Dresner, 1992).

Comprehension and Production of Words in Sentences. The last aspect of language development that we discuss is multiword comprehension and production. One needs semantic and pragmatic knowledge, as well as syntax, to comprehend multiword utterances. Therefore, when we examined this phase of language development, we measured all these aspects.

Comprehension was tested using sentences requiring comprehension of the relation between utterances and real-world events ("smell flower") and knowledge of word meaning ("kiss teddy" and "tickle car"). Development of sentence production was evaluated through the language produced by the children at each visit after they began producing multiword utterances.

The age at which the multiword utterances were comprehended varied as a function of the relations expressed in these utterances. Items testing predictable action–object, as in "roll ball," were comprehended at 20 months, agents acting on an object ("make the bunny kiss") items at 21 months, and anomalous-relation items ("tickle car") at 23 months. On the average, the children could comprehend all the items at 23 months. The age by which all the items were completed ranged from 20 to 26 months. The girls were ahead of the boys in completing this sentence comprehension task. On the average, girls completed the task at 22.6 months, whereas the boys, on the average, did not complete it until 25.5 months. However, if we give the boys the benefit of the doubt, this may well have been a function of the boys unwillingness to comply with requests rather than lack of knowledge of the meaning of the utterances.

There were many measures taken of multiword production. We measured both the communicative functions and structural content of these utterances. We found that the pragmatic functions of these utterances changed very little over time. However, the proportional use of different sentence types did change over the period from 22 to 35 months rather dramatically, and, therefore, the proportional use of utterances for different functions changed in time.

Throughout this developmental period, the most frequently used sentence type in conversational interactions was the declarative. The proportion of yes–no questions and declaratives rose over this period, and the proportion of imperatives and "indicators" ("That a book.") declined. The proportion of Wh- questions rose slightly from 22 to 29 months, and then fell slightly from 29 to 35 months. These findings indicate that as the children become more sophisticated in their communicative interactions, they are no longer simply limited to demanding and ascribing.

The use of complex sentence types also grew during this period. There was a dramatic change in proportional use of complex sentences, from a mean of 3.6% at 25 months to a mean of 30.3% at 35 months. Of course, the MLU grew as well. The MLU at 22 months was 1.5 words; at 35 months, the MLU was 3.7 words. There was a great deal of variation among the children in this measure. There was a range from 1 to 4 words at 22 months and from 1.5 to 5 words at 35 months. As is true with other measures, our findings are quite similar to those of other studies. In addition to individual variation in mean length of utterance, boys and girls in this study systematically differ from each other as well. The girls produced significantly longer utterances at each of the ages examined over the 22- to 35-month period.

In summary, we repeat the initial assertion: There is a great deal of variation among the children we observed in the rate at which they develop different aspects of language. For the most part, these differences in rate of development did not result in apparent problems in language development. Most of the differences in rate of development occur in production of language. There are also gender differences in production, with girls being faster than boys in development. There appear to be no gender differences in measures of compehension of language. The one outstanding exception is the difference in the age at which all types of items in the sentence comprehension task are completed. However, we believe this gender difference may be attributable to the unwillingness of the boys to comply with what they may have perceived as demands. We are not sure about this.

We found no evidence that SES caused any systematic variations in rates of development of the differing aspects of language that we measured. This result departs from what is usually found. The difference may stem from the fact that none of the children in our study came from welfare families.

COMPARISONS OF PREMATURE AND FULL-TERM INFANTS

In our sample, the premature infants were less than half the average weight of the full-term babies, and had significantly poorer Apgar scores. Despite these starting differences in the two groups of children, the intellectual and language measures we obtained on the children did not, in many instances, show significant differences between the two groups.

There were significant differences in favor of the full-term infants in the MDI of the Bayley test given at 13 months, and the PDI of the Bayley test given at 28 months. These differences disappear when scores are corrected for gestational age in the premature infants. However, by the 28-month Bayley, and on the 29- month McCarthy test, both groups of children were above the normative scores for their ages. Exactly the same pattern of results on cognitive measures is obtained when only our VLB infants are compared to our full-term babies.

Comparisons of premature and full-term infants on the language measures produced similar results. Overall, our premature babies were equal to their full-term peers on all measures. When comparisons are made on the basis of gestational age, rather than chronological age, the premature infants were ahead on many measures. Although there was no significant difference between the two groups on age of comprehension of 10 words, the premature children were significantly ahead for the age at which 50 words were comprehended (prematures 12.6 months, full-terms 13.1 months), and on age at which 100 words were comprehended (15.5 months vs. 16.1 months). Premature infants were significantly faster than terms in the rate at which they acquire comprehension of a lexicon from 10 to 100 words. Prematures acquired 25.8 words per month, whereas full-terms acquired 17.9 words per month.

Similar patterns appear for word production. Significant differences are found only when the gestational age, not chronological age, of the prematures are used in comparisons. Prematures produce 10 words and 50 words at significantly earlier ages than do full-terms (13.5 months vs. 14.9 months, and 17.6 months vs. 19 months). The groups show no significant differences in the age at which they complete the procedure examining comprehension of two-part relations. Both groups, premature and full-term, perform better than average on the comprehension and production outcome measures. On these measures, the prematures do significantly better than full-terms on the comprehension outcome measures when the groups are compared on the basis of chronological age (premature 8.2 months ahead vs. full-term 5.8 months ahead of age expectation). There were no significant differences between the groups on expressive language outcome measures regardless of the basis of comparison. In summary, the premature infants are significantly ahead of their full-term matches on a number of language development measures when the groups are compared on the basis of gestational age; they are equal when compared on the basis of chronological age.

When comparisons are made between the full-term infants and the 12 smallest premature infants (whose birthweight was less than 1,550 grams), an only somewhat different picture emerges. The chronological age at which 10 words are comprehended favors full-term babies, but the gestational age at which 50 words are comprehended favors the "small" premature babies. On outcome measures, this premature group is behind the full-term babies by 3.5 months (although still performing above normal expectations) in receptive language and in expressive language. Thus, although on some language measures they are behind their full-term peers, prematures are, on others, similar to their full-term peers and clearly functioning normally (within normal range) in terms of outcome measures. Overall, we found early catch-up by our premature children who look like our full-term children by about 1 year. It should be noted that the full-term children, as a group, and the premature children, as a group, were significantly ahead of the norm populations on the outcome measures.

As stated earlier, it is possible that the somewhat surprising results of our study are due to a combination of three factors. The first is the overall health of the population, both premature and full-term. This we think is a very important contributor to the results but we don't know, nor do others, what parameters of illness would lead to different outcomes except for very obvious and severe damage. The second and third factors we discuss are highly speculative. The second factor may be the experiment itself. That is, we may have carried out an intervention by our monthly visits. These visits lent support to the mothers by allowing them to discuss questions about their children's development with persons they considered knowledgeable. It also focused their attention on their children's accomplishments in language development. They were able to observe remarkable changes over a fairly short period of time. Earlier, we indicated that there is a big question about this effect. Finally, because we frequently engaged the children in language-processing tasks during our monthly visits, which the mothers may have duplicated between visits, we may have modeled appropriate procedures for eliciting more complex language, which they then proceeded to do. This may account for the performance above age expectation on tests of language comprehension and production by both the premature and full-term infants in our study. These latter two suggestions are only that, and need to be bolstered by further research on the effect of home visits that include mild language elicitation procedures on infants' course of language development.

HOW MOTHERS TALK TO CHILDREN

Without question, how mothers and others in the child's environment talk to their children plays a very important role in how children get to listen and talk. Obviously, children learn the language or languages they are exposed to and no others. But outside of these facts, it is not always clear what caregivers' input does do for the language development of children. Can it make language acquisition faster, or in some sense, better? What effect does it have on the language development of children who look like they are in trouble? These are some of the questions that we and other researchers have asked about the role of input on children's language development. Our tentative answers to these questions are presented here.

Can Input Make Language Development Faster?

The language behavior of our children's caregivers varied as much as the language behavior of the children. We had mothers who talked a lot to the children and those who talked comparatively little. In terms of the complexity of the language they used, we had mothers who were generally more in tune with the children's language functioning and mothers who were less so. The question we asked was, then: Do differences among the mothers either in the amount of talking or structural input (as measured by how much they simplified their language to the children) make a difference in the children's rate of development? The children's language behaviors we used to answer this question were rate of shift from vocalizations to speech sound vocalizations; rate of lexical acquisition; rate of growth of the length of multiword utterances; and rate at which children comprehend all types of multiword utterances as measured by our nonpublished, nonnormative, newly constructed test.

Our overall finding was that neither the amount of talking nor the degree to which the mothers simplified the structure of their language had any differential effect on the language development of their children. For example, a mother's MLU was unrelated to the rate at which her child increased the mean length of his or her multiword utterances. What seemed to be occurring is that mothers' conversational behaviors were more significantly related to the child language behaviors listed earlier than were measures of the amount and structure of her talk. Further, the child's language behaviors seemed to affect mothers' behaviors more significantly than the reverse.

Recall that we found a group of EFDs, a group of LFDs, and a group of SDs when we examined the age at which the shift from vocalization to speech sound vocalization (true babbling) occurred, and the rate at which words were acquired. We asked whether the mothers of EFDs were more responsive to their children's babbling than were the mothers of LFDs and SDs.

Overall, we found that mothers of EFD children were indeed more responsive to their children's vocalizations than the mothers of LFD children and mothers of SD children. However, we also found that this seems to be a product of what the mothers of these respective groups of children are given to respond to. That is, when the children were producing equivalent amounts of structure, the mothers of EFD children were less responsive than mothers of LFD children who, in turn, were less responsive than mothers of SD children. Under the condition of equivalent structure, the mothers of SD children were in fact most reponsive. Perhaps this indicates an awareness on the part of the latter group of mothers that their children need more input. This is only one example of the many conversational behaviors of the mothers that we found were affected by the rate of their children's language development (Chesnick, Menyuk, Liebergott, & Ferrier, 1983). At any rate, these findings make clear that the more rapid rate of development on the part of the EFD children cannot be accounted for by the amount of their mothers' responsiveness.

Despite the information just presented (and keeping it in mind), we also found that although the structural characteristics of mothers' input had little effect on the rate of the children's language development, some conversational–interactional factors were more successful in predicting rate of development. Consider our examination of the effect of mothers' conversational devices on the rate of acquisition of language milestones. The measures we used included age of shift to true babbling; age at 50 words of production; rate of development of MLUs; rate of development of mastery of markers of number, tense, etc. (14 morphemes); rate of growth of vocabulary; and rate of growth of complex sentences.

We found that the children who showed the greatest amount of growth between 12 and 16 months had mothers who spoke more often about persons and objects that were present rather than absent. These mothers did not attempt to elicit imitation but, rather, made requests for action that the children were frequently in the process of carrying out (so-called protodirectives). Further, these requests for action were accompanied by focusing gestures. It seemed that talking about the here and now and indicating how this talk is related to the here and now speeded up lexical acquisition. This makes sense.

The children who made the greatest progress from 22 to 25 months were those whose mothers had more frequently paraphrased the baby, partially repeating what the baby had just said and less frequently repeating themselves. These mothers responded to their babies' vocalizations and extended the conversation. The children who made the greatest progress from 29 to 35 months had mothers who more frequently elicited imitation, paraphrasing the baby, and responding to the baby while less frequently requesting action. This reduction in requests for action probably meant an increase in requests for information, although the latter behavior did not significantly affect progress in the measures we used.

These results indicate that mothers who provide situations that are within the processing abilities of their babies, and who provide opportunities for interaction that result in "successful" turns, and who then switch to providing more challenging situations as their children mature have babies who more rapidly achieve structural language milestones. The switch that occurs from the 12- to 16-month period to the 25- to 29-month period indicates that mothers are increasing conversational challenges (Liebergott, Menyuk, Schultz, Chesnick, & Thomas, 1984).

Can Input Make Language Development Better?

Clearly, the term *better* is open to many interpretations. Our definition in this discussion, outside of rate of development of various language milestones, is based on outcome measures of comprehension and production of language. These criteria, in a very limited sense, might be considered measures of the quality of language development. The effect of input on these aspects of language development now comes into focus.

There are a few environmental factors that account for variation in performance on the outcome measures of production and comprehension of language for both premature and full-term children in our study. For the premature children, mothers' education accounts for variation on comprehension and production performance on exit tests, and mothers' age for variation in comprehension performance on these tests. For the full-term children, fathers' education and age accounts for variation in comprehension and production performance on outcome measures. Mothers' education accounts for variation in performance on the outcome measure of language production only. Socioeconomic status accounts for variation in outcome performance on the language production measure for the premature children only.

These findings indicate that there are possible effects of input on how well children do on standard test measures of language development. However, these effects seem to be very indirect and difficult to determine. Specific maternal language measures, having to do with amount and structure of input, were not related to rate of development of language milestones nor with the ability of the children to participate in communicative interaction. Fathers' age and education and mothers' age and education are probably related to aspects of interaction not measured in our study. In any case, these possible differences in interaction do not make a crucial difference on the measures of language development we obtained at the end of the study. All of the children in our study performed above expected age norms on the tests used to measure language comprehension and production.

The effect of the varying measures of mothers' conversational interaction with their children on the various outcome measures was also examined. We selected the 10 children with the highest scores on the comprehension and production outcome measures, and the 10 children with the lowest scores. We then observed how successfully the interactional measures could predict the assignment of the children to the lowest and highest score groups. Using the mothers' conversational measures at 12 months, we could succesfully predict 75% of the assignments in outcome measures; using the 22-month measures, we could successfully predict 90% of the assignments on outcome measures. It seems that mothers' techniques for communicative interaction with their children have a much greater effect on their children's rate and "quality" of language development than does the amount and structure of their talking.

Input and Children at Risk

The literature on caregiver interaction with premature as compared to full-term infants indicates that there is a great deal of difference in the input to the two groups. Our findings did not show these differences, despite the fact that the early histories of these two groups were clearly different. Others, in observing differences, have attributed them to a variety of factors, among them the abnormal separation between the premature infant and his or her family due to longer hospitalization and the anxiety created in the family because of the infant's illness. Obviously, these conditions also existed with the premature infants in our study. Further, one of our premature children was diagnosed as having cerebral palsy at 1 year of age, and another had been placed on a respiratory monitor after instances in which he had stopped breathing. Still another was on seizure medication.

Several factors might account for this difference in our findings as compared to the findings of others. The families in our study may have been different from those of the other studies, in such factors as the mean age of mothers (and fathers), SES (there were no welfare families in our study), and ethnicity (our families were primarily White, and all were English-speaking). Our measures may have been too gross or taken too infrequently in the early months to reveal the types of differences that can be observed only by using microanalytic procedures with videotape. Our use of a comparatively large sample of children followed longitudinally revealed the wide variance in dyadic interaction that can exist with both full-term and premature infants and their mothers. This wide overall variation probably prevented any one child or small group of children from looking remarkably different.

Just as there were no remarkable differences in language development that could be attributed to prematurity, neither were there marked differences in the communicative interaction of the mother–infant dyads in our study attributable to the factor of prematurity. Mothers of premature children interacted with their children as much as mothers of full-term children, and, according to the measures we used, they were neither more nor less responsive.

Despite the fact that our overall numbers indicated no differences, our intuitive feeling was that those children who may have been on the borderline of having language development difficulties were prevented from having them by having very interactive families. One of the children we discussed earlier (Kate) may be such a child. Our analysis did not support this intuition. However, there are a number of studies that are pursuing this question by examining interaction between mothers and their at-risk infants with more fine-grained tasks and analyses. Thus far, no conclusive answer has been obtained to the question.

To summarize, our findings concerning the role of caregiver language input on language development indicated wide variation in the amount of input, in the language structure of the input, and in the conversational styles or types of interactions that our children received. These differences had no apparent significant effect on whether children were going to perform well (within the range of normal on standard tests of language comprehension and production) at age 30 or 36 months. The few exceptions are discussed in the final section of this chapter.

Although there was a great deal of variation in patterns of interaction between individual children and their mothers, there was also a great deal of similarity. All mothers interacted with their children and all mothers showed mostly similar behaviors. The variation primarily concerned the relative amounts of specific behaviors. This was discussed when we examined the effects of either proportional use of structural simplification or proportional use of certain conversational techniques or both on rate of language development in children.

In general, conversational or communicative techniques have a greater effect on rate of development that the particular structure of the input. That is, those aspects that, early on, appear to have a positive effect on rate of development are mothers' expansions of the child's verbal and nonverbal contributions, her acknowledgments of and responses to the child's contributions, her providing responses rather than demanding them, her setting the stage for the child to take a turn. All of these behaviors organize opportunities for the child to take a successful turn. Later on, mothers' asking for imitation, action and responses have the most positive effects. At this later time the child can, does, and, apparently, should take greater responsibility in the interaction.

Most of the mothers and children in our study interacted successfully because most of the mothers and children were interacting. That is, both mothers and children were sensitive to the cues provided by their conversational partners. The few exceptions are discussed later.

PREDICITING LANGUAGE DEVELOPMENT OUTCOMES

In this section, we discuss predictions: specifically, the early language behaviors that predict later language behaviors, the risk factors that predict outcome measures of language production and comprehension and the language behaviors that predict these outcome measures. The early signs that may predict children who are in trouble and need special intervention are discussed in the next section, and in the last section. Keep in mind that we initially followed our children only to the ages of 30 and 36 months. It is possible that our early data contained predictive information of still later oral and written language development of the children in our study. We pursued the relations of earlier and later language characteristics to a limited extent in a later research study, and some of the findings of that study are reported on in the Epilogue section of this chapter.

Predicting Later Language Behavior
From Earlier Behaviors

We examined many language behaviors that other studies found useful for predicting the course of language development in children. We found some of these behaviors predictive; others we found not to be predictive. We found still others that had not been discussed in the literature, but were also predictive.

We examined duration, amplitude, and pitch characteristics of early cries, but did not find that differences in these cry characteristics were at all predictive of later speech or language functioning. We did find as a result of acoustic analysis that the four children who did not acquire a high–low distinction ("heat" vs. "hot") among the vowels before they acquired a front–back ("hit" vs. "hoot") developed later speech articulation problems. There was a relation between the combination of the age at which the children completed a speech discrimination test and the rate at which they matched consonants to an adult target, and whether they showed the presence of an articulation problem. Thus, early discrimination may predict later production. This is not surprising but, nevertheless, reassuring.

We believe there to be a speech development chain. The rate at which the children shifted from vocalization to true babbling related to the rate at which they achieved articulation mastery of consonantal sounds, in particular those of final consonants. This behavior, in turn, was related to the rate of word acquisition and morpheme development. Speech sound discrimination and production appear to be related to lexical acquisition which, of course, makes sense.

None of the measures of turn-taking behaviors or conversational participation behaviors was predictive of lexical or structural aspects of language development. We found a group of children in our population who could be characterized as referrers (grossly, those who spend more time labeling objects and events than using language for social purposes) and a group of expressers (those who do the inverse), but the distinction was unrelated to later language development or to outcome measures.

Cry, rate of lexical acquisition, and proportion of language used to refer and express were all nonpredictive of later language development, nor did they predict outcome measures of language comprehension and production. Other studies had indicated that these were likely to be important predictive measures. We did not find them so.

We did find that sequential speech production measures were highly related to each other and, in turn, were highly related to word and morpheme production. The rate of development of speech discrimination was related to several measures of the development of speech production. There was a sequential relation between word comprehension, comprehension of two-part relations, and outcome measures. That is, children showing superior performances on one measure showed superior performance on all. On the whole, the reception or comprehension measures seemed to be more predictive of the course of language development than production or expressive measures. This is explored further in the following sections.

Outcome and Risk Factors

We have already discussed some of the risk factors in the section on input factors. In addition to mothers' and fathers' ages, educations, and SES, the effect of other risk factors such as 1-minute and 5-minute Apgars, birthweight, evidence of intraventricular hemorrhaging, respiratory distress, reported occurrences of episodes of otitis media, mothers' smoking, and gender (the literature indicates that boys are at greater risk than girls) were examined. The literature on the development of premature infants indicates that these are important factors in predicting outcome measures of linguistic and cognitive developments.

Our findings indicate that for premature children (outside of mothers' education and age and the SES of the family), the gender of the child and the lack of respiratory distress best predict outcome performance on the comprehension measures. For production performance, 1-minute and 5-minute Apgar and gender, as well as mothers' education, best predict outcome. In general, then, the best predictors of comprehension outcome for the premature infant are environmental factors, and the best predictors of production outcome are state-of-the-baby measures. Child's gender may lead to biological or input differences or both. These possibilities are discussed more fully when we talk about children in trouble.

For full-term children, gender, fathers' education and age, and mothers' smoking best predict comprehension performance. Mothers' education and age, fathers' education and age, and gender best predict production outcome. It is possible that these paternal factors are important because they determine SES and this may influence maternal attitudes and interactions. However, the role of fathers in the language development of their children has seldom been examined. It is clear from our results that this is an area worthy of much greater exploration.

Language Factors and Outcome

For both premature and full-term children, we examined which language measures best predicted the children's performance on outcome measures. As might be suspected, the earlier language measures were more highly correlated with outcome language measures than were risk factors, although these were also highly correlated to outcome. For premature children, the correlations between risk factors and production outcome ranged from .39 to .59. For comprehension outcome, they ranged from .48 to .64. For full-term children, the correlations between risk factors and production outcome measures ranged from .50 to .63. For comprehension outcome, they ranged from .45 to .59. The correlations between language measures and outcome measures were significantly higher, ranging overall from .63 to .84.

In this order of most to least important, the full-term children's performance on the comprehension portions of the outcome measures could significantly be accounted for by the age at which they completed the agent–action portion of the comprehension test, the rate at which they acquired word comprehension from their 10th to their 100th word, the age at which they comprehended 50 words, the age at which they completed the predictable items on the sentence comprehension test, and the proportion of items they had correct on this test at 22 months. For the production portions of the outcome measures, in the same order of most to least important, the best predictors are the proportion of items they had correct on the sentence comprehension test at 25 months, the age at which they comprehended 100 words, the proportion of items on the comprehension test they had correct at 22 months, and the rate at which they gained from 10 to 100 comprehension words. Performance on the sentence comprehension test and rate of mastering comprehension of words are powerful predictors of both comprehension and production outcomes for the full-term children.

A very similar pattern emerged for the premature children. Those language behaviors that significantly accounted for comprehension outcome measures, in order of highest to lowest predictiveness, were age of comprehension of the predictable items on the sentence comprehension test, the age at which they produced 50 words (a departure from the pattern), the proportion of items they had correct on the sentence comprehension test at 22 months, and the age at which they completed the whole test. For productive outcome measures, the language behaviors that were predictive were, in order, the age at which the whole comprehension test was completed, the age at which they completed the predictable items on the test, the age at which they comprehended 100 words, and the proportion of items on the comprehension test that were correct at 25 months. The single best predictor of both comprehension and production outcomes for both groups of children is their performance on the comprehension of two-part relations that we began giving the children at 14 months of age. We think this is an important finding that needs to be followed up. If such task performance is so highly predictive of language outcome measures at later ages then a powerful evaluative tool would have been found.

We examined those factors that best predict later language behavior and performance on tests of comprehension and production at ages 30 and 36 months. We found that there were straightforward patterns of relations between early and later language behaviors that apparently tied together early and later speech development as well as early and later language development. The relation between early and later speech development is that those children who were early in shifting to syllabic or speech sound vocalizations were early in mastering consonantal production and, in turn, were early in word and grammatical morpheme production. However, these developments, in turn, are accounted for by performance on the speech discrimination task.

The relations between early and later language behaviors also were found. On the whole, early measures of comprehension of language seemed better predictors of later production, as well as later comprehension of language for both premature and full-term infants. However, the course of language development for premature children seemed somewhat more affected by productive factors than that of full-term children. Overall, however, performance on the test of comprehension of two-part relations was the best single predictor of language development outcome. The child's performance on this single brief task may be a very good indicator to pediatrician, clinician, or nursery school teacher of the language competence of a child.

Environmental factors, and in the case of premature children, initial state of the infant, also play a role in predicting performance on outcome measures. For the premature children, the environmental factor that was predictive of comprehension performance was mothers' age, perhaps a reflection of mothers' degree of security in dealing with the premature infant. The two most predictive factors of production outcome for these children was mothers' education (a correlation of .58), and 5-minute Apgar (a correlation of .59), indicating the very important role of both environment and state for these children.

For full-term children, the most predictive factors of comprehension outcome were mothers' smoking (.58) , which may be a state-of-the-baby factor, and fathers' age (.59). The most predictive factors for production outcome were, interestingly, gender (.58) (state or environment) and fathers' education (.63). Fathers' age and education may, as suggested, have either a direct or indirect (perhaps subtle SES factors) effect on language development. This could also be true of the factor of gender. Boys in our study were slower than girls in some aspects of language development, which can be a product of either biology or environment, or both.

In this next section, we discuss prediction and outcome in the context of children who turned out to be in some trouble in language development.

Troubles With Language Development

There were some, among the children we studied, who either had frank language problems or who, we felt, might have some difficulties eventually.

There were 2 children who were receiving speech therapy because of artic-ulation problems. There was 1 child who began receiving language therapy at 2 1/2 years old. The child with cerebral palsy was receiving physical therapy and was in an infant stimulation program. There were 4 children, among them 1 who was the tiniest baby in our population (birthweight 794 grams), who we considered to be at risk for language problems, but these children had not received any direct intervention.

The 2 children with articulation problems were not among the lowest scoring children on outcome measures of language comprehension and production. This may have been because we did not include a speech discrim-ination or speech production test in our battery of outcome measures. We had earlier found that the age at which a short speech discrimination test was completed by all the children largely accounted for the variance in the speech production patterns of the children. The 6 other children (excluding the 2 with articulation problems) were the 6 lowest scoring children on outcome measures. In this section, we discuss these 6 children in comparison to the 6 highest scoring children on outcome measures.

The 6 highest scoring children included 3 who were full-term and 3 who were premature. The 6 lowest scoring included 4 who were full-term and 2 who were premature. The mean birthweight of the 6 highest scoring was 2,626 grams, and that of the 6 lowest was 2,792 grams. Again, we find that prematurity and even low birthweight are not good predictors of poor language outcomes.

The measured IQs of the two groups of children did indicate differences between them. At 13 months, the higher functioning group had a mean Bayley MDI score of 118 and PDI score of 98. The lower functioning children had, at this age, a mean MDI score of 97 and a PDI score of 78. The differences between the two groups became even more marked with time. At 28 months, the higher functioning children had an MDI score of 135 and a PDI score of 124. The lower functioning children had an MDI score of 103 and a PDI score of 83. However, we found that IQ scores were not good predictors of language outcome measures in the total group. Further, on the Uzgiris–Hunt test of cognitive functioning, given to the children when they were 19 months, there were no significant differences between the two groups. The higher functioning group was 1.8 months ahead of age norms, whereas the lower functioning group was 1.7 months ahead of age norms at test time.

On language outcome measures the groups were very distinct, being separated by about 15 months. The higher functioning group achieved an overall language age score 14.2 months ahead of age norms, the lower functioning group a score 1.5 months behind age norms. On the receptive language tests, the higher functioning group was 14.6 months ahead of age norms, the lower functioning group 2.2 months behind. On production language measures the higher functioning group was 13.8 months ahead of age norms, whereas the lower functioning group was 1 month behind.

Given the fact that prematurity, low birthweight, and measured IQ scores were not predictive of language outcome measures, we asked whether there were differences in patterns of language development between the two groups that might forecast the lower performance scores achieved on the outcome battery. What we found was that the language behaviors predictive of outcome for the entire population were just those behaviors that were markedly different between the higher functioning and lower functioning group.

The higher functioning children were 3 months ahead of the lower functioning children in the age at which they comprehended 100 words (15.2 months vs. 18.6 months) and 2 months ahead in the age at which they produced 50 words (19 months vs. 21 months). The MLU of the higher functioning children was longer than that of the lower functioning children at the same ages. At 22 months, the former had produced utterances with a mean length of 1.7, whereas those of the latter had a mean length of 1.2. At 25 months, the higher functioning children produced utterances with a mean length of 2.3, whereas the MLU of the lower functioning group was 1.7. These differences, however, were not the most dramatic differences in patterns of development between the groups.

The higher functioning children increased their comprehension from 10 to 50 words at the rate of 18.3 words per month, whereas the lower functioning children did so at the rate of 13.6 per month. A more striking difference is that the higher functioning children further increased their rate of acquisition; they went from 50 to 100 words comprehended at a rate of 23.3 words per month, whereas the lower functioning group continued to acquire words at the same rate of 13.6 words per month. The higher functioning children completed all the items on the two–part comprehension test just as the lower functioning children were starting to respond correctly. Further, on the three–part comprehension test, the higher functioning children had 61% of the items correct, whereas the lower functioning group had only 28.6% of the items correct.

In summary, there were 3 children in our population of 53 children who had speech and language problems and were receiving therapy. There were 4 who were slow in reaching various developmental milestones and might be followed to see if they developed problems later. For the children with problems, the most outstanding difference between them and the higher functioning children was the rate at which they developed discrimination of sounds, comprehension of words and comprehension of multiword utterances. As with all of our children, these children foreshadow their later performance most directly by their earlier receptive language development.

Recent research indicates that early difficulties in production of language can forecast later language difficulties. There have been a number of studies that have examined the longer term effects of early expressive language delay. These are children who at 2 years have normal nonverbal intellectual development and age-appropriate receptive abilities. This research suggests that about half of this population still have marked expressive language delay at 3 years (Paul, 1991; Rescorla & Schwartz, 1990; Thal, 1994), and that approximately half again still have delays at 4 years in syntactic and discourse skills (Paul & Alforde, 1993).

The one child we discuss at great length, Lee, who showed abnormally protracted delay in both word and sentence development showed a different developmental pattern, we believe, than the children described in the previous paragraph. Lee appeared to be developing the noun phrases and then the verb phrases separately. That is, he eventually developed modifier + noun (happy boy) and verb + noun or adjective (be sick, be a boy) but not noun + verb + noun constructions. This may indicate that he is not storing information about the meaning of nouns that includes the syntactic roles they can play nor storing information about verbs that includes knowledge about the arguments (nouns) that they can take. The process is called syntactic or semantic *bootstrapping* (Hirsh-Pasek, Reeves, & Golinkoff, 1993). This, as stated previously, is what normally developing children do. To do this, the whole sentence must be kept in mind and Lee may have difficulty in doing this. In turn, however, the difficulty may initially be related to a language perception problem, an inability to segment clauses, then phrases, and finally words. Logically, lexical segmentation plays a very important role in lexical acquisition (Plunkett, 1993). It is very likely that children with expressive language delay are different from eachother. After all some of them recover by age 4. However, the possibility that expressive language problems are in fact related to perception problems of the kind described should be explored in future studies of children with marked language delay.

EPILOGUE

A number of studies have found that a significantly higher proportion of premature than full-term children have academic and social problems in the school years (Gregoriou-Serbaneau, 1984). It has been found that at 9 years old, preterm children have significantly lower scores in math than their full-term peers but significantly lower reading scores that are unrelated to measured IQ differences (Klein, Hack, & Breslau, 1989). These lower scores in math have been attributed to perceptual–motor difficulties. However, differences in language-processing abilities have been found to be related to math problem solving, and differences in language development could account for these social and academic differences. The important question that still needs to be answered is: What specific factors in these premature infants' histories best predict academic and social development outcomes?

The results of the initial study we carried out, as you have read, indicated that there were no significant differences between premature and full-term infants in language development outcomes. This was true of the VLB premature infants as well as the premature infants as a whole, although these VLB children were significantly different from their full-term peers on some of the outcome measures. There were, however, biological factors, early language behaviors, and environmental factors that appeared to account for differences among premature children on outcome measures. Those factors that accounted for the most variance in language comprehension and language production outcome measures were language comprehension measures (rate and age of acquisition of comprehension of words and comprehension of two-part relations). Included among the most predictive measures of language outcomes for the premature children as a whole were language comprehension measures, mother's age and education, and family SES.

A second study (Menyuk et al., 1991) was carried out, which included some of the premature children in our original study as part of the study population. One of the questions asked in that study was whether or not the low birthweight premature children, who appeared on the whole to be developing normally, and who, for the most part, did not display any overt language problems at age 3 were, in fact, performing well on measures of both oral and written language development at age 7 to 8. A further question asked was whether other randomly selected VLB prematurely born children with no overt sign of expressive language delay would have difficulty on oral language-processing tasks and reading tests at age 7 to 8.

In the population of the second study were children with diagnosed language disorder, control children (developing language normally), 10 of the VLB infants in the original study, and an additional number of prematurely born children whose birthweights were also less than 1,500 grams. Thirty four children composed the entire premature group. The average birthweight for this group was 1,113 grams with a range of 652 to 1,500 grams. Socioeconomic status for the children in this group was calculated on the same bases as those described in chapter 1. Of the premature children, 6 came from upper middle-class families, 14 from middle-class, 12 from lower middle-class, and 2 from lower class families. Again, none of the children were in welfare families. Information was available on the added children's birth and hospitalization histories as well as their environmental backgrounds. The medical histories of the additional premature children in this later study were similar to those in the original study, and none of the additional premature, like our original children had outstanding medical problems.

All the children in the study were given an intake battery of speech and language tests, an IQ test, and a sweep check test of their hearing. All the premature children were of normal intelligence and had normal hearing. At the beginning of the study and each 6 months thereafter until 3 years later, at the end of the study, they were given an experimental battery of language-processing tasks to carry out. The premature children did not do as well as the control children on the intake measures but, on the whole, did significantly better on these tasks than did children with frank language disorder (SLI), and did remarkably better than them on some of the oral language-processing tasks . However, a cluster analysis indicated that 4 of the children in the premature group were performing as poorly as SLI children on the intake battery. The comparisons of the three groups of children on intake measures are shown in Table 7.5.

The performance of the three groups of children on the language-processing tasks is shown in Table 7.6. Again, the premature children did not do as well as the control children but, on the whole did better than the SLI children on some of these tasks and remarkably better on others. However, again, when a cluster analysis was carried out, 9 of the premature children did as poorly as the SLI children on these tasks.

At the end of the study the children were given an oral language test (the TOLD primary; Newcomer & Hammill, 1982) and three reading tests, the

TABLE 7.5
Mean Scores of Control, Premature, and Control Children on Standard Intake Tests in Study 2

Tests	Groups		
	Control	Premature	SLI
Wisc	114.3	106.9	93.6
Receptive Tests			
Token	85.7	69.2	45.7
Tacl (percentile)	75.8	67.8	35.8
PPVT	70.4	69.3	51.1
Expressive Tests			
DSS	67.7	59.1	39.0
Reporters	2.3	2.2	.2
ITPA	87.9	78.1	52.9
Gardner	79.7	79.8	53.7
Speech Tests			
TOLD Discrim.	78.5	66.6	55.3
Templin Darley	70.0	69.3	41.7
Verbal Fluency	67.8	61.6	52.9

WRAT (Jastak & Jastak, 1976), the Gray oral reading test (Gray & Robinson, 1963), and the TORC (Brown, Hammill, & Weiderholt, 1978). The premature children did significantly better than children with frank language disorders on all these tests. However, 9 of the premature children were found to be borderline or deficient readers on the WRAT. Despite many questions about this test in measuring reading ability, this test's scores were used to identify problem readers because many of the children in the SLI group did not do well enough on the Gray or the TORC to use those scores for comparison and identification of problem readers. Two of the children who were found to be possibly at risk for reading failure were in our original study. One of these 2 children was in language therapy at the end of the study and 1 was considered at risk and to be followed. These 2 children were among those identified as low functioning at the end of our 3-year study.

A regression analysis was carried out to determine which background and language behavior measures accounted for significant variance in scores on the oral language test and the reading test for the 10 children from our original study, and for the population as a whole. The results of the analysis are shown in Table 7.7. As can be seen in this table, some background measures, mother's education and SES, as well as some language-processing measures account for variance in performance on the WRAT for these children from the original study. Variation in oral language performance, as measured by the TOLD, is best accounted for by a word perception measure (the PPVT) and the Apgar at 5 minutes. In the population as a whole, only language-processing measures accounted for variance on these two tests.

The results at this later age for the children followed from birth indicate that mother's education again figures as an important factor for our 10

TABLE 7.6

Comparison of Premature and SLI Children's Scores on First Presentation of Metalinguistic Tasks

Task	Maximum Value	Premature	SLI
Syllable segment	20	10.9	11.2
Phoneme segment	20	6.9	5.6
Grammat. judge.	54	28.6	23.6
Complex sent. peocess.	16	7.7	6.7
Word recall	16	8.2	7.1
RAN[a]			
Colors		.63	.58
Letters		.72	.60
Numbers		.70	.70
Objects		.54	.53
CLOZE	30	12.8	7.7
Story recall	45	27.3	6.0

[a]RAN scores = number of correct names, minus errors, divided by time. Larger scores mean more accurate and faster responses

TABLE 7.7
Multiple Regression Analysis of Factors that Account for Variance in Language Performance
at Age 7 to 8 years for Total Sample and Subsample of Premature Children

| | Groups | | | | | |
| | Subsample | | | Total | | |
Outcome Measures	F	Factors p value	r^2	F	Factors p value	r^2
WRAT Standard Score	Letter Rate Templin-Darley SES Gardner Mother's Education			Letter Rate Story Accuracy Token Standard Score Number Rate		
	42.95	.001	.98	12.80	.0001	.67
TOLD Spoken Language Quotient	PPVT Apgar 5 minutes			PPVT CLOZE Total Score		
	17.51	.002	.83	18.15	.0001	.57

children but now in reading as measured by the WRAT. The Apgar at 5 minutes again figures as an important factor but now in oral language performance as measured by a particular test. However, for them, as well as for the population as a whole language–processing measures accounted for the most variance on these outcome measures at 7 to 8 years. Our findings in this second study concerning VLB prematurely born children indicate two things. First, that within a population of prematurely born VLB children, without serious and lasting health problems and from nonpoverty families, risk for reading difficulties can emerge. Nine of the premature children (28%) in the study were at borderline in reading on a particular test. Second, the factors that continue to account most adequately for variance in performance on standard tests of language are measures of language processing. Further, because the 2 children from our original study who were having difficulty in reading were those we found at age 3 to be in difficulty we think that some of these early measures of language comprehension might be quite helpful in predicting language performance outcomes, both oral and written, at school age. Apgar at 5 minutes might successfuly predict some oral language production measures both early and late but not language comprehension at 3 or at 7 years nor reading at 7 years.

Within our population of premature children other biological measures, such as birthweight, IVH, and RDS, did not predict any language outcomes. Again, the general healthiness of our premature children might have brought about this result. Environmental factors such as mothers' education and SES together with a child's capacity to comprehend words and sentences early were most predictive for the children in our original study but not for the premature children in the later study. The important finding, in terms of development of procedures for prediction of later language problems, is that early language comprehension measures stand out as being most predictive of oral and written language outcome measures given to the children 4 years later.

SOME IMPLICATIONS

We think the results of our study have implications in terms of answers to the questions we asked initially; that is, what effect does biology, cognition and input have on the course of language development. We are aware that our findings can only be generalized to populations of the kind we studied. However, we hypothesize that the results of our study also have implications for assessment and intervention.

Factors That Affect Language Development

Clearly, there are birth defects that accompany prematurity that can signficantly affect language development. The findings in our study, however, indicated that even though premature infants are at biological risk in that they suffer RDS and IVH, as long as there are no long-lasting health problems that follow from this experience, this biological risk does not seriously affect the course of early language development. That development appears to be quite robust.

Cognitive development, as measured by the tests we used, was not significantly related to the language outcome measures at 3 years. However, there were significant differences between our 6 highest functioning and 6 lowest functioing children on the Bayley, especially the PDI scores. On the Uzgiris–Hunt test there were no significant differences between the groups. These results suggest that delayed perceptual–motor development can have an effect on performance on our language outcome measures but that within the measured intelligence range of the children in our population there was no detrimental effect of this delay on language outcomes at age 3. These factors, in conjunction with others discussed later, might have an effect on later reading measures.

Finally, our results indicated that SES did not affect the course of development of the many aspects of language we looked at. However, with our full-term and premature children, the short-term effects of mother input, and parental education and age, did account for variance in outcome measures at 3 years old. These factors and SES accounted for variance in the performance of the 10 VLB children followed to age 7 to 8 years. These factors seem to be interrelated. We hypothesize that the ages of the parents, their education, and family SES had an effect on input.

In a recent volume on the psychological development of VLB (primarily premature) infants, the editors summarize recent findings in the following way, "Research findings in the 80s have revealed that proximal social variables, such as the quality of the mother–child interaction and of the home environment have a major influence on the outcome of low-birthweight children" (Friedman & Sigman, 1992, p. 8). Certainly, both our short-term and long-term findings support this conclusion. It was not what mothers said to their children that had an effect on their rate of development but, rather, the structure of the communication interaction that took place. Mothers who used their child's focus of attention to comment on, and used directives concerning objects and actions that were there and ongoing, had children who became earlier developers of language and participants in conversation. The mothers were not modelers of language but, rather, providers of opportunities.

In summary, within our population of essentially normally developing children, the biological and cognitive variation that existed had little effect on the course of development. Environmental input had little direct effect but did have subtle effects. There was a great deal of individual variation among the children in their course of language development. There was also a great deal of variation among the mothers in their language input behaviors. However, the frquency with which the child was allowed and encouraged to participate in conversation, under conditions that clarified the ongoing activity appeared to speed up the process.

Assessment Implications

Assessment of the discrimination and comprehension of language categories and relations seem to be the best predictors of early language development outcomes. We found that perception of speech sound differences played an important role in speech production mastery and, also, in word comprehension. Word comprehension, in turn, played an important role in comprehension of two-word utterances. In addition to understanding the meaning of the words, we believe that children are simultaneously learning about the syntactic roles that words can play. Comprehension of the relations expressed by words within clauses and within phrases follows from learning about the semantic properties and syntactic roles of words. It is possible that children who are delayed in language expression as well as in comprehension have initial difficulty in segmenting utterances and then in learning about the relations among words in clauses and phrases. Earlier language comprehension measures were the best predictors of both comprehension and production outcome measures at 3 years. Language-processing measures best accounted for variation on an oral language test and a reading measure at ages 7 to 8 years.

Implications for Intervention

We found that mothers who provided opportunities for their children to take a turn successfully had babies who developed language more rapidly. We also found that providing these opportunities was also a function of what the child was doing. That is, mothers appeared to depend on their children to give them cues about what opportunities they should provide and what they should expect. When the children were slow in, for example, lexical development, mothers tried hard to elicit words but needed some feedback to continue to try. Indeed these children were not making clear what kinds of support they needed to participate in the conversation.

Because almost all our children were developing language normally, most of the mothers were successful in engaging their children in conversational interaction. There are children who are not successful language acquirers, both premature and full-term, and it is these children for whom intervention needs to be planned. In our study, the researchers visited the homes of the children at bimonthly or, in some instances, monthly intervals. During these visits attention was, primarily, on the child's language development. Not only did the researchers record the language interaction but they also periodically assessed aspects of the child's language development in the home, and in this way made clear to the caregivers important developments that were occurring in lexical acquisition and syntactic development. We provided these mothers with inexpensive materials and techniques to assess their children's language development on their own, which, as we have said, might have elicited more complex language from the children. In addition, as stated previously, mothers were asked to focus on the child's language development by keeping a diary of the children's lexical acquisition and having this diary checked periodically. The recordings and assessments could have been carried out by trained observers, and not necessarily by trained researchers. Although much of the data obtained on the effectiveness of home visits for intellectual, communicative, social, and emotional outcomes point to the necessity for programs that include more than one focus, home visits that focus on the techniques that the mothers used in our study to engage the child in conversation and to elicit more complex language behavior might be useful. What we did cannot solve the language development problems of children with such problems but might be helpful in guiding the design of more appropriate interventions.

Appendix A: Parents' Lexical Diary—Description and Coding Materials

MOTHER'S LOG OF BABY'S FIRST WORDS

Some time between 9 and 15 months of age, most babies show many signs of language development: You may notice that your baby is listening *more* carefully to what you say, understanding *more* of what you say, and beginning to say *some* words.

We would like to make a list of the words your baby says at this point in development and we need your help. Each week, we would like you to write down as many of the words your baby knows how to say as you can. Try to notice whenever your baby uses a word with meaning, then write down the word and when your baby uses the word. Each word only needs to be listed once. When children are first learning words, they sometimes imitate or copy words after hearing them. Do not write down words that are copied. We want you only to write words your child says without having heard someone else say them first.

To help you write the words, we have made a chart you can fill in. To show you some ways you can fill it in, we have provided examples from the lists of other parents whose babies were the same age.

word	when says
ball	when plays with ball
light	as pointed to ceiling
baby	when sees picture of baby
allgone	when can't find toy, looking around
car	when going to get in car
keys	playing with keys
oof off	when asked "what does the doggie say?"
Hi	on phone

The chart is set up so it makes two copies of the list, one for our research team and one for you to keep. We hope making this list is fun for you.

WORD CHECKLIST

On this list, we would like to know which words your child understands. You have already completed a list of the words he or she says. This list is *different* because we are interested in only *those words he or she understands when you* or *another person says* them.

There are many ways to tell if your child understands a word. For example, to show comprehension of an object word, your child may look at the object, get it, or start playing with it. For an action word, if your child consistently does what you ask, you know he or she understands that word. For example, your child usually *gives* you *something* even if it is not the correct object when you use the word "give." In some cases, he or she can show understanding indirectly, such as going to the door when you say, "Let's *go outside,*" or running to the refrigerator when you ask if he or she wants to *eat* (showing understanding of the words "go outside" and "eat").

It is important to list only words you are certain your child understands. If you are unsure or, if you notice that he or she only understands the word if you also point to the object or do the action (e.g., he or she only understands bye-bye when you wave as you say it, do not list it).

Read the list carefully. If you see a word he or she understands, put a check in the space provided. If you use a word that has the same meaning but a different form of the word in the list (e.g., your child knows "kitty" for cat) write the word you use in this space. Sometimes your child will understand more than one word for the same thing (such as knowing that both "puppy" and "dog" mean dog). When this is true, write all of the similar words he or she understands in the space. At the end of each group of words, there are spaces for other words that your child knows that are not on the list. You would add words like "pretzel" at the end of the food list or "choo-choo" at the end of the vehicle list.

For each week following Week 1 you only need check new words that your baby understands.

Name _____

Group _____

DIARY PRODUCTION

Date	Word	Interpretation	Context	Code	Age
1.					
2.					
3.					
4.					
5.					
6.					
7.					
8.					
9.					
10.					
11.					
12.					

DIARY COMPREHENSION CHART

Name _____

CATEGORIES   DATE WORD UNDERSTOOD   CONTEXT IN WHICH WORD UNDERSTOOD

ACTIONS:

get _____

give _____

throw _____

other _____

ACTIONS

get
give
throw
put in
kiss
shake
hi
want to
snow
find
open
close
pull
where's
sit down
eat
stop
kick
sing

go out
bathe
drink
jump

UTENSILS
bottle
cup
spoon
pacifier

PEOPLE
mother
father
grandmother
grandfather
boy
girl
baby
child names
adult names

ANIMALS
pet's name(s)
dog
cat
duck
horse
bird
bear
cow

FOOD AND DRINK
juice
milk
cookie
water
toast
apple
cake
banana
drink
bread
butter
cheese
egg
peas

VEHICLE
truck
car
boat

bus
train

GAMES
bye-bye
night-night
so big
patty cake
peek-boo
do nice
all gone
come here
clap hands
do a dance
no
tickle

OTHER
cold
more
pretty
hot
dirty
wait a minute
downstairs
upstairs
outside
up
down
another

FURNITURE
clock
light
blanket
chair
door

BODY PARTS
eye
nose
mouth
hair
hand
foot
belly button

PERSONAL
key
book
watch

telephone
ring
comb
brush

CLOTHES
shoes
hat
socks
boots
belt
coat

TOYS
ball
block
doll
teddy bear
bike

OUTDOOR
snow
flower
house
moon
rock

CODING CATEGORIES FOR LEXICAL DIARY

I. Nominals: words that refer to "things."
   A. Specific nominals: words that refer to only one exemplar of a category, usually but not necessarily limited to proper names.
      1. People (Daddy)
      2. Animals (Cappy—name of pet)
      3. Objects (Roscoe—name of toy dog)
   B. General nominals: words that refer to all members of a category.
      1. Inanimate objects (common subcategories include toys, clothes, body parts, food, household items)
      2. Animate objects (people or animals)
      3. Pronouns (e.g., this, that, he)
II. Action Words: words that elicit specific actions from the child or that accompany actions of the child.
   A. Social-action games: words that elicit one and only one action response involving no more than one specific object (usually no object is involved) always in a social-game relationship.
      1. Action games: games that elicit a motor response (e.g., clap hands, peek-a-boo)

2. Verbal games: games that elicit a verbal response (e.g., what does the doggie say?)

B. Event words: words that elicit an action sequence or an activity (e.g., *eat* where the response is to run to the kitchen and climb into the high chair).

C. Locatives: words that require locating something or putting something in a specific location.

    1. Locative search words: *where's, look at*

    2. Locative actions: *put in*

D. General action words

    1. Object-related: get, give, find, show, kiss

    2. Nonobject-related: dance, jump

E. Action inhibitors: words that inhibit actions (no, don't touch).

III. Modifiers: words that refer to properties or qualities of things or events.

A. Attributes (big, pretty)

B. States (all gone, hot, dirty)

C. Locatives (there, outside)

D. Possessives (mine)

IV. Personal-Social: words that express affective states and social relationships.

A. Assertions (yes, no, want)

B. Social expressive actions (bye-bye, hi, night-night)

Appendix B: Multiword Comprehension Test

MULTIWORD COMPREHENSION SCORE SHEET

Baby ID _____
Date of Visit _____
Session Month _____
Age _____
Criteria: 80 Words Comprehended

PRETEST	CORRECT	INCORRECT
1. Give me bunny		
2. Give me ball		
3. Give me flower		
4. Give me car		
5. Give me horn		
6. Give me teddy		
7. Give me doll		

Criteria 2/7 _____

1. Pat the doll (animal)		
2. Kiss the doll		
3. Hug the doll		
4. Tickle the doll		
5. Wash the doll		

Criteria 2/7 _____

SEMANTICALLY ANOMALOUS

	Correct	Incorrect	Partially Correct	Non-contingent	DNT
1. Pat the horn					
2. Blow the bunny					
3. Smell the car					
4. Push the flower					
5. Smell the horn					
6. Blow the flower					
7. Smell the teddy					
8. Kiss the flower					
9. Smell the doll					
10. Hug the flower					
11. Push the teddy					
12. Kiss the car					
13. Push the doll					
14. Hug the car					
15. Blow the teddy					
16. Kiss the horn					
17. Blow the doll					
18. Hug the horn					

#Correct _____   #Incorrect _____
#Partially Correct _____   #Noncontingent _____
#Did Not Test _____

AGENT ACTION (give all)

	Correct	Incorrect	Partially Correct	Non-contingent	DNT
1. Bunny kiss					
2. Car go					
3. Doll sleep					
4. Teddy jump					
5. Flower fall					
6. Horn toot					

#Correct _____   #Incorrect _____
#Partially Correct _____   #Noncontingent _____
#Did Not Test _____

SEMANTICALLY PREDICTABLE (give all)

	Correct	Incorrect	Partially Correct	Non-contingent	DNT
1. Pat the bunny					
2. Smell the flower					
3. Push the car					
4. Blow the horn					
5. Kiss the teddy					
6. Hug the doll					
7. Kiss the bunny					
8. Hug the teddy					

#Correct _____   #Incorrect _____
#Partially Correct _____   #Noncontingent _____
#Did Not Test _____

Appendix C:
Definitions of
Semantic Categories

Action: A perceivable movement or activity engaged in by an
                   agent, animate or inanimate. Other systems distinguish
                   action, process, change of state, and state categories.

Entity: Any labeling of the present person or object regardless
                   of the occurrence or nature or action being performed
                   on or by it.

Locative: The place where an object or action was located or
                   toward which it moved.

Negation: The impression of any of the following meanings with
                   regard to someone or something, or an action or a state:
                   nonexistence, rejection, cessation, denial, disappear-
                   ance.

Agent: The performer, animate or inanimate, of an action.
                   Body parts and vehicles, when used in conjunction with
                   action verbs, were coded agent.

Object: A person or thing, marked by the use of a noun or
                   pronoun, that received the force of the action.

Demonstrative: The use of demonstrative pronounds or adjectives,
                   "this," "that," "these," "those," and the words
                   "there," "right there," "here," "see," when stated for
                   the purpose of pointing out a particular referent.

Recurrence: A request for a comment on an additional instance or
                       amount; the resumption of an event; or the reappear-
                       ance of a person or an object.

Attribute: An adjectival description of the shape, size, or quality of
                       an object or person; also noun adjuncts that modified
                       nouns for a similar purpose (e.g., *gingerbread* man).

Possessor: A person or thing, marked by the use of a proper noun
                       or pronoun, that an object was associated with or to
                       which it belonged, at least temporarily.

State: A passive condition experienced by a person or object.
                       This category implies involuntary behavior on the part
                       of the experiencer (q.v.), in contrast to the voluntary
                       action performed by an agent (q.v.).

Adverbial: This represents a collapse of semantic categories of
                       words representing modifiers, including time, distance,
                       duration, frequency, intensity, and manner. Included in
                       this category are two subcategories of action/attribute
                       and state/attribute.
                       Action/Attribute: A modifier of an action indicating
                       time, manner, duration, distance, or frequency. (Direc-
                       tion or place of action was separately coded as locative,
                       repetition, or recurrence.)
                       State/Attribute: A modifer indicating time, manner,
                       quality, or intensity of a state.

Quantifier: A modifier that indicated amount or number of a person
                       or object. Prearticles and indefinite pronouns such as "a
                       piece of," "lots," "any," "every," and "each" were
                       included.

Experiencer: Something or someone that underwent a given experi-
                       ence or mental state. Body parts, when used in conjunc-
                       tion with state verbs, were coded experiencer.

Recipient: One who received or was named as the recipient of an
                       object (person or thing) from another.

Beneficiary: One who benefited from or was named as the benefi-
                       ciary of a specified action.

Name: The labeling or requesting for naming a person or thing
                       using the utterance forms: "my (his, your, etc.) name is
                       _____ " or "what's _____ name?"

Commitative: One who accompanied or participated with an agent in carrying out a specified activity.

Created Object: Something created by a specific activity, for example, a song by singing, a house by building, a picture by drawing.

Instrument: Something that an agent used to carry out or complete a specified action.

Appendix D:
Functions of Language
in Mothers' Speech

I. Description: represents observable or verifiable aspects of the environment. Included in this category are:
    A. Identification: "That's a ball." "That's a kitty."
    B. Events: I'm drawing a house.
    C. Properties: "That's a bear with a wheel."
    D. Location: "I put the dollar in the bank." "Here's your milk."

II. Statements: express facts, beliefs, attitudes, or emotions. Also subjective states—interpretation of internal states, motives, wishes, etc. Also includes:
    A. Evaluations: "That's right." "Good."
    B. Internal Reports: "I'm tired."
    C. Attributions: "He wants me to go." (Internal state of other)
    D. Rules: "You can't ride the horse here." "No."

III. Request for information: the utterance seeks an informational response from the child. "What's that?" "Where's the kitty going?" Also includes all utterances followed by a tag with rising intonations.

IV. Request for permission: the speaker seeks the right to do or accept something. "Can I tie your shoe?"

V. Request for action: the utterance seeks a behavioral response from the addressee. Such requests can occur in any of five forms:
    A. Prohibition: request for nonaction. "Don't eat."
    B. Question form: "Why don't you feed him a carrot?"
    C. Command form: "Get a purple block." "Sit down."

D. Embedded Command form: "Let's look at this." "Let's do a puzzle."

E. Statement form: "It would be nice if . . ." (indirect form)

VI. Organizational device: utterances that regulate contact and conversation. Included are:

A. Boundary marker: Indicates openings, closings, and other significant points in the conversation (e.g., topic switches). "Hi." "Bye." "Okay." "By the way."

B. Calls: solicit attention. "John."

C. Speaker selections: explicitly label speaker of the next turn. "John." "You."

D. Politeness markers: indicate ostensible politeness. "Thanks." "Sorry." "Please."

E. Accompaniments: maintain verbal contact, typically conveying information redundant with respect to context. "Here you are." "There." "There you are." "There you go." "OK." "Oh." "Let's see." "Oh wow." "Whoops." "Huh?" "Mm?" "Never mind." Also accidental markers: "Uh oh."

VII. Performance play: any riddle, nursery rhyme, or reading from a book, as well as ritualized games (e.g., peek-a-boo, patty cake).

VIII. Elicit imitation: the utterance explicitly asks for an imitation from the addressee: "Say night-night." "Can you say shoe?"

IX. Repetition of other: the utterance is an exact repetition of a remark, including prosodic characteristic.

Appendix E: Three-Part Comprehension Test

NAME _____   + = correct

DATE _____   − = incorrect

MONTH _____   0 = noncontingent

(N.B. The sentence order is illustrative. Each child was given the comprehensive test in a unique order)

PART A	1	2	3	Description of incorrect response
1. Doll eat Cheerio.				
2. House push the doll.				
3. House eat the doll.				
4. Doll push the truck.				
5. Doll push the house.				
6. Truck push the doll.				
7. Doll eat the house.				
8. Truck run over the doll.				
PART B				
1. Big doll push truck.				
2. Doll push big truck.				
3. Little truck push doll.				
4. Truck push little doll.				
5. Doll on the box push the truck.				
6. Doll push the truck on the box.				

Appendix F:
Speech Discrimination

Name _____

Baby ID # _____

K = Known
T = Taught
X = Not Learned

PRODUCTION
Write test phoneme phonetically
What's this?

Session (months): Date:	18	21	24	27	29	31	33
1. rock							
2. lock							
3. book							
4. sock							
5. cup							
6. duck							

Criteria: 2 of 3

PERCEPTION
Show me

Session (months) Date:	18	21	24	27	29	31	33
1. rock							
2. lock							
3. book							
4. sock							
5. cup							
6. duck							

Criteria: 2 of 3

SPEECH DISCRIMINATION

Name _____

Baby ID# _____

TRAINING STRING   Criteria: 7 of 8

Date_____   Date_____

1. dog _____   1. shog _____
2. dog _____   2. dog _____
3. shog _____   3. shog _____
4. dog _____   4. dog _____
5. shog _____   5. dog _____
6. shog _____   6. shog _____
7. dog _____   7. dog _____
8. shog _____   8. shog _____

Date_____   Date_____

1. dog _____   1. dog _____
2. shog _____   2. shog _____
3. shog _____   3. shog _____
4. dog _____   4. dog _____
5. dog _____   5. dog _____
6. shog _____   6. shog _____
7. dog _____   7. shog _____
8. shog _____   8. dog _____

Date_____   Date_____

1. shog _____   1. shog _____
2. dog _____   2. shog _____
3. shog _____   3. shog _____
4. shog _____   4. dog _____
5. dog _____   5. shog _____
6. dog _____   6. dog _____
7. shog _____   7. dog _____
8. shog _____

Date_____

1. dog _____
2. shog _____
3. shog _____
4. shog _____
5. dog _____
6. dog _____
7. shog _____

SPEECH DISCRIMINATION

Randomize knowns and test

Name _____

Baby ID# _____

ROCK–ZOCK   Criteria 7 of 8

Month 18
  Date_____

1. zock _____
2. zock _____
3. zock _____
4. rock _____
5. rock _____
6. rock _____
7. rock _____
8. zock_____

Month 21
  Date_____

1. zock _____
2. zock _____
3. rock _____
4. zock _____
5. rock _____
6. zock _____
7. rock _____
8. rock _____

Month 24
  Date_____

1. rock _____
2. zock _____
3. zock _____
4. rock _____
5. zock _____
6. zock _____
7. rock _____
8. rock _____

Month 27
  Date_____

1. rock _____
2. rock _____
3. zock _____
4. zock _____
5. zock _____
6. rock _____
7. rock _____
8. zock _____

Month 29
  Date_____

1. zock _____
2. rock _____
3. zock _____
4. zock _____
5. rock _____
6. rock _____
7. rock _____
8. zock _____

Month 31
  Date_____

1. rock _____
2. zock _____
3. rock _____
4. zock _____
5. rock _____
6. zock _____
7. rock _____
8. zock _____

Month 33
  Date_____

1. rock _____
2. zock _____
3. zock _____
4. rock _____
5. rock _____
6. rock _____
7. zock _____
8. zock _____

SPEECH DISCRIMINATION

Name _____

Baby ID# _____

LOCK–DOCK   Criteria 7 of 8

Month 18   Month 21
  Date_____   Date_____

1. dock _____   1. dock _____
2. lock _____   2. lock _____
3. dock _____   3. lock _____
4. dock _____   4. dock _____
5. lock _____   5. lock _____
6. lock _____   6. dock _____
7. dock _____   7. dock _____
8. lock _____   8. lock _____

Month 24   Month 27
  Date_____   Date_____

1. lock _____   1. lock _____
2. lock _____   2. dock _____
3. dock _____   3. lock _____
4. dock _____   4. lock _____
5. dock _____   5. dock _____
6. lock _____   6. dock _____
7. dock _____   7. dock _____
8. lock _____   8. lock _____

Month 29   Month 31
  Date_____   Date_____

1. dock _____   1. dock _____
2. dock _____   2. dock _____
3. lock _____   3. lock _____
4. dock _____   4. dock _____
5. lock _____   5. lock _____
6. dock _____   6. lock _____
7. lock _____   7. lock _____
8. lock _____   8. dock _____

Month 33
  Date_____

1. dock _____
2. lock _____
3. lock _____
4. dock _____
5. lock _____
7. lock _____
8. dock _____

SPEECH DISCRIMINATION

Name _____

Baby ID# _____

BOOK–DOOK   Criteria 7 of 8

Month 18
Date_____

1. dook _____
2. book _____
3. book _____
4. dook _____
5. dook _____
6. dook _____
7. book _____
8. book _____

Month 24
Date_____

1. book _____
2. dook _____
3. dook _____
4. book _____
5. dook _____
6. book _____
7. dook _____
8. book _____

Month 29
Date_____

1. dook _____
2. book _____
3. dook _____
4. book _____
5. dook _____
6. book _____
7. book _____
8. dook

Month 33
Date_____

1. dook _____
2. dook _____
3. book _____
4. dook _____
5. book _____
6. book _____
7. book _____
8. dook _____

Month 21
Date_____

1. dook _____
2. book _____
3. book _____
4. book _____
5. dook _____
6. dook _____
7. book _____
8. dook _____

Month 27
Date_____

1. book _____
2. book _____
3. dook _____
4. dook _____
5. dook _____
6. book _____
7. book _____
8. dook _____

Month 31
Date_____

1. dook _____
2. dook _____
3. book _____
4. book _____
5. book _____
6. book _____
7. dook _____
8. dook _____

SPEECH DISCRIMINATION

Name _____

Baby ID# _____

SOCK–SHOCK   Criteria 7 of 8

Month 18   Month 21
    Date_____   Date_____

1. sock _____   1. sock _____
2. sock _____   2. sock _____
3. shock _____   3. shock _____
4. shock _____   4. shock _____
5. sock _____   5. shock _____
6. sock _____   6. sock _____
7. shock _____   7. sock _____
8. shock _____   8. shock _____

Month 24   Month 27
    Date_____   Date_____

1. sock _____   1. shock _____
2. sock _____   2. sock _____
3. sock _____   3. sock _____
4. shock _____   4. sock _____
5. shock _____   5. shock _____
6. sock _____   6. shock _____
7. shock _____   7. sock _____
8. shock _____   8. shock _____

Month 29   Month 31
    Date_____   Date_____

1. shock _____   1. shock _____
2. shock _____   2. shock _____
3. sock _____   3. shock _____
4. sock _____   4. sock _____
5. shock _____   5. sock _____
6. sock _____   6. sock _____
7. sock _____   7. sock _____
8. shock _____   8. shock _____

Month 33
    Date_____

1. shock _____
2. sock _____
3. shock _____
4. shock _____
5. sock _____
6. shock _____
7. sock _____
8. sock _____

SPEECH DISCRIMINATION

Name _____

Baby ID# _____

CUP–GUP   Criteria 7 of 8

Month 18   Month 21
    Date_____   Date_____

1. cup _____   1. gup _____
2. gup _____   2. cup _____
3. gup _____   3. gup _____
4. cup _____   4. cup _____
5. gup _____   5. gup _____
6. cup _____   6. cup _____
7. cup _____   7. cup _____
8. gup _____   8. gup _____

Month 24   Month 27
    Date_____   Date_____

1. cup _____   1. gup _____
2. gup _____   2. gup _____
3. gup _____   3. cup _____
4. gup _____   4. cup _____
5. cup _____   5. cup _____
6. cup _____   6. gup _____
7. cup _____   7. cup _____
8. gup _____   8. gup _____

Month 29   Month 31
    Date_____   Date_____

1. cup _____   1. gup _____
2. gup _____   2. gup _____
3. gup _____   3. cup _____
4. cup _____   4. gup _____
5. cup _____   5. gup _____
6. gup _____   6. cup _____
7. gup _____   7. cup _____
8. cup _____   8. cup _____

Month 33
    Date_____

1. gup _____
2. cup _____
3. gup _____
4. cup _____
5. cup _____
6. gup _____
7. cup _____
8. gup _____

SPEECH DISCRIMINATION

Name _____

Baby ID# _____

DUCK–JUCK   Criteria 7 of 8

Month 18
Date_____

1. juck _____
2. duck _____
3. juck _____
4. duck _____
5. juck _____
6. juck _____
7. duck _____
8. duck _____

Month 21
Date_____

1. duck _____
2. juck _____
3. duck _____
4. juck _____
5. duck _____
6. juck _____
7. juck _____
8. duck _____

Month 24
Date_____

1. juck _____
2. juck _____
3. duck _____
4. duck _____
5. juck _____
6. juck _____
7. duck _____
8. duck _____

Month 27
Date_____

1. juck _____
2. duck _____
3. juck _____
4. juck _____
5. duck _____
6. duck _____
7. duck _____
8. juck _____

Month 29
Date_____

1. juck _____
2. duck _____
3. duck _____
4. duck _____
5. juck _____
6. duck _____
7. juck _____
8. juck _____

Month 31
Date_____

1. duck _____
2. juck _____
3. juck _____
4. duck _____
5. duck _____
6. juck _____
7. duck _____
8. juck _____

Month 33
Date_____

1. duck _____
2. duck _____
3. juck _____
4. duck _____
5. juck _____
6. duck _____
7. juck _____
8. juck _____

Appendix G:
Vocal Turntaking—
Transcription Rules

SAMPLE SELECTION

Code 25 minutes of continuous interaction.

* Zero the tape deck immediately after the identifying information. Discount the first 15 minutes of the tape (approximately 250–300 on the foot counter) and then begin coding. Code only the next 25 minutes on the tape (approximately 700 on the foot counter when finished).

  Where baby is noninteractive (which would be coded 4 or 5 under "Turn") for more than 1 minute, exclude that noninteractive portion from the sample. Similarly, exclude continuous cry sequences or sequences in which the infant's eyes are closed.
* Enter counter numbers sequentially in the counter boxes.
* Code all utterances by the baby and directed at the baby plus incidental utterances to which the baby responds. Discount all others. Ignore unclear utterances unless there is enough information/content to make an educated guess.

DIVISION INTO UTTERANCES

Use 1. syntactic form
    2. intonation
    3. juncture or pause to determine utterance boundaries.

Polarity markers, yes–no, vocatives, and expletives may be included in an utterance, where they are produced on one breath,

example: Yes, I want you to do that.
          No, don't do that.
          Hey, Kate, d'you want some more?
          Mmm, that's delicious.

These items may also occur in isolation and be counted as separate utterances.

Enter each utterance or relevant nonverbal act on a new line. If two utterances by two different speakers overlap, code separately, giving a new line to each. Do *not* omit any lines. Do not omit any numbers. Every utterance *must* be entered in each column; however, only the baby utterances require an utterance number, to be entered in the second column, "Baby Utterance Number." Number the baby utterances sequentially. Do *not* give any baby nonverbal acts a number.

"WHO" COLUMN

Enter the corresponding number for the person who produced the utterance or nonverbal act. 1 = Baby, 2 = Mother, 3 = Sibling, 4 = Father, 5 = Other (Also includes the researcher), and 6 = Both (for overlap).

CONTEXT

1. Subject alone = subject out of sight of others and beyond conversational distance (researcher present but neutral).
2. Subject with Mom = subject interacting with Mom or within conversational distance (normally within the same room).
3. Subject with other = subject with siblings, Dad, neighbors, etc., or experimenter if experimenter is interacting with subject.
4. Subject playing alone with object = subject playing out of sight of others and beyond conversational distance, but is playing with objects (experimenter present but neutral).
5. Subject interacting both with mother and some other, for example, a sibling.
6. Subject interacting with father.

NONVERBAL

Any nonverbal act, reported on the contextual commentary, which serves, either alone or in conjunction with a vocalization, to initiate or terminate a sequence, or maintain the interaction.

0 = yes (nonverbal act occurs)
1 = no (no nonverbal act)
2 = both (verbal and nonverbal act produced simultaneously)

Code all nonverbal acts as 7 under "Type" (other). Do *not* code nonverbal activities that are ongoing and not related to verbal/vocal production.

TURN

The unit of analysis, which includes one or more utterances is the sequence. A sequence is a unit of discourse with unitary topic or purpose. A new topic (signaled by the introduction of new lexical information into the text) or a new purpose (signaled by the beginning of a new activity) initiates a new sequence. When dividing the discourse into sequences, err in the direction of *more* rather than *less* sequences. Where the topic changes but the purpose remains the same, consider that the sequence has changed. A sequence may be initiated verbally or nonverbally by either partner. Sequences are terminated by a 2-second or longer pause, or the beginning of a new sequence. They may be terminated by either partner. Each sequence must have a terminating utterance whether or not the purpose of the sequence is achieved.

1 = the utterance or nonverbal act that initiates a new sequence. 2 = the utterance or nonverbal act that terminates a sequence. 3 = an utterance or act that serves to maintain the sequence. 4 = noninteractive. Baby is in a different room from mother or any other potential co-conversationalist. 5 = noninteractive. Utterances by the baby without communicative intent, to which no one responds. Any utterance or act by the baby that elicits a response cannot, therefore, be coded in this category.

Examples of Sequences

A. The one-utterance sequence. Where one partner initiates a sequence that is ignored by co-conversationalist.

	Who	Turn	
Seq. 1	Mother	1	Why don't you show the nice lady a book?
Seq. 2	Baby	1	Voc (pulls herself up on mother's skirt)
	Mother	3	You wanna be picked up?
	Mother	2	(Picks up baby)

B. Baby-initiated sequences. Because infants do not have the verbal means to change topics, they often initiate or terminate sequences nonverbally.

Who	Turn	
Who	*Turn*	
Mother	2	I don't think you're in a good mood
Baby	1	(reaches for her coffee)
Mother	3	Oh no you don't.
	3	Hot
	3	But maybe you need a drink

C. Baby vocalizations or discomfort sounds that mom ignores (and that are therefore coded either 4 or 5 as noninteractive) are not considered part of a sequence. Where the infant produces a long string of such sounds, the last of which the mother responds to, consider that the last sound, to which mother makes a response, as the sequence initiator, and mother's response as ongoing, for example:

Who	*Turn*	*Type*	
1	5	2	
1	5	2	
1	5	2	
1	5	2	
1	5	2	
1	1	2	
2	3	6	OK Grouchy.
2	3	6	What's up?

Sequence Terminators

Provided there has been at least one ongoing utterance following a sequence initiation there *must* be a sequence terminator. Following are some examples of sequence terminators.

A. Verbal/vocal terminators: Mothers often signal the end of sequences with markers such as "OK," "All done." Sequence are also frequently terminated by laughter (by mother and others in response to antics of baby).

B. The self-terminated sequence: The self-terminated sequence occurs when mothers terminate sequences that they themselves initiated when they fail to elicit the hoped-for response.

	Who	Turn	
	Who	*Turn*	
Sequence 1	Mother	1	Give me a smile
	"	3	Come on, give me a smile
	"	3	Just a little one
	"	2	OK, no smiles today
Sequence 2	"	1	Shall we play with Raggedy?

A sequence terminator may therefore be an eliciting utterance, such as a question or demand that does not achieve a response. It is simply the last turn on a particular topic.

C. Baby terminators, using the 2-second pause rule: If the baby produces a string of vocalizations within a sequence, the last vocalization before a 2-second pause is considered to terminate the sequence. Subsequent vocalizations, which are not responded to are treated as noninteractive.

D. Ambiguous sequence boundaries (The Ritarule): Where it is unclear whether the infant is nonverbally terminating a previous sequence or beginning a new one, invoke the Ritarule and consider his or her act a sequence terminator. Mother's response to that act then begins the new sequence.

	Who	*Turn*	
Sequence 1	Mother	3	OK, put your leg over the giraffe.
	Baby	2	(Baby loses interest in giraffe, gets down and crawls toward TV)
	Mother	1	Oh, that's what you're interested in.

TYPE OF UTTERANCE

1. *Cry.* Continuous cry segments, associated with acute distress.
2. *Discomfort.* Discontinuous distress noises, of lower amplitude than cry sequences, but also highly nasal. Both cry and discomfort sounds should be verified by reference to the visual information coded in the contextual commentary.
3. *Physiological or vegetative* sounds. Generally reflexive behaviors. Include sounds associated with feeding, burps, sneezes, coughs, choking, spitting up, hiccoughing, and sighing. Exclude sucking and lip-smacking during eating, and breathing noises.
4. *Vocalization* by infant associated with a comfort state. Any voluntary sound or speech attempt *on the part of the* infant. Include grunts.
5. *Vocalization by mom or other.* Any intentional nonlinguistic utterance directed at the infant, by mother or other, treat as vocalizations: uh! uh! = accident marker, nuh! nuh! = don't or warning, sh! = be quiet, mmm? = question intonation.

Appendix H: Measurement and Coding Rules of Mother's Speech

The Sample

1. Begin by checking tape to see if transcript is accurate.
2. Analyze first 100 utterances.
3. At the point where the sample includes more than 10 idioms, toss idioms. Code for MLU, discourse feature and function only.
4. Don't include any songs or nursery rhymes if they are given in their entirety.
5. Exclude laughs but include mom vocalizations.

Coding Instructions

A. Well-Formedness
  - 0 = Unanalyzable: utterances that are incomplete and broken off in midstream or were partially or wholly unintelligible.
  - 1 = Grammatical: utterances that are complete and colloquially acceptable: include utterances that begin with a false start but end with a complete and correct utterance; exclude the false start from the MLU count.
  - 2 = Ungrammatical: utterances that are ill-formed even in colloquial speech. "Tarzan talk," as in baby, reductions count here.
  - 3 = Fragment: utterances that consist only of isolated constituents or phrases.
  - 4 = Interjections: utterances that are one of the following:
    yes, no, uh-huh, uh-uh, right, okay, hi, thank you, hmm, huh?

These are generally items that are incapable of structural change.

5 = Vocalizations: utterances that are mom vocalizations.

SOME ADDITIONAL RULES:
1. If a sentence is elipsed it is well-formed if the preceeding utterance contains the information also.
2. If there is only an aux and/or subject deleted in requests for information, that is, rising intonation, the utterance is well-formed.
   Example: Wanna . . . . . ? is well-formed
3. Person names are counted as fragments.
4. Animal sounds like woof-woof, meow are fragments.

B. MLU
1. Follow Brown's rules.
2. Count all irregular pasts as one morpheme.
3. Count pronouns like everybody, nobody, etc. as two.
4. Count diminuitives by mom as two. Example: doggie is two, but kitty is one.
5. Do not count "huh' and "hmm," etc. at all when they are part of a larger utterance, but count when they stand alone as a separate utterance.

C. Number of Propositions = Number of underlying sentences/utterances. This means that there must be a verb for each proposition.

SOME ADDITIONAL RULES:
1. Tag questions are counted as one proposition because they are essentially repetitions.
2. Sentences containing catenatives (e.g., gonna, wanna, haveta, etc.) have one proposition, coded by the main verb following these. Treat these as auxiliary verbs.

D. Syntactic Complexity
0 = Unanalyzable (i.e., not a sentence)
1 = Simple
2 = Conjoined
3 = Embedded
4 = Conjoined and embedded
5 = Adjoined as in tags that are fully syntactic (e.g., You wanna come, don't you? [hmm? and mmm?]).

SOME ADDITIONAL RULES:
1. Treat sentences containing catenatives gonna, hafta, wanna or going to, have to, etc., as simple.

2. Treat sentences that have "come eat," "go get," etc., as conjoined (i.e., as if they were "Come and eat" or "Go and get").

E. Sentence Type (Mood)
   0 = Unanalyzable
   1 = Declarative
   2 = Yes–no question
   3 = Wh question
   4 = Imperative
   5 = Deixis

   SOME ADDITIONAL RULES:
   1. Deixis: an utterance is coded 5 when, and only when, it says
      "That is a _____ " or "That is not a _____ " or is a "that is" question.
      Basically these are items that fulfill the labeling function.
   2. Imperatives include hortatives, "Let's"
   3. If order of surface structure is subject then verb, even if intonation rises it is a declarative.
   4. When aux plus subject are omitted as in "wanna eat?" treat it as unanalyzable.

F. Number of morphemes per noun phrase:
   Count the number of morphemes in each NP and record on a separate line.
   A personal pronoun or a possessive pronoun may be counted as an NP.

   SOME ADDITIONAL RULES:
   1. Prepositions are not counted in the NP (e.g., "on the table" = two morphemes).
   2. Locatives "here" and "there" do not count.
   3. "Wh" anythings do not count.
   4. Conjoined NP's count separately:
      "I see Andy and Teddy" = 1,1,1
      NP   NP   NP

G. Complex VP/NP
   If the verb contains anything more than the main verb it is coded as complex. Code infinitives as complex verbs.

   SOME ADDITIONAL RULES:
   1. Verb plus particle is simple.
   2. Third-person indicative is simple.

3. Catenatives or "going to" are counted as one complex verb (e.g., Are we gonna eat? = one complex).

4. "Come eat" or "Go hide" would be two simples, as if the utterance were "come and eat," This makes the scoring consistent with calling the utterance conjoined.

H. Discourse Feature

In analyzing discourse feature use the preceding utterance as your frame of reference except where there is an interjection like "huh."

Example: 'What's your name?"

        "Huh?"

        "What's your name?" (would be exact repetition)

1 = New: it means exactly that. Exclude "huh" from this category and score it as other.

2 = Partial repetition of self. This is a reduction. A maternal utterance that repeated any phrase, or phrases, of a preceding utterance, but was not an exact repetition.

Example: "Do you want juice?"

        "Want juice?"

3 = Exact repetition of self: a maternal utterance that repeats exactly the mother's preceding utterance. Include utterances in this category if there is only one intervening baby voc or mom "Hmm?"

4 = Expansion of self: a maternal utterance that repeated any phrase or phrases of the preceding utterance, and added new lexical items.

        Example: "Get the truck." "Get the big truck."

5 = Paraphrase of self: an utterance that altered any lexical item contained in the original, but that was restricted to reiterating the sense of any preceding maternal utterance and was not a partial repetition or a paraphase.

6 = Partial repetition of baby

7 = Exact repetition of baby

8 = Expansion of baby

9 = Paraphrase of baby

10 = Other

I. Time

Utterances are coded for time when there is a marking of time in the utterance either by a verb or by a time adverbial. Code for contextual time (i.e., use your head!).

0 = Unanalyzable: when there is no time adverbial or verb, or it is a rule like "You must never shout at your mother!"

1 = Present ongoing: this category included all imperatives

2 = Immediate past: within the taping session

3 = Immediate future: within the taping session. Also treat "going to" as future.

4 = Remote past: outside the taping session

5 = Remote future: outside the taping session

J. Subject

Use main clause. Because any wh word may be fronted in wh questions, take the underlying subject (e.g., in "Where is Teddy?" Teddy is the subject)

0 = Unanalyzable (includes indefinite pronouns, e.g., "Nobody")

1 = Animate

2 = Inanimate (includes toys)

K. Verb

Use main clause. Must be realized in the surface structure and only code the first verb.

0 = Unanalyzable

1 = Active

2 = Static: includes the copula and verbs of state, but watch out for what is really going on.

Example: "I am sitting" if the person is already sitting down, code as static; if the person is in the act of sitting, code as active

L. Object

Must be realized in the surface structure. If it is a demonstrative, code it as 0.

0 = Unanalyzable

1 = Animate

2 = Inanimate (includes toys)

SOME ADDITIONAL RULES:

1. Nominalized objects (i.e., kiss, a hug), prepositional phrases, and clauses are not counted as objects.

2. In predicate nominatives (e.g., where the referent of the subject is the same as the objects—"That is a balloon" assign object code but not subject code.

M. Child-Controlled/Mother-Controlled

0 = Unanalyzable

1 = Child-controlled: any maternal utterance that refers to any activity that the child either has just completed or is currently engaged in, or to any object that the child is manipulating or holding just prior to or at the same time as the utterance was produced.

2 = Mother-controlled: as above except the activity or object was related to the mother's ongoing manipulations.

N. Action
    Code only if the verb was coded as active
    0 = Unanalyzable
    1 = Ongoing
    2 = Absent
    3 = Next turn (i.e., the action coded in the verb is required in the next
        turn)

O. Persons or Objects Present
    0 = Unanalyzable
    1 = Present: code as present any maternal utterance that referred to
        any person or object that was present in the immediate recording
        situation (i.e., the room where the recording was taking place.)
        Imperatives may be coded as subject present.
    2 = Absent: those utterances that are neither of the above.

P. Functions—See Appendix D for description.

Q. Conversational Moves—See Table 2.10 for description.

CODING SHEET—MOTHERS' SPEECH

Well-Formedness[a]	MLU	Number of Propositions	Syntactic Complexity[b]	Sentence Type[c]	Morphemes per Noun Phrase
From 0 To 5		From 0 To 5	From 0 To 5	From 0 To 5	

[a]0 = Unanalyzable; 1 = grammatical; 2 = ungrammatical; 3 = fragment; 4 = interjections;
   5 = Vocalizations
[b]0 = unanalyzable; 1 = simple; 2 = conjoined; 3 = embedded; 4 = conjoined & embedded;
   5 = adjoined
[c]0 = unanalyzable; 1 = declarative; 2 = yes–no question; 3 = who question; 4 = imperative;
   5 = deixis

Complex VP/NP	Discourse Feature[d]	Time[e]	Subject[f]	Verb[g]	Object[f]
	From 1 To 10	From 0 To 5	From 0 To 2	From 0 To 2	From 0 To 2

[d]1 = new; 2 = partial repetition of self; 3 = exact repetition of self; 4 = expansion of self; 5
   = paraphrase of self; 6 = partial repetition of baby; 7 = exact repetition of baby; 8 =
   expansion of baby; 9 = paraphrase of baby; 10 = other.
[e]0 = unanalyzable; 1 = present ongoing; 2 = immediate past; 3 = immediate future; 4 =
   remote past; 5 = remote future.
[f]0 = unanalyzable; 1 = animate; 2 = inanimate.
[g]0 = unanalyzable; 1 = active; 2 = static.

Child/Mother Controlled[h]	Action[i]	Persons or Objects Present[j]	Functions[k]	Conversational Moves[l]
From 0 to 2	From 0 To 3	From 0 To 2	From 1 to 13	From 1 To 9

[h]0 = unanalyzable; 1 = child-controlled; 2 = mother-controlled.

[i]0 = unanalyzable; 1 = ongoing; 2 = absent; 3 = next turn.

[j]0 = unanalyzable; 1 = present; 2 = absent.

[k]1 = description; 2 = statement; 3 = request for information; 4 = request for permission; 5 = request for action; 6 = organizing device; 7 = performative play; 8 = elicitation; 9 = repetition; 10 = response; 11 = acknowledgment; 12 = label; 13 = other.

[l]1 = elicit; 2 = continue; 3 = respond to self; 4 = respond to baby; 5 = acknowledge; 6 = give; 7 = continue to vocalization; 8 = response to vocalization; 9 = acknowledge vocalization.

Appendix I: Mothers' Requests for Nonverbal Action Coding Sheet

Weightings		Definitions
Gestures:	one point for single gesture.	Clumps = More than one sub-act
	two points for multiple gestures.	Subact = gesture, intonation, or repetition
Clumps:	One point for each.	
Repetitions:	One point for each	
Intonation:	One point for each rise.	
One point given for each episode.		

Episode	Type[a]	Outcome[b]	Focus[c]	Sub-Acts	Gestures[d]
number	From 1 to 4	From 0 to 2	1 or 2	number per episode	From 0 To 3

[a]1 = directive; 2 = protodirective (mom); 3 = protodirective (prompt); 4 = protodirective (baby doing).
[b]0 = irrelevant; 1 = inappropriate; 2 = appropriate.
[c]1 = within; 2 = outside.
[d]0 = none; 1 = focus; 2 = demonstrative; 3 = multiple.

Nonverbal[e]	Explicitness[f]	Intonation[g]	Clumps	Repetitions
From 0 To 2	From 0 To 4	From 0 To 2	number per episode	number per episode

[e]0 = yes; 1 = no; 2 = both.
[f]0 = none; 1 = imperative; 2 = embedded imperative; 3 = indirect imperative; 4 = other.
[g]0 = indeterminate or nonapplicable; 1 = rise; 2 = nonrise.

References

Aram, D., Hack, M., Hawkins, S., Weissman, B., Borawski-Clark, E. (1991). Very-low-birthweight children and speech and language development. *Journal Speech and Hearing Research*, *34*, 1169–1179.

Bailey, D., & Wolery, M. (1989) *Assessing infants and preschoolers with handicaps*. Columbus, OH: Merrill.

Barnes, S., Gutfreund, M, Satterly, D., & Wells, G. (1983). Characteristics of adult speech which predict children's language development. *Journal of Child Language*, *10*, 65–84.

Barsky, V., & Siegel, L. (1992). Predicting future cognitive, academic and behavioral outcomes for very-low-birth weight infants. In S. Friedman & M. Sigman (Eds.), *The psychological development of low-birthweight children* (pp. 275–298). Norwood, NJ: Ablex.

Bates, E. (1976). *Language and context: The acquisition of pragmatics*. New York: Academic Press.

Bates, E., Bretherton, I., & Snyder, L. (1988). *From first words to grammar: Individual differences and dissociable mechanisms*. New York: Cambridge University Press.

Bates, E., O'Connell, B., & Shore, C. (1987). Language and communication in infancy. In J. Osofsky (Ed.), *Handbook of infant development* (2nd ed., pp. 149–203). New York: Wiley.

Bayley, N. (1969). *Bayley Scales of Infant Development*. New York: The Psychological Corp.

Bayley, N. (1993). *Bayley Scales of Infant Development* (2nd ed.). San Antonio, TX: The Psychological Corp., Harcourt Brace.

Behrman, R. (Ed.). (1993). *Home visiting* (Vol. 3, No. 3). Los Angeles, CA: Center for the Future of Children, The David and Lucille Packard Foundation.

Bell, S., & Ainsworth, M. (1972). Infant crying and maternal responsiveness. *Child Development*, *43*, 1171–1190.

Benedict, H. (1979). Early lexical development: comprehension and production. *Journal of Child Language*, *6* , 183–200.

Berko-Gleason, J. (1958). The child's learning of English morphology. *Word, 14*, 150–177.

Bernstein Ratner, N. (1984). Patterns of vowel modification in mother–child speech. *Journal of Child Language*, *11*, 557–578.

Bloom, L. (1991). *Language development from two to three*. New York: Cambridge University Press.

Brown, J., & Bakeman, R. (1980). Relationships of human mothers with their infants during the first year of life. In R. Bell & W. Smotherman (Eds.), *Maternal influences on early behavior* (pp. 437–447). New York: Spectrum.

Brown, R. (1973). *A first language*. Cambridge, MA: Harvard University Press.

Brown, U., Hammill, D., & Weiderholt, J. (1978). *Test of Reading Comprehension: A method of assessing the comprehension of written language*. Austin, TX:Pro-Ed.

Buium, N., Rynders, J., & Turnure, J. (1974). Early maternal linguistic environment of normal and Down's syndrome language learning children *American Journal of Mental Deficiency, 79,* 52–58.

Carey, S. (1978). The child as word learner. In M. Halle, J. Bresnan, & G. Miller (Eds.), *Linguistic theory and psychological reality* (pp. 264–293). Cambridge, MA: MIT Press.

Chesnick, M., Menyuk, P., Liebergott, J., & Ferrier, L. (1983). *Who leads whom in language development*. Paper presented at the biennial meeting of The Society for Research in Child Development, Detroit, MI.

Crnic, K., Ragozin, A., Greenberg, M., Robinson, N., & Basham, R. (1983). Social interaction and developmental competence of pre-term and full-term infants during the first year of life. *Child Development, 54,* 1199–1210.

Cross, T. (1977). Mother's speech adjustments: The contribution of selected child-listener variables. In C. Snow & C. Ferguson (Eds.), *Talking to children: Language input and acquisition.* Cambridge, England: Cambridge University Press.

DeHirsch, K., Jansky, J., & Langford, W. (1964). Oral language performance of premature children and controls. *Journal of Speech and Hearing Disorders, 20,* 60–69.

Dore, J. (1974). A pragmatic description of early language development. *Journal of Psycholinguistic Research, 4,* 343–350.

Dorval, B., & Eckerman, C. (1984). Developmental trends in the quality of conversation achieved by small groups of acquainted peers. *Monographs of the Society for Research in Child Development, 29,* No. 206.

Dunn, L., & Dunn, L. (1981). *Peabody Picture Vocabulary Test*. Minneapolis: American Guidance Service.

Dunst, P. (1980). *Uzgiris and Hunt scales of psychological development*. Champaign: University of Illinois Press.

Eilers, R., & Oller, K. (1975). The role of speech discrimination in developmental sound substitutions. *Journal of Child Language, 2,* 319–329.

Fenson, L., Dale, P., Reznick, J. S., Thal, D., Bates, E., Hartung, J., Pethick, S., & Reilly, J. (1993). *Macarthur Communicative Development Inventories*. San Diego, CA: Singular.

Ferguson, C., & Farwell, C. (1975). Words and sounds in early language acquisition: initial English consonants in the first fifty words. *Language, 51,* 419–439.

Fernald, A. (1984). The perceptual and affective salience of mothers' speech to infants. In L. Feagans, C. Garvey, & R. Golinkoff (Eds.), *The origins and growth of communication.* New Brunswick, NJ: Ablex.

Fernald, A., & McRoberts G. (1992, May). *Prosodic features and early word recognition*. Paper presented at the eighth International Conference on Infancy Studies, Miami FL.

Field, T., Dempsey, J., & Shumar , H. (1981). Developmental follow-up of pre- term and post-term infants. In M. Sigman & S. Friedman (Eds.), *Preterm birth and psychological development* (pp. 299–312). New York: Academic Press.

Fisher, C., & Tokura, H. (May 1992). *Prosodic structure and turn- taking in mother–infant dialogues*. Paper presented at the eighth International Conference on Infancy Studies, Miami, FL.

Folger, J. P., & Chapman, R. S. (1978). A pragmatic analysis of spontaneous imitations. *Journal of Child Language, 5,* 25–38.

Friedman, S., & Sigman, M. (Eds.). (1992). *The psychological development of low-birthweight children*. Norwood, NJ: Ablex.

Furrow, D., & Nelson, K. (1984). Environmental correlates of individual differences in language acquisition. *Journal of Child Language, 11,* 523–534.

Gleitman, L., Newport, E., & Gleitman, H. (1984). The current status of the motherese hypothesis. *Journal of Child Language, 11,* 43–79.

Golinkoff, R. (1986). "I beg your pardon?": The preverbal negotiation of failed messages. *Journal of Child Language, 13*, 455–476.

Golinkoff, R., Hirsh-Pasek, K, Cauley, K., & Gordon, L. (1987). The eyes have it: Lexical and syntactic comprehension in a new paradigm. *Journal of Child Language, 14*, 23–45.

Gopnik, A., & Meltzoff, A. (1986). Relations between semantic and cognitive development in the one-word stage: The specificity hypothesis. *Child Development, 57*, 1040–1053.

Gray, W., & Robinson, T. (1963). *Gray's Oral Reading Test*. Los Angeles, CA: Western Psychological Services.

Greenberg, M., & Crnic, K. (1988). Longitudinal predictors of developmental status and social interaction in premature and full-term infants at age two. *Child Development, 59*, 554–570.

Gregoroiu-Serbaneau, M. (1984). Intellectual and emotional development and school adjustment in pre-term children at six and seven years of age. *International Journal of Behavioral Development, 7*, 307–320.

Hedrick, D., Prather, E., & Tobin, A. (1975). *Sequenced inventory of communication development*. Seattle: University of Washington Press.

Hirsh-Pasek , K. (1989, April). *Infants perception of fluent speech: implications for language development*. Paper presented at the annual meeting of the Society for Research in Child Development, Kansas City, MO.

Hirsh- Pasek, K., Reeves, L., & Golinkoff, R. (1993). Words and meanings: From primitives to complex organization. In J. Berko-Gleason & N. Bernstein-Ratner (Eds.), *Psycholinguistics* (pp. 134–199). Fort Worth, TX: Holt, Rhinehart & Winston.

Hoff-Ginsburg, E. (1991). Mother–child conversation in different social classes and communication settings. *Child Development, 62*, 782–796.

Ingram, D. (1981). *Procedures for phonological analysis of children's language*. Baltimore, MD: University Park Press.

Jastak, S., & Jastak, S. (1976). *Wide range achievement test*. Wilmington, DE: Guidance Associates.

Jusczyk, P., & Kemler-Nelson, D. (1992, May). *When does sensitivity to prosodic marking lead to syntactic development?* Paper presented at the eighth International Conference on Infant Studies, Miami, FL.

Jusczyk, P., Pisoni, D., Mullenix, I. (1992). Effects of talker variability on speech perception of 2 month-old infants. *Cognition, 43*, 253–291.

Kavanaugh, J., & Jenkins J. (Eds.). (1986). *Otitis media and child development*. Parkton, MD: York Press.

Kemler-Nelson, D., Hirsh-Pasek, K., Jusczyk, P., & Cassidy, K. (1989). How the prosodic cues in motherese might assist language learning. *Journal of Child Language,16*, 55–68.

Klein, N., Hack, M., & Breslau, N. (1989). Children who are very low birthweight: Development and academic achievement at nine years of age. *Developmental and Behavioral Pediatrics, 10*, 32–37.

Kuhl, P. (1990). Toward a new theory of the development of speech perception. In H. Fujisaki (Ed.), *Proceedings of the 1990 International Conference on Spoken Language Processing*. Acoustical Society of Japan.

Lee, L. (1969). *Northwestern syntax screening test*. Evanston, IL: Northwestern University Press.

Lee, L., & Canter, S. (1971). Developmental sentence scoring: A clinical procedure for estimating syntactic development in children's spontaneous speech. *Journal of Speech and Hearing Research, 36*, 315–340.

Leonard, L. (1989). Language learnability and specific language impairment in children. *Applied Psycholinguistics, 3*, 109–125.

Lester, B. (1987). Developmental outcome prediction from acoustic cry analysis in term and preterm infants. *Pediatrics, 80*, 529–534.

Lewis, M., & Freedle, R. (Eds.). (1972). *Mother–infant dyad: The cradle of meaning*. Princeton, NJ: Educational Testing Service.

Liebergott, J., Menyuk, P., Schultz, M., Chesnick, M., & Thomas, S. (1984). *Individual variation and the mechanisms of interaction.* Paper presented at Southeastern Regional Meeting, Conference for Children's Development, Athens, GA.

Lieberman, P. (1980). On the development of vowel production in young children. In G. Yeni-Komshian, J. Kavanaugh, & C. Ferguson (Eds.), *Child phonology, Vol. I: Production* (pp. 113–142). New York: Academic Press.

Lieven, E., Pine, J., & Dresner, H. (1992). Individual differences in vocabulary development: Redefining the referential–expressive distinction. *Journal of Child Language, 19,* 287–310.

MacWhinney, B. (1991). *The CHILDES project: tools for analyzing talk.* Hillsdale, NJ: Lawrence Erlbaum Associates.

MacWhinney, B., & Snow, C. (1992). The wheat and the chaff: Or four confusions regarding CHILDES. *Journal of Child Language, 19,* 459–471.

Markman, E. (1991). Initial constraints on word meaning. In S. Gelman & J. Byrnes (Eds.), *Perspectives on language and thought* (pp. 72–106). Cambridge: Cambridge University Press.

McCarthy, D. (1970). *McCarthy scales of children's ability.* New York: The Psychological Corp.

McCarthy, D. (1930). *The language development of the preschool child* (Institute of Child Welfare Series, No. 4) Minneapolis: University of Minnesota Press.

McCormick, L., & Schiefelbusch, R. (1990). *Early language intervention: An introduction* (2nd ed.). Columbus, OH: Merrill.

McDonald, L., & Pien, D. (1982). Mother conversational behavior as a function of interaction intent. *Journal of Child Language, 9,* 337–358.

Menyuk, P. (1979). Methods used to measure linguistic competence during the first five years of life. In R. Kearsley & I. Siegel (Eds.), *Infants at risk: Assessment of cognitive functioning.* Hillsdale, NJ: Lawrence Erlbaum Associates.

Menyuk, P. (1980). Effects of persistent otitis media on language development. *Annals of Otology, Rhinology, Laryngology* (Supp. 68), *89,* 257–263.

Menyuk, P. (1988). *Language development: Knowledge and use.* New York: Harper Collins.

Menyuk, P. (1992a). Early communicative and language behaviors. In J. Rosenblith (Ed. and Author) *In the beginning: development from conception to age two* (2nd ed., pp. 428–455). Newbury Park, CA: Sage Publications.

Menyuk, P. (1992b). Relationship of otitis media to speech processing and language development. In J. Katz, N. Stecker, & D. Henderson (Eds.), *Central auditory processing: A transdisciplinary view* (pp. 187–198). St. Louis: Mosby.

Menyuk, P., Liebergott, J., Chesnick, M., Korngold, B., D'Agostino, R., & Belanger, A. (1991). Predicting reading problems in at risk children. *Journal of Speech and Hearing Research, 34,* 893–903.

Miller, J., & Chapman, R. (1981). The relation between age and mean length of utterance in morphemes. *Journal of Speech and Hearing Research, 24,* 154–161.

Miller, J. F. (1981). *Assessing language production in children.* Baltimore, MD: University Park Press.

Morgan, J., & Saffron, J. (1992, October). *Integration of segmental and suprasegmental information in early speech segmentation.* Paper presented at the 17th annual Boston University Conference on Language Development, Boston, MA.

Moslin, B. (1979). *The role of phonetic input in the child's acquisition of the voiced–voiceless contrast in English stops: A VOT analysis.* Unpublished doctoral dissertation, Brown University, Providence, RI.

Nelson, K. (1973). Structure and strategy in learning to talk. *Monograph of the Society for Research in Child Development, 38,* No. 149.

Newcomer, P., & Hammill, D. (1982). *Told-P.* Austin, TX: Pro-Ed.

Nicolich, L. (1981). Toward symbolic functioning: Structure of early pretend games and potential parallels with language. *Child Development, 52,* 785–797.

Oller, K. (1980). The emergence of the sounds of speech in infancy. In G. Yeni-Komshian, J.

Kavanaugh, & C. Ferguson (Eds.), *Child phonology, Vol. 1: Production* (pp. 93–112). New York: Academic Press.

Paul, R. (1991). Profiles of toddlers with slow expressive language development. *Topics in Language Disorder, 11*, 1–13.

Paul, R., & Alforde, S. (1993). Grammatical morpheme acquisition in 4-year olds with normal, impaired and late developing language. *Journal of Speech and Hearing Research, 36*, 1271–1275.

Pisoni, D. (1992). Some comments on invariance, variability and perceptual normalization in speech perception. In J. Ohala, T. Neary, B. Derwing, M. Hodge, & G. Wiebe (Eds.), *Proceedings 1992 conference on speech processing*. Alberta, Canada: University of Alberta.

Plunkett, K. (1993). Lexical segmentation and vocabulary growth in early language acquisition. *Journal of Child Language, 20*, 43–60.

Prechtl, H., Theorell, K., Gramsbergen, A., & Lind, J. (1969) A statistical analysis of cry patterns in normal and abnormal newborn infants. *Developmental Medicine and Child Neurology, 11*, 142–152.

Rescorla, L., & Goosens, M. (1992). Symbolic play development in toddlers with expressive specific language impairment. *Journal of Speech and Hearing Research, 35*, 1290–1302.

Rescorla, L., & Schwartz, E. (1990). Outcome of toddlers with specific expressive language delay. *Applied Psycholinguistics, 11*, 393–407.

Retherford, K. S., Schwartz, B. C., & Chapman, R. S. (1981). Semantic roles and residual grammatical categories in mother and child speech: Who tunes into whom? *Journal of Child Language, 8*, 583–608.

Reynell, J. (1969). *Reynell developmental language scales*. Slough, Bucks: N. F. E. R.

Rosenblith, J. F. (1992). *In the beginning: Development from conception to age two* (2nd ed.). Newbury Park, CA: Sage.

Sachs, J., & Truswell, L. (1978). Comprehension of two word structures by children in the one word stage. *Journal of Child Language, 5*, 17–24.

Sameroff, A., & Chandler, M. (1975). Reproductive risk and the continuum of caretaking causality. In F. Horowitz (Ed.), *Review of child development research* (Vol. 4, pp. 187–224). Chicago: University of Chicago Press.

Schlesinger, I. (1982). *Steps to language*. Hillsdale, NJ: Lawrence Erlbaum Associates.

Siegel, L. (1982). Reproductive, perinatal, and environmental factors in the cognitive and language development of pre-term and full-term infants. *Child Development, 53*, 963–973.

Silber, R. (1992). *Variability and intelligibility of clarified speech to different listener groups*. Unpublished doctoral dissertation, Boston University, Boston, MA.

Teele, D., Klein, J., Chase, C., Menyuk, P., & Rosner, B. (1990). Otitis media in infancy and development of intellectual ability, school achievement, speech and language at age seven years. *Journal of Infectious Diseases, 162*, 685–694.

Templin, M. (1957). *Certain language skills in children*. Minneapolis: University of Minnesota Press.

Thal, D. (1994). Relationships between language and gesture in normally developing and late talkers. *Journal of Speech and Hearing Research, 37*, 157–170.

Tyack, D., & Gottslaben, R. (1974). *Language sampling analysis training*. Palo Alto, CA: Consulting Psychologist Press.

Ungerer, J., & Sigman, M. (1983). Developmental lags in pre-term infants from one to three years of age. *Child Development, 54*, 1217–1229.

Uzgiris, I., & Hunt, J. (1975). *Assessment in infancy: Ordinal scales of psychological development*. Champaign: University of Illinois Press.

Waxman, S. (1990). Linguistic biases and the establshment of conceptual hierarchies: Evidence from pre-school children. *Cognitive Development, 5*, 123–150.

Wells, C. G., MacLure, M., & Montgomery, M. (1979). Adult–child discourse: outline of a model of analysis. *Journal of Pragmatics, 3*, 337–380.

Werker, J., & Lalonde, C. (1988). Cross-language speech perception: initial capabilities and developmental change. *Developmental Psychology, 24*, 672–683.

Whitehurst, G., Fischel, J., Lonigan, C., Valdez- Menchaca, M., Arnold, D., & Smith, M., (1991). Treatment of early language expressive delay: If, when and how. *Topics in Language Disorders, 11*, 55–68.

Yeni-Komshian, G. (1993). Speech perception. In J. Berko-Gleason & N. Bernstein-Ratner (Eds.), *Psycholinguistics* (pp. 90–133). Fort Worth, TX: Harcourt Brace, Jovanovich.

Author Index

238

Subject Index